Mac OS® X Tiger™ For Dummies®

D1635488

Top Six Things You Should Never Do

6. Never clean your monitor with Windex (or other product not designed to be used on video display). And nix on the paper towels and tissues, too — use a soft cloth (microfiber is best) if you want to avoid scratching the display.

5. Never pay attention to anyone who says that Windows is just like the Mac. Yeah, right. And Yugo is the Eastern-European cousin of BMW.

4. Never bump, drop, shake, wobble, dribble, drop-kick, or play catch with a hard drive (or PowerBook or iBook, which contain hard drives) while it's running. Don't forget: Your desktop Mac has a hard drive inside it, too.

3. Never shut off your Mac by pulling the plug or flipping the power switch. Always use the Shut Down command from the Apple menu (or press the Power button and then click the Shut Down button).

2. Never get up from your Mac without saving your work. Just before your butt leaves the chair, your fingers should be pressing ⌘+S. Make it a habit.

1. Never keep only one copy of your important documents. Make at least two backup copies and keep one of them in another location. Period.

Do I Need an Antivirus Program?

"Do I need an antivirus program?" Even though Mac OS X viruses have been rarer than hens' teeth of late, you probably do need antivirus software if you're at risk. How do you know you're at risk? Well, you are if you

- Download files from the Internet.

- Receive e-mail with attachments (and open the attachments).

- Are on a network and share files with others.

- Use disks — floppy, Zip, Jaz, Orb, CD-R, CD-RW, DVD-R, DVD-RW — or any other type of storage medium that has ever been inserted into (or in any way connected to) anyone else's Mac.

These are the routes that viruses use to spread; if any or all of them apply to you, you'd be well served to run an antivirus program (such as Virex or Norton AntiVirus for Macintosh). That said, I have to add that we Mac users are exposed to significantly fewer viral threats than our Windows-using counterparts.

Mac OS® X Tiger™ For Dummies®

Cheat Sheet

Five Awesome Web Sites for Mac OS X Lovers

`www.apple.com/support/`: This is the Apple support site and Knowledge Base — a treasure trove of tech notes, software update information, troubleshooting tips, and documentation for most Apple products.

`www.MacInTouch.com`: This is the preeminent Mac news and information site, full of tips, hints, and troubleshooting information. Many users consider MacInTouch (along with MacSurfer and MacFixit) a must-read every day.

`www.versiontracker.com`: VersionTracker is the place to go to find freeware, shareware, and software updates for Mac OS X. If VersionTracker doesn't have it, it probably doesn't exist.

`www.macminute.com`: This site is where those in the know go for up-to-the-minute Mac news. Just the facts — usually in a single paragraph, with a link to more information.

`www.doctormacdirect.com`: Doctor Mac Direct (okay, I'm proud of it) is, in effect, my day job. We have a team of Mac experts with over 100 person-years of Mac experience providing technical help and training via telephone, e-mail, and/or our unique Internet-enabled remote control software. We (usually) offer same-day service and our prices are quite reasonable.

Keyboard Shortcuts

Make these shortcuts second nature. All these shortcuts work in the Finder, and many of them work in other application programs as well. See those perforations over there? That's so you can tear this cheat sheet out and memorize these shortcuts. Ready? Fold at the perforations, crease, RIP!

Command	Keyboard Shortcut	Command	Keyboard Shortcut
New Finder Window	⌘+N	Find	⌘+F
New Folder	⌘+Shift+N	Undo	⌘+Z
New Smart Folder	⌘+Option+N	Cut	⌘+X
Open	⌘+O	Copy	⌘+C
Close Window	⌘+W	Paste	⌘+V
Close All Windows	⌘+Option+W	Select All	⌘+A
Get Info	⌘+I	Next Window	⌘+`
Open Inspector	⌘+Option+I	Eject Disk	⌘+E
Duplicate	⌘+D	Help	⌘+Shift+?
Make Alias	⌘+L		

For Dummies: Bestselling Book Series for Beginners

Mac OS® X Tiger™

FOR

DUMMIES®

by Bob LeVitus

WILEY

Wiley Publishing, Inc.

Mac OS® X Tiger™ For Dummies®

Published by
Wiley Publishing, Inc.
111 River Street
Hoboken, NJ 07030-5774
www.wiley.com

WILEY

About the Author

Bob LeVitus, often referred to as "Dr. Mac," has written nearly 50 popular computer books, including *Dr. Mac: The OS X Files* and *Mac OS 9 For Dummies* for Wiley Publishing, Inc.; *Stupid Mac Tricks* and *Dr. Macintosh* for Addison-Wesley; and *The Little iTunes Book*, 3rd Edition and *The Little iDVD Book*, 2nd Edition for Peachpit Press. His books have sold more than a million copies worldwide.

Bob has penned the popular Dr. Mac column for the Houston *Chronicle* for more than six years and has been published in dozens of computer magazines over the past 15 years. His achievements have been documented in major media around the world. (Yes, that was him juggling a keyboard in *USA Today* a few years back!)

Bob is known for his expertise, trademark humorous style, and ability to translate techie jargon into usable and fun advice for regular folks. Bob is also a prolific public speaker, presenting more than 100 Macworld Expo training sessions in the U.S. and abroad, keynote addresses in three countries, and Macintosh training seminars in many U.S. cities. (He also won the Macworld Expo MacJeopardy World Championship three times before retiring his crown.)

Bob is considered one of the world's leading authorities on Mac OS. From 1989 to 1997, he was a contributing editor/columnist for *MacUser* magazine, writing the Help Folder, Beating the System, Personal Best, and Game Room columns at various times.

In 2004, LeVitus founded his most ambitious undertaking yet, Doctor Mac Direct LLC (www.doctormacdirect.com), a company that provides expert technical help and training to Mac users, in real time and at reasonable prices, via telephone, e-mail, and/or its own unique Internet-enabled remote control software. If you're having problems with your Mac, you ought to give them a try!

Prior to giving his life over to computers, LeVitus spent years at Kresser/ Craig/ D.I.K. (a Los Angeles advertising agency and marketing consultancy) and its subsidiary, L & J Research. He holds a B.S. in Marketing from California State University.

Dedication

This book is dedicated to my wife, Lisa, who taught me almost everything I know about almost everything except computers.

Author's Acknowledgments

Special thanks to everyone at Apple who helped me turn this book around in record time: Keri Walker, Pam Bennett, Nathalie Welch, Greg (Joz) Joswiak, and all the rest. I couldn't have done it without you.

Thanks also to super-agent Carole "Swifty-for-life" McClendon, for deal-making beyond the call of duty, again. You've been my agent nearly 20 years, and I want you to know that you're a treasure.

Big-time thanks to the gang at Wiley: Bob "Is the damn thing done yet?" Woerner, Nicole "Whipcrcker VI" Sholly, Andy "Big Boss Man" Cummings, Barry "Still no humorous nickname" Pruett, technical editor Dennis R. Cohen, who did a rocking job, and all the others.

And additional extra special thanks to Dennis R. Cohen for technical support and for updating several chapters for me when time got short. It's been an honor and a privilege to work with the only guy I know who's been using OS X longer than me. You rock, dude!

Thanks also to my family and friends, for putting up with me during my all-too lengthy absences during this book's gestation. And thanks to Saccone's Pizza, Lucky Dog Chicago-style hot dogs, John Muller Texas BBQ, Taco Cabana, Bass Ale, Sam Adams, and ShortStop for sustenance.

And finally, thanks to you, gentle reader, for buying this book.

Publisher's Acknowledgments

We're proud of this book; please send us your comments through our online registration form located at www.dummies.com/register/.

Some of the people who helped bring this book to market include the following:

Acquisitions, Editorial, and Media Development

Project Editor: Nicole Sholly

Senior Acquisitions Editor: Bob Woerner

Senior Copy Editor: Barry Childs-Helton

Technical Editor: Dennis R. Cohen

Editorial Manager: Kevin Kirschner

Media Development Manager: Laura VanWinkle

Media Development Supervisor: Richard Graves

Editorial Assistant: Amanda Foxworth

Cartoons: Rich Tennant (www.the5thwave.com)

Composition Services

Project Coordinator: Maridee Ennis

Layout and Graphics: Carl Byers, Andrea Dahl, Lauren Goddard, Denny Hager, Joyce Haughey, Melanee Prendergast, Heather Ryan

Proofreaders: Jessica Kramer, Linda Morris, Joe Niesen, Carl William Pierce

Indexer: TECHBOOKS Production Services

Publishing and Editorial for Technology Dummies

 Richard Swadley, Vice President and Executive Group Publisher

 Andy Cummings, Vice President and Publisher

 Mary Bednarek, Executive Acquisitions Director

 Mary C. Corder, Editorial Director

Publishing for Consumer Dummies

 Diane Graves Steele, Vice President and Publisher

 Joyce Pepple, Acquisitions Director

Composition Services

 Gerry Fahey, Vice President of Production Services

 Debbie Stailey, Director of Composition Services

Contents at a Glance

Table of Contents

Introduction

*Y*ou made the right choice twice: Mac OS X Tiger and this book.

Take a deep breath and get ready to have a rollicking good time. That's right. This is a computer book, but this is going to be fun. What a concept! Whether you're brand spanking new to the Mac or a grizzled old Mac vet, I guarantee that discovering the ins and outs of Mac OS X Tiger will be fun and easy. Wiley, Inc. (the publisher of this book) couldn't say it on the cover if it weren't true!

About This Book

This book's roots lie with my international bestseller *Macintosh System 7.5 For Dummies,* an award-winning book so good that now-deceased Mac cloner Power Computing gave away a copy with every Mac clone they sold. *Mac OS X Tiger For Dummie*s is the latest revision and has been, once again, completely updated to include all the cool new features found in Mac OS X Tiger. In other words, this edition combines all the old, familiar features of the previous books (*Mac OS 7.6 For Dummies, Mac OS 8 For Dummies, Mac OS 8.5 For Dummies,* and *Mac OS 9 For Dummies,* plus the three previous editions of *Mac OS X For Dummies* with cat names) — but once again expanded and updated to reflect the latest and greatest offering from Apple.

Why write a *For Dummies* book about Tiger? Well, Tiger is a big, somewhat complicated personal-computer operating system. So I made *Mac OS X Tiger For Dummies* a not-so-big, not-very-complicated book that shows you what Tiger is all about without boring you to tears, confusing you, or poking you with sharp objects.

In fact, I think you'll be so darned comfortable that I wanted the title to be *Mac OS X Tiger Without Discomfort,* but the publishers wouldn't let me. Apparently we *For Dummies* authors have to follow some rules, and using "Dummies" and "Mac OS X Tiger" in this book's title are among them.

And speaking of "dummies," remember that it's just a word. I don't think you're dumb — quite the opposite! My second choice for this book's title was *Mac OS X Tiger For People Smart Enough to Know They Need Help with It,* but you can just imagine what Wiley thought of that. ("C'mon, that's the whole point of the name!" they insisted. "Besides, it's shorter this way.")

Anyway, the book is chock-full of information and advice, explaining everything you need to know about Mac OS X in language you can understand — along with timesaving tips, tricks, techniques, and step-by-step instructions, all served up in generous quantities.

What You Won't Find in this Book

Another rule we *For Dummies* authors must follow is that our book cannot exceed a certain number of pages. (Brevity is the soul of wit, and all that.) So there are some things I wish I could have included, but they didn't fit. Although I feel confident you'll find everything you need to know about Mac OS X Tiger in this book, some things bear further looking into, including these:

✔ **Information about many of the applications (programs) that come with Mac OS X Tiger**

An installation of Mac OS X Tiger includes more than 50 separate applications, mostly found in the Applications folder and the Utilities folder within it. I'd love to walk you through each one of them, but that would have required a book a whole lot bigger, heavier, and more expensive than this one.

This book is, first and foremost, about using Mac OS X, so I brief you on the small handful of bundled applications essential to using Mac OS X Tiger and keep the focus there. Reserved for independent study elsewhere are the iLife application suite (iTunes, iMovie, iPhoto, iDVD, and GarageBand), as well as other programs that aren't essential to OS X (such as Stickies, TextEdit, Chess, DigitalColorMeter, and the like). Programs you need to know about to configure or use Mac OS X Tiger (for example, System Preferences, Printer Setup Utility, Activity Monitor and such) are covered in full and loving detail.

For what it's worth, there are many books about the applications included with Mac OS X Tiger; the two my publisher suggested I recommend are *Mac OS X Tiger All-in-One Desk Reference,* written by Mark L. Chambers, and *iLife 04 All-in-One Desk Reference,* written by Tony Bove and Cheryl Rhodes, which are both (sheer coincidence) published by Wiley.

✔ **Information about Microsoft Office, AppleWorks, Photoshop, Quicken, and most other third-party applications**

Okay, if all the gory details of all the bundled (read: *free*) Mac OS X Tiger applications don't fit here, I think you'll understand why digging into third-party applications that cost extra was out of the question.

✔ **Information about programming for the Mac**

This book is about *using* Mac OS X Tiger, not writing code for it. There are dozens of books about programming on the Mac, most of which are two or three times the size of this book.

✔ **My world-famous Mojito recipe**

I make perhaps the finest Mojito you'll ever find outside of Cuba, but my editor insists it would be inappropriate to include it in this book (food stains would make the text hard to read). So if you like a good Mojito, send me an e-mail at MojitoExpert@doctormacdirect.com and I'll send you a Mojito recipe that will knock your socks off. (If you don't know what a Mojito is, here's a chance to find out.)

Conventions Used in This Book

To get the most out of this book, you need to know how I do things and why. Here are a few conventions used in this book to make your life easier:

✔ When I want you to open an item in a menu, I write something like "Choose File➪Open," which means, "Pull down the File menu and choose the Open command."

✔ Stuff you're supposed to type appears in bold type, **like this.**

✔ **Sometimes an entire a sentence is in bold,** as you'll see when I present a numbered list of steps. **In those cases, I** debold **what you're supposed to type,** like this.

✔ Web addresses, programming code (not much in this book), and things that appear onscreen are shown in a special monofont typeface, `like this.`

✔ When I refer to the menu, I'm referring to the menu in the upper-left corner of the Finder menu bar that looks like a blue or graphite Apple (called the *Apple menu*). For example, I may say, "From the menu, choose File➪Open." I do *not* use the symbol to refer to the key on your Mac keyboard that may or may not have both the ⌘ and symbols on it. I refer to that key (called the *Command key*) with the equally funky ⌘ symbol and write something like, "Press the ⌘ key." So, when you see , think Apple menu.

✔ For keyboard shortcuts, I write something like ⌘+*A*, which means to hold down the ⌘ key (the one with the little pretzel and/or symbol on it) and then press the letter A on the keyboard. If you see something like ⌘+*Shift*+*A*, that means to hold down the ⌘ and Shift keys while pressing the A key. Again, for absolute clarity, I never refer to the ⌘ key with the symbol. I reserve that symbol for the menu *(Apple menu)*. For the Command key, I use only the ⌘ symbol. Got it? Very cool.

What You're Not to Read

The first few chapters of this book are where I describe the basic everyday things that you need to understand in order to operate your Mac effectively.

Even though Mac OS X Tiger is way different from previous Mac operating systems, this first part is so basic that if you've been using a Mac for long, you may think you know it all — and you may know most of it. But hey! — not-so-old-timers need a solid foundation. So here's my advice: Skip through the stuff you know; you'll get to the better stuff faster.

Other stuff that you can skip over (if you're so inclined) is any sidebar or section marked with a Technical Stuff icon, which I talk about in a moment.

Foolish Assumptions

Although I know what happens when you make assumptions, I've made a few anyway. First, I assume that you, gentle reader, know nothing about using Mac OS X — beyond knowing what a Mac is, that you want to use OS X, that you want to understand OS X without digesting an incomprehensible technical manual, and that you made the right choice by selecting this particular book.

And so, I do my best to explain each new concept in full and loving detail. Maybe that's foolish, but . . . oh well.

Oh, and I also assume that you can read. If you can't, ignore this paragraph.

How This Book Is Organized

Mac OS X Tiger For Dummies is divided into five logical parts, numbered (surprisingly enough) 1 through 5. By no fault of mine, they're numbered using those stuffy old Roman numerals, so you'll see I–V where you (in my humble opinion) ought to see Arabic numbers 1–5. Another rule, I think.

Anyway, it's better if you read the parts in order, but if you already know a lot — or think you know a lot — feel free to skip around and read the parts that interest you most.

Part 1: Introducing Mac OS X

This first part is very, very basic training. From the mouse to the Desktop, from menus, windows, and icons to the snazzy-but-helpful Dock, it's all here. A lot of what you need to know to navigate the depths of Mac OS X safely and sanely will be found in this section. And although old-timers may just want to skim through it, you newcomers should probably read every word. Twice.

Part 11: Rounding Out Your Basic Training

In this part, I build on the basics of Part I and really get you revving with your Mac. Here I cover additional topics that every Mac user needs to know, coupled with some hands-on, step-by-step instruction. It starts with a closer look at the program you'll be using most, the OS X Finder, followed by a chapter about how to open and save files (a skill you're sure to find handy). Next comes a chapter about managing your files for maximum efficiency followed by a quick look at using removable media (which means *ejectable disks* — CDs, DVDs, and even oldies but goodies such as Zip drives). Last, but certainly not least, is a chapter about the importance of backing up your data — and how to do it painlessly.

Part 111: Doing Stuff with Your Mac

This part is chock-full of ways to do cool stuff with your Mac. In this section, you'll discover the Internet first — how to get it working on your Mac, and what to do with it after you do. Next, I show you the ins and outs of printing under OS X. You also read about some of the more important OS X-related applications and features, plus how to make your Tiger look and feel just the way you like it. That's all followed by the lowdown on the Classic Environment, and possibly the most useful chapter in the whole book, Chapter 13, which details each and every gosh-darned System Preference, filled with useful observations and recommendations.

Part 1V: Networking and Troubleshooting

Here I get into the nitty-gritty underbelly of Mac OS X, where I cover somewhat more advanced topics, such as file sharing, creating and using multiple users (and why you might want to), and the all-important troubleshooting chapter, Chapter 15.

Part V: The Part of Tens

Finally, it's The Part of Tens, which may have started life as a Letterman rip-off, although it does include heaping helpings of tips, optional software, great Mac Web sites, and hardware ideas.

The Appendix

Last, but certainly not least, I cover installing Mac OS X Tiger in the Appendix. The whole process has become quite easy with this version of the system software, but if you have to install Tiger yourself, it would behoove you to read this helpful Appendix first.

Icons Used in This Book

You'll see little round pictures (icons) off to the left side of the text throughout this book. Consider these icons as miniature road signs, telling you a little something extra about the topic at hand. Here's what the different icons look like and what they all mean.

Look for Tip icons to find the juiciest morsels: shortcuts, tips, and undocumented secrets about Tiger. Try them all; impress your friends!

When you see this icon, it means that this particular morsel is something that I think you should memorize (or at least write on your shirt cuff).

Put on your propeller-beanie hat and pocket protector; these parts include the truly geeky stuff. It's certainly not required reading, but it must be interesting or informative or I wouldn't have wasted your time with it.

Read these notes very, very, very carefully. (Did I say *very*?) Warning icons flag important information. The author and publisher won't be responsible if your Mac explodes or spews flaming parts because you ignored a Warning icon. Just kidding. Macs don't explode or spew (with the exception of a few choice PowerBook 5300s, which won't run Tiger anyway). But I got your attention, didn't I? I'll tell you once again: It is a good idea to read the Warning notes very carefully.

These icons represent my ranting or raving about something that just bugs me. Imagine foam coming from my mouth. Rants are required to be irreverent, irrelevant, or both. I try to keep them short, more for your sake than mine.

Well, now, what could this icon possibly be about? Named by famous editorial consultant Mr. Obvious, this icon highlights all things new and different in Mac OS X Tiger.

Where to Go from Here

Go to a comfortable spot (preferably not far from a Mac) and read the book.

I didn't write this book for myself. I wrote it for you and would love to hear how it worked for you. So please drop me a line or register your comments through the Wiley Online Registration Form located at www.dummies.com.

You can send snail mail care of Wiley, Inc. (the mailroom there will see that I receive it), or if you want me to see it sometime in this century, you might want to send e-mail to me directly at

Tigerfordummies@doctormacdirect.com

Did this book work for you? What did you like? What didn't you like? What questions were unanswered? Did you want to know more about something? Did you want to find out less about something? Tell me! I have received more than 100 suggestions about previous editions, most of which are incorporated here. So keep up the good work!

I appreciate your feedback, and I *try* to respond to all reasonably polite e-mail within a few days.

So what are you waiting for? Go — enjoy the book!

Part I

Introducing Mac OS X Tiger

The 5th Wave   By Rich Tennant

"Brad! That's not your modem we're hearing! It's Buddy!! He's out of his cage and in the iMac!!"

In this part . . .

Mac OS X Tiger sports tons of new goodies and features. I'll get to the hot new goodies soon enough, but the standard approach is crawl first, we walk later.

In this part, you discover the most basic of basics, such as how to turn on your Mac. Next, I acquaint you with the Mac OS X Desktop: windows, icons, menus, and the Dock — you know, the whole shmear. To finish things up, I describe each and every OS X menu in full and loving detail. (Yum.)

So get comfortable, roll up your sleeves, fire up your Mac if you like, and settle down with Part I, a delightful little section I like to think of as "The Hassle-Free Way to Get Started with Mac OS X Tiger."

Chapter 1

Mac OS X Tiger 101 (Prerequisites: None)

....

In This Chapter

▶ Defining Mac OS X Tiger

▶ Finding help if you're a beginner

▶ Turning on your Mac

▶ Shutting down your Mac without getting chewed out by it

▶ Knowing what you should see when you turn on your Mac

▶ Taking a refresher course on using a mouse

▶ Touring the Desktop

▶ Sniffing out the default Desktop icons

▶ Beautifying your Desktop

....

Congratulate yourself on choosing Mac OS X, which stands for Macintosh Operating System X — that's the Roman numeral *ten,* not the letter *X* (pronounced *ten,* not *ex*). You made a smart move because you scored more than just an operating system upgrade. Mac OS X version 10.4 Tiger includes dozens of new or improved features to make using your Mac easier as well as dozens more that help you do more work in less time. Now you can use these new features to be more productive, have fewer headaches, reduce your cholesterol level, and fall in love with your Mac all over again.

In this chapter, I start at the very beginning and talk about Mac OS X in mostly abstract terms. After the basics are out of the way, I get right down to the real nitty-gritty about the Mac OS X Desktop — the place where you start doing stuff with your Mac.

Those of you who've been using Mac OS X for a while may find some of the information in this chapter hauntingly familiar; some features that I describe haven't changed from earlier versions of Mac OS X.

Besides, if you decide to skip this chapter — just because you think you have all the new stuff figured out — I assure you that you'll miss out on sarcasm, clever wordplay, shortcuts, awesome techniques, a bad pun or two, and some good advice on making the Desktop an easier place to be. If that's not enough to convince you, I also provide a bunch of stuff that Apple didn't bother to tell you (as if you read every word in Mac OS X Help, which is the only user manual Apple provides anyway!).

Those of you who are about to upgrade to Mac OS X Tiger from an earlier version of Mac OS — in particular, Mac OS 9 or a previous Mac OS X release such as Panther or Jaguar — should read the Appendix right about now. It contains important information about installing Tiger that can make upgrading a more pleasant experience.

If you are about to upgrade to Tiger, I feel obliged to mention a major pitfall to avoid: One very specific misplaced click in the wrong place, done while installing your new OS, could erase every file on your hard drive. The Appendix describes it. So if you aren't running Tiger yet, I urge you to read the Appendix before you install — it could save your bacon.

To sum things up: This chapter contains some important information that you need to know in order to use Mac OS X Tiger successfully. If you're a total beginner to the Mac experience, you should probably read every word in this chapter. Even if you're past the beginner stage, you may want to skim these sections anyway to refresh your memory.

Tantalized? Let's rock.

Gnawing to the Core of OS X

Along with the code in its read-only memory (ROM), the operating system (that is, the *OS* in *Mac OS X*) is what makes a Mac a Mac. Without it, your Mac is a pile of silicon and circuits — no smarter than a toaster.

"So what does an operating system do?" you ask. Good question. The short answer is that an *operating system* controls the basic and most important functions of your computer. In the case of Mac OS X and your Mac, the operating system

- ✔ Manages memory.
- ✔ Controls how windows, icons, and menus work.
- ✔ Keeps track of files.
- ✔ Manages networking.
- ✔ Does housekeeping. (No kidding!)

Other forms of software, such as word processors and Web browsers, rely on the operating system to create and maintain the environment in which that software works its magic. When you create a memo, for example, the word processor provides the tools for you to type and format the information. In the background, the operating system is the muscle for the word processor, performing crucial functions such as the following:

- ✔ Providing the mechanism for drawing and moving the on-screen window in which you write the memo
- ✔ Keeping track of a file when you save it
- ✔ Helping the word processor create drop-down menus and dialogs for you to interact with
- ✔ Communicating with other programs
- ✔ And much, much more (stuff that only geeks could care about)

So, armed with a little background in operating systems, take a gander at the next section before you do anything else with your Mac.

Don't let that UNIX stuff scare you. It's there if you want it, but if you don't want it or don't care (like most of us), you'll rarely even know it's there. All you'll know is that your Mac just runs and runs and runs without crashing and crashing and crashing.

One last thing: As I mention in the Introduction (I'm only repeating it for those of you who don't read Introductions), Mac OS X Tiger comes with more than 50 applications. And although I'd love to tell you all about each and every one, I can only tell you about the small handful of bundled applications

The Mac advantage

Most of the world's PCs use Windows. You're among the lucky few to have a computer with an operating system that's intuitive, easy to use, and (dare I say) fun. If you don't believe me, try using Windows for a day or two. Go ahead. You probably won't suffer any permanent damage. In fact, you'll really begin to appreciate how good you have it. Feel free to hug your Mac. Or give it a peck on the CD-ROM drive slot — just try not to get your tongue caught.

As someone once told me, "Claiming that the Macintosh is inferior to Windows because most people use Windows is like saying that all other restaurants serve food that's inferior to McDonald's."

We may be a minority, but we have the best, most stable, most modern all-purpose operating system in the world, and here's why: UNIX — on which Mac OS X is based — is widely regarded as the best industrial-strength operating system. For now, just know that being based on UNIX means that a Mac running OS X will crash less often than an older Mac or a Windows machine, which means less downtime. But perhaps the biggest advantage OS X has is that when an application crashes, it doesn't crash your entire computer, and you don't have to restart the thing to continue working.

essential to using Mac OS X Tiger. If you need more info on the programs I don't cover, may I (again) recommend *Mac OS X Tiger All-in-One Desk Reference For Dummies,* written by Mark L. Chambers, or *iLife '04 All-in-One Desk Reference For Dummies,* written by my old friends Tony Bove and Cheryl Rhodes (both from Wiley).

A Safety Net for the Absolute Beginner (Or Any User)

In this section, I deal with the stuff that the manual that came with your Mac doesn't cover — or doesn't cover in nearly enough detail. If you're a first-time Macintosh user, please, *please* read this section of the book carefully — it could save your life. Okay, okay, perhaps I'm being overly dramatic. What I mean to say is that reading this section could save your *Mac.* Even if you're an experienced Mac user, you may want to read this section anyway. Chances are you'll see at least a few things you may have forgotten (and that may come in handy).

Turning the dang thing on

Okay. This is the big moment — turning on your Mac! Gaze at it longingly first and say something cheesy, such as "You're the most awesome computer I've ever known." If that doesn't turn on your Mac (and it probably won't), keep reading.

Apple, in its infinite wisdom, has manufactured Macs with power switches and buttons on every conceivable surface: on the front, side, and back of the computer itself, and even on the keyboard or monitor. So if you don't know how to turn on your Mac, don't feel bad — just look in the manual or booklet that came with your Mac.

Some Macs (including most older PowerBooks) even hide the power button behind a little plastic door. Because of the vast number of different configurations, I can't tell you where the switch is without devoting a whole chapter just to that topic. (Can you say b-o-o-r-r-ring?)

 These days some Macs have a power-on button on the keyboard; if so, it usually looks like the little circle thingie you see in the margin.

 Don't bother choosing Help⇨Mac Help, which opens the Help Viewer program because it can't tell you where the switch is either. Although the Help program is good for learning a lot of things, the location of the power switch isn't among them. Of course, if you haven't found the switch and turned on the Mac, you can't access Help anyway. (D'oh!)

What you should see on startup

When you finally do turn on your Macintosh, you set in motion a sophisticated and complex series of events that culminates in the loading of Mac OS X and the appearance of the Mac OS X Desktop. After a small bit of whirring, buzzing, and flashing (meaning that the operating system is loading), OS X first tests all your hardware — slots, ports, disks, random-access memory (RAM) — and so on. If everything passes, you hear a pleasing musical tone and see the tasteful gray Apple logo in the middle of your screen, along with a small spinning-pinwheel cursor somewhere on the screen. Both are shown in Figure 1-1.

Figure 1-1:
No more smiley-Mac or multicolored beach-ball cursors at startup. These are their OS X replace-ments.

✔ **Everything is fine and dandy:** Next, you see the soothing graphite Apple logo, the words *Mac OS X,* and a status indicator with messages that tell you the Mac is going through its normal startup motions. Makes you feel kind of warm and fuzzy, doesn't it? If all this fanfare shows up on-screen, Mac OS X is loading properly. In the unlikely event that you don't see the gray Apple logo, the soothing messages, and/or the familiar Desktop, see Chapter 15 (where I show you how to troubleshoot your system).

Next, you may or may not see the Mac OS X login screen, where you enter your name and password. If you do, press the Enter or Return key (after you type your name and password, of course) and away you go.

If you don't want to have to type your name and password every time you start or restart your Mac (or even if you do), check out Chapter 13 for the scoop on how to turn the login screen on or off.

Either way, the Desktop soon materializes before your eyes. If you haven't customized, configured, or tinkered with your Desktop, it should look something like Figure 1-2. Now is a good time to take a moment for positive thoughts about the person who convinced you that you wanted a Mac. That person was right!

Figure 1-2:
The Mac OS X Desktop after a brand-spanking-new installation of OS X.

✔ **Sad Mac:** If any of your hardware fails when it's tested, you could see a black or gray screen that may or may not display the dreaded Sad Mac icon (shown in the left margin) and/or hear a far less pleasing musical chord (in the key of F-minor, I believe), known by Mac aficionados as the *Chimes of Doom.*

Some older Macs played the sound of a horrible car wreck instead of the chimes, complete with crying tires and busting glass. It was exceptionally unnerving, which may be why Apple doesn't use it anymore.

The fact that something went wrong is no reflection on your prowess as a Macintosh user. Something inside your Mac is broken, and it probably needs to go in for repairs (usually to an Apple dealer). If any of that's already happened to you, check out Chapter 16 to try to get your Mac well again.

If your computer is under warranty, dial 1-800-SOS-APPL, and a customer-service person can tell you what to do. Before you do anything, though, skip ahead to Chapter 15. It's entirely possible that one of the suggestions there can get you back on track without you having to spend even a moment on hold.

✔ **Prohibitory sign (formerly known as the flashing-question-mark disk):** Although it's unlikely that you'll ever see the sad Mac, most users eventually encounter the prohibitory sign shown in the left margin (which replaced the flashing question-mark-on-a-disk icon and flashing folder icon back in OS X 10.2 Jaguar). This icon means your Mac can't find a startup disk, hard drive, network server, or CD-ROM containing a valid Macintosh operating system. See Chapter 15 for ways you can try to ease your Mac's ills.

How do you know which version of the Mac OS your computer has? Simple. Just choose About This Mac from the menu (that's the menu with the symbol in the upper-left corner of the Finder menu bar). The About This Mac window pops up on your screen, as shown in Figure 1-3. The version you're running appears just below *Mac OS X* in the center of the window. Click the More Info button to launch the System Profiler application, which has much more information, including processor speed, bus speed, number of processors, caches, installed memory, networking, storage devices, and much more. You can find more about this useful program in Chapter 11.

Figure 1-3:
See which version of Mac OS X you're running.

The legend of the boot

Boot this. *Boot* that. "I *booted* my Mac and. . . ." or "Did it *boot*?" and so on. Talking about computers for long without hearing the *boot* word is nearly impossible.

But why *boot*? Why not *shoe* or *shirt* or even *shazam*?

Back in the very olden days — maybe the 1960s or a little earlier — starting up a computer required you to toggle little manual switches on the front panel, which began an internal process that loaded the operating system. The process became known as *bootstrapping* because if you toggled the right switches, the

computer would "pull itself up by its bootstraps." This phrase didn't take long to transmogrify into *booting* and finally to *boot*.

Over the years, *booting* has come to mean turning on almost any computer or even a peripheral device, such as a printer. Some people also use it to refer to launching an application: "I booted Excel."

So the next time one of your gearhead friends says the *b*-word, ask whether he knows where the term comes from. Then dazzle him with the depth and breadth of your (not-quite-useful) knowledge!

Shutting down properly

Turning off the power without shutting down your Mac properly is one of the worst things you can do to your poor Mac. Shutting down your Mac improperly can really screw up your hard drive, scramble the contents of your most important files, or both.

If a thunderstorm is rumbling nearby or if you're unfortunate enough to have rolling blackouts where you live, you may *really* want to shut down your Mac. (See the next section where I briefly discuss lightning and your Mac.)

To turn off your Mac, always use the Shut Down command on the menu (which I discuss in Chapter 3), or you can shut down in one of these kind-and-gentle ways:

- ✔ Press the Power key once and then click the Shut Down button.

- ✔ On Apple Pro keyboards, which don't have a Power key, press Control+Eject instead, and then click the Shut Down button that appears (or press the Return key, which does the same thing).

Of course, most of us have broken this rule several times without anything horrible happening — but don't be lulled into a false sense of security. Break the rules one time too many (or under the wrong circumstances), and your most important file *will* be toast. The only times you should turn off your Mac without shutting down properly is if your screen is frozen or if you crash and you've already tried everything else. (See Chapter 15 for what those "everything elses" are.) A really stubborn crash doesn't happen often — and less often under OS X than ever before — but when it does, turning your Mac off

---

Eternally yours . . . *now*

Mac OS X is designed so you never have to shut it down. You can configure it to sleep after a specified period of inactivity. (See Chapter 13 for more info on the Energy Saver features of OS X.) If you do so, your Mac will consume very little electricity when it's sleeping and will be ready to use just a few seconds after you awaken it (by pressing any key or clicking the mouse). On the other hand, if you're not going to be using it for a few days, you may want to shut it down anyway.

Note: If you leave your Mac on constantly and you're gone when a lightning storm or rolling

blackout hits, your Mac may get wasted. So be sure you have adequate protection (say, a decent surge protector designed specifically for computers) if you decide to leave your Mac on and unattended for long periods. See the section "A few things you should definitely NOT do with your Mac" (elsewhere in this chapter) for more info on lightning and your Mac. Frankly, if I plan to be away from mine for more than a day, I usually shut it down, just in case. But because OS X is designed to run 24/7, I don't shut it down at night unless it's dark and stormy.

and then back on may be the only solution. Sometimes even that doesn't work, and you may have to unplug the computer from the power outlet, wait a moment or two, and then plug it back in to get it to reboot.

A few things you should definitely NOT do with your Mac

In this section, I deal with the bad stuff that can happen to your computer if you do the wrong things with it. If something bad has already happened to you — I know . . . I'm beginning to sound like a broken record — see Chapter 15.

✔ **Don't unplug your Mac when it's turned on.** Very bad things can happen, such as having your operating system break. See the preceding section, where I discuss shutting your system down properly.

✔ **Don't use your Mac when lightning is near.** Here's a simple life equation for you: Mac + lightning = dead Mac. 'Nuff said. Oh, and don't place much faith in inexpensive surge protectors. A good jolt of lightning will fry the surge protector right along with your computer — as well as possibly frying your modem, printer, and anything else plugged into it. Some surge protectors can withstand most lightning strikes, but these warriors aren't the cheapies that you buy at your local computer emporium. Unplugging your Mac from the wall during electrical storms is safer and less expensive. (Don't forget to unplug your external modem, network hubs, printers, or other hardware that plugs into the wall as well — lightning can fry them, too.)

✔ **Don't jostle, bump, shake, kick, throw, dribble, or punt your Mac, especially while it's running.** Your Mac contains a hard drive that spins at 4,200+ revolutions per minute (rpm) or more. A jolt to a hard drive while it's reading or writing a file can cause the head to crash into the disk, which can render many (or all) files on it unrecoverable. Ouch!

✔ **Don't forget to back up your data!** I beg you: Please read Chapter 8 now before something horrible happens to your valuable data! If the stuff on your hard drive means anything to you, you must back it up. Not maybe. You must. Even if your most important file is your last saved game of Tony Hawk Pro Skater 2, you still need to realize how important it is to back up your files.

In Chapter 8, I discuss how to back up your files, and I *strongly* recommend that you read Chapter 8 sooner rather than later — preferably before you do any significant work on your Mac. Dr. Macintosh sez: "There are only two kinds of Mac users: Those who have never lost data and those who will." Which kind will you be?

✔ **Don't kiss your monitor while wearing stuff on your lips.** For obvious reasons! Use a soft cloth and/or the Klear Screen polish and wipes that Apple recommends if you need to clean your display.

Point-and-click boot camp

Are you new to the Mac? Just learning how to move the mouse around? Now is a good time to go over some fundamental stuff that you need to know for just about everything you'll be doing on the Mac. Spend a few minutes reading this section, and soon you'll be clicking, double-clicking, pressing, and pointing all over the place. If you think you've got the whole mousing thing pretty much figured out, feel free to skip this section. I'll catch you on the other side.

Still with me? Good. Now for some basic terminology.

✓ **Point:** Before you can click or press anything, you have to *point* to it. Place your hand on your mouse and move it so that the cursor arrow is over the object you want — like on top of an icon or a button. Then click the mouse to select the object or double-click it to run it (if it's an application or an icon that starts up an application). You point and then you click — *point-and-click,* in computer lingo.

✓ **Click:** (Also called *single-click.*) Use your index finger to push the mouse button all the way down and then let go so it produces a satisfying clicking sound. (If you have one of the new optical Apple Pro mice, you push down the whole thing to click.) Use a single-click to highlight an icon, press a button, or activate a check box or window.

✓ **Double-click:** *Click twice* in rapid succession. With a little practice, you can perfect this technique in no time. Use a double-click to open a folder or to launch a file or application.

✓ **Control-click:** Hold down the Control key while single-clicking. Control-clicking is the same as right-clicking on a Windows system and displays a menu (called a *contextual menu*) where you Control-clicked. In fact, if you are blessed with a two-or-more-button mouse (I personally use the four-button Kensington Expert Mouse Pro Trackball, and recommend it highly), you can right-click and avoid having to hold down the Control key.

✓ **Drag:** *Dragging* something usually means you have to click it first and hold the mouse button down. Then you move the mouse on your desk or mouse pad so the cursor — and whatever you select — moves across the screen. The combination of holding down the button and dragging the mouse it is usually referred to as *click-and-drag.*

✓ **Press:** A *press* is half a click. Instead of letting go of the mouse button to finish the click, keep holding it down. In most cases, your next step is to drag the mouse somewhere — say, down a menu to choose a command, or across the screen to move an object.

✓ **Choosing an item from a menu:** To get to Mac OS menu commands, you must first open a menu and then pick the option you want. Point at the name of the menu you want with your mouse cursor, press your mouse button down, and then drag your mouse downward until you select the command you want. When the command is highlighted, finish selecting by letting go of the mouse button.

If you're a long-time Mac user, you probably hold down the mouse button the whole time between clicking the name of the menu and selecting the command you want. You can still do it that way, but you can also click once on the menu name to open it, release the mouse button, and then drag down to the item you want to select *and then click again*. In other words, OS X menus stay open for a few seconds after you click them, even if you're not holding down the mouse button. Go ahead and give it a try . . . I'll wait.

Touring the Desktop

Just about everything you do on your Mac begins and ends with the Desktop. This is where you manage files, store documents, launch programs, adjust the way your Mac works, and much more. If you ever expect to master your Mac, the first step is to master the Desktop.

Some folks use the terms *Desktop* and *Finder* interchangeably to refer to the total Macintosh environment you see — icons, windows, menus, and all that other cool stuff. Just to make things confusing, the background you see on your screen — the backdrop behind your hard drive icon and open windows — is also called the Desktop. In this book, I refer to the *Finder* as the Finder, which I discuss in Chapters 4 and 5. When I say *Desktop,* I'm talking about the background behind your windows and Dock.

Got it? The Desktop is convenient and fast. Put stuff there.

Check out the default Mac Desktop for OS X in Figure 1-4.

The Desktop is the center of your Mac OS experience, so before I go any farther, here's a quick description of its most prominent features:

✔ **Desktop:** The *Desktop* is the area behind the windows and the Dock, where your hard drive icon (ordinarily) lives. The Desktop isn't a window, yet it acts like one. Like a folder window or drive window, the Desktop can contain icons. But unlike most windows, which require a bit of navigation to get to, the Desktop is a great place for things you use a lot, such as folders, applications, or particular documents. The next section discusses the default icons you see on the Desktop when you first load up OS X.

✔ **Dock:** The *Dock* is the Finder's main navigation shortcut tool. It makes getting to frequently used icons easy, even when you have a screen full of windows. Like the Desktop, the Dock is a great place for things you use a lot, such as folders, applications, or particular documents. Besides putting your frequently used icons at your fingertips, it's almost infinitely customizable, too; read more about it in Chapter 2.

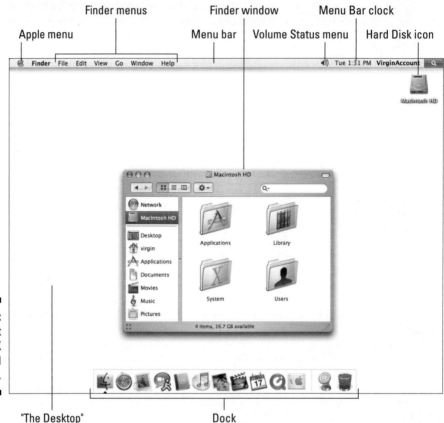

Apple menu   Finder menus   Finder window   Menu Bar clock

Menu bar   Volume Status menu   Hard Disk icon

Figure 1-4:
The default
Mac OS X
Finder and
Desktop.

"The Desktop"   Dock

If you used an earlier version of Mac OS, think of the Dock as the OS X version of the Apple menu in Mac OS versions of the past. Yes, the OS X Finder *does* have an Apple menu, but it doesn't work at all like the Apple menu in earlier versions of Mac OS. See Chapter 3 for more info on the Apple menu.

✔ **Icons:** *Icons* are the little pictures you see in your windows and even on your Desktop. Most icons are containers that hold things you work with on your Mac, such as programs and documents, which are also represented by — you guessed it — icons. In Chapter 2, I cover icons in detail, and the next section discusses the icons you see on the OS X Desktop when you first boot up your Mac.

✔ **Aliases:** Use *aliases* of things that you use often so you can keep the originals tucked away in one of your perfectly organized folders. Check out aliases in Chapter 2.

✔ **Windows:** Opening most icons (by double-clicking them) makes a window appear. Windows in the Finder show you the contents of hard drive and folder icons, and windows in applications usually show you the contents of your documents. For the full scoop on Tiger windows, which are very different from Mac windows in previous OS releases, check out Chapter 3.

✔ **Menus:** *Menus* let you choose to do things, such as create new folders; duplicate files; cut, copy, or paste text; and so on. Find out all about them in Chapter 3.

If all these new terms such as *alias, Dock,* and so on seem strange to you, don't worry — I explain them all in detail in the rest of Part I.

Sniffing Out the Default Desktop Icons

Icons on the Desktop behave the same as icons in a window. You move them and copy them just like you would an icon in a window. The only difference is that Desktop items aren't in a window: They're on the Desktop, which makes them more convenient to use.

Actually, if you look at your Home directory (click the Home button on any Finder window toolbar or use the shortcut ⌘+Shift+H to open a window displaying Home), you see a folder named *Desktop,* which contains the same icons you place on the Desktop (but not the hard-drive icons). The reason for this folder is that each user has an individual Desktop. But I'm getting ahead of myself. You find out much more about Home, users, and all that jazz in upcoming chapters.

To move an item to the Desktop, simply click its icon in any window and then, without releasing the mouse button, drag it out of the window and onto the Desktop; then release the mouse button. If you don't see a disk icon on your Desktop, skip ahead to Chapter 3, where I discuss Finder Preferences. That's where you can choose whether to see disks on your Desktop.

✔ **Hard drive icons:** The first icon you should get to know is the icon for your hard drive (refer to Figure 1-4). You can usually find it on the upper-right side of the desktop when you first start the Mac. Look for the name Macintosh HD, iMac HD, or something like that, unless you've already renamed it. (I renamed my hard drive TigerDisk in Figure 1-5.)

There are two ways to rename your hard drive:

• **Single-click the icon's name. When the name highlights (as shown in the middle icon in Figure 1-5), type its new name.**

If you click directly on the icon instead of its name, the icon will be selected but the name won't become highlighted for editing, as shown in the icon on the right in Figure 1-5.

or

• **Single-click the icon itself, press Return or Enter, and then type in a new name for the drive.**

Figure 1-5:
An
unselected
icon (left); an
icon with its
name
selected
(middle); an
icon that is
selected
(right).

Macintosh HD   TigerDisk   Macintosh HD

✔ **Disk icons:** These appear on the Desktop by default. When you insert a CD or DVD, its icon appears on the Desktop just below your hard-drive icon (space permitting).

Picture This: A Picture on Your Desktop

I'd be remiss if I didn't mention that you can change the background picture of your Desktop.

In Figure 1-6, you can see my Desktop with a background picture I made to celebrate the release of the book before this one, *GarageBand For Dummies* (Wiley). If you want a reminder of what the default Desktop background looks like, refer to Figure 1-4.

Here's how you can change your Desktop picture if you care to:

1. **From the Desktop, choose ⌘➪System Preferences or click the System Preferences icon in the Dock.**

   The System Preferences window appears.

2. **Click the Desktop & Screen Saver icon.**

   The Desktop & Screen Saver Preferences pane appears as shown in Figure 1-7.

3. **Click on any picture in your Home/Pictures folder.**

   I'm clicking a picture called `drmacandbandtxt` in Figure 1-7. You can see it's one of the items in my Home/Pictures folder, which is also shown in Figure 1-7.

Figure 1-6:
My
beautified
Desktop.

Figure 1-7:
Selecting a
Desktop
picture from
my Home/
Pictures
folder.

There are at least two other ways to change your Desktop picture:

✔ Drag a picture file from the Finder onto the *picture well* (the little rectangular picture to the left of the picture's name (`drmacandbandtxt` in Figure 1-7).

or

✔ Select the Choose Folder item in the list of folders on the left side of the Desktop & Screen Saver System Preference pane and then select a folder using the standard Open File dialog. That folder then appears in the list; you can use any picture files it contains for your Desktop picture.

If you don't know how to choose a folder that way, look in Chapter 5. And for more info on using System Preferences, check out Chapter 13.

Chapter 2

I Think Icon, I Think Icon . . .

*I*n this chapter, I start with the Dock — a special, always-running application that displays icons for quick access to frequently used applications, folders, and even disks. (Dock icons are also a quick way to bring a hidden window or application to the front so you can work with it again.) I also show you how to customize your Dock so it works and looks just the way you want it to.

Then we delve deeper into icons, which are a fundamental part of what makes a Mac a Mac. I may have said a word or two about icons already, but this time I'm giving you the real nitty-gritty — everything you need to know about all the icons you'll encounter while using Mac OS X Tiger.

What You Get (In a Stock Dock)

Take a minute to look at the row of icons at the bottom of your display. That row, ladies and gentlemen, is the Dock (shown in Figure 2-1), and those individual pictures are known as icons (which I will discuss in greater detail momentarily).

 Dock icons are odd ducks — they're activated with a single-click. You'll find that most other icons are *selected* (highlighted) when you single click, and *opened* when you double-click. So Dock icons are kind of like links on a Web page — you only need a single click to open them.

Figure 2-1:
The Dock
and all its
default
icons.

A quick introduction to using the Dock

Single-click a Dock icon to open the item it represents. If the item is an application, the application will open and become active; if the item is a document, that document will open in its appropriate application, which will become the active application; if it's a folder icon, the folder will open and the Finder will become the active application. If the item is open already when you click its Dock icon, it becomes active.

You can tell whether an application is open (running) by looking for the small triangle beneath its Dock icon; you can see one under the Finder icon at the far left in Figure 2-1.

When you press (click but don't let go) Dock icons, a menu appears, as shown in Figures 2-2 and 2-3.

Figure 2-2:
Press and
hold on an
Application
icon in the
Dock and
a menu
appears.

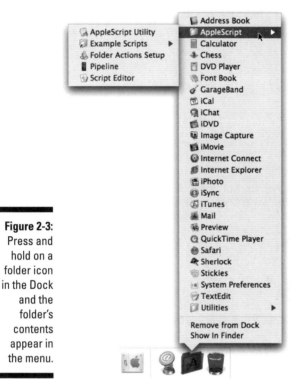

Figure 2-3:
Press and
hold on a
folder icon
in the Dock
and the
folder's
contents
appear in
the menu.

In addition to useful program-specific commands (as you see in the iTunes Dock menu in Figure 2-2), Dock menus for applications that have multiple windows offer a list of windows in their menus, as shown in Figure 2-4.

Figure 2-4:
If an
application
has multiple
windows, its
Dock menu
lets you
choose the
one you
want.

Control-clicking a Dock icon gives you the same result as press-and-hold. The cool part is that the menu pops up immediately when you Control-click.

The default icons of the Dock

By default, the Dock contains a number of commonly used Mac OS X applications, and you can also store your own applications, files, or folders there. (I show you how to do that in the "Adding an icon to the Dock" section later in this chapter.)

But first, look at the items you find on a stock OS X Tiger Dock. If they aren't familiar to you, they certainly will be as you get to know Mac OS X.

In the Introduction to this book, I said I couldn't do justice to all the programs that come with Mac OS X Tiger that aren't, strictly speaking, part of the operating system. Alas, some of the programs in the default Dock are ones we won't be seeing much more of. But I'd hate to leave you wondering what all those icons in the Dock are, so Table 2-1 gives you a brief description of each stock Dock icon (moving from left to right on-screen). If there is additional coverage of an item elsewhere in the book, the table tells you where.

Table 2-1		**Icons on the Dock**	
Icon	*Name*	*What It Is*	*Go Here for More Info*
	Finder	The always-running application that manages the Desktop, files, folders, disks, and more.	Chapters 3 and 4
	Dashboard	Apple's layer containing small special-use applications called "widgets."	Chapter 11
	Mail	Apple's e-mail program.	Chapter 9
	Safari	Apple's Web browser.	Chapter 9
	iChat	Apple's instant messaging program.	Chapter 9
	Address Book	Apple's address book application.	n/a

Icon	Name	What It Is	Go Here for More Info
	iTunes	Apple's audio player and iPod manager. (Part of iLife package.)	n/a
	iCal	iCal is Apple's calendar program.	n/a
	QuickTime Player	Apple's multimedia player for movies, audio, and streaming audio and video.	n/a
	System Preferences	The System Preferences application lets you configure many aspects of the way your Mac works so they're just the way you like them.	Chapter 13
	Apple — Mac OS X	The Apple — Mac OS X icon launches your Web browser (Safari) and takes you to the Mac OS X section of Apple's Web site.	n/a
	Trash	The Trash icon is not a file or application that you open. Instead, you drag files and folders onto this icon to get rid of them, or drag removable discs onto it to eject them.	The next section

If you bought a new Mac with Tiger pre-installed, you may or may not see icons for the iLife applications — iMovie, iDVD, iPhoto, and GarageBand — in your Dock. It was unclear at press time if EVERY new Mac shipped with Tiger on it was going to also include the iLife suite.

Don't want it? Trash it

The Trash icon is unique among Dock items: It's not a file or application that you open. Instead, you drag things to this icon to get rid of them.

The *Trash* is a special container where you put the icons that you no longer want on your hard drive or removable media storage device (such as Zip or floppy disk). Got four copies of TextEdit on your hard drive? Drag three of them to the Trash. Tired of tripping over old letters that you don't want to keep? Drag them to the Trash, too. To put something in the Trash, just drag its icon on top of the Trash icon and watch it disappear.

Like other icons, you know that you've connected with the Trash while dragging when the icon is highlighted. And like other Dock icons, the Trash icon's name appears when you move the cursor over the icon.

You know how the garbage in the can in your garage sits there until the sanitation engineers come by and pick it up each Thursday? The Mac OS X Trash works the same. When you put something in the Trash, it sits there until you choose the Finder⇨Empty Trash command or use the keyboard shortcut ⌘+Shift+Delete.

While items sit in the Trash waiting for you to empty it, the Trash basket shows you that it has files waiting for you there . . . as in real life, your unemptied Trash is full of crumpled papers.

You can also empty the Trash from the Dock by pressing the mouse button and holding it down on the Trash icon for a second or two. The Empty Trash menu pops up like magic. Move your mouse over it to select it and then release the mouse button.

Think twice before you invoke the Empty Trash command. After you empty the Trash, the files that it contained are (usually) gone forever. My advice: Before you get too bold, read Chapter 8 and back up your hard drive several times. After you get proficient at backups, chances improve greatly that even though the files are technically gone forever from your hard drive, you can get them back if you like (at least in theory).

As with all icons, you can open the Trash to see what's in there — just click its icon in the Dock. If you decide that you don't want to get rid of an item that's already in the Trash, just drag it back out, either onto the Desktop or back into the folder where it belongs.

Delving Deeper into the Dock

In this section, I tell you all about the Dock — how to use it, how to customize it, how to resize it, and more.

The Dock is a convenient way to get at oft-used icons. By default, the Dock comes pre-stocked with icons that Apple thinks you'll need most frequently (refer to Table 2-1), but you can customize it to contain any icons that you choose, as you'll see in the following sections.

More about Dock icons

Dock icons work like other icons — except instead of double-clicking them, you single-click them. Note that when you single-click a Dock, it moves up and out of its place on the Dock for a moment, letting you know that you've activated it. Check out Figure 2-5 to see an animated Dock icon — it's still on the Dock, but it appears raised higher than the inactive icons.

Figure 2-5:
A raised
Dock icon
(middle)
with before
(left) and
after (right)
shots.

Many Dock icons also do a little bouncy dance when that program isn't active (that is, its menu bar isn't showing and it's not the frontmost program) to inform you that it desires your attention. If you notice that the icon for an open application is dancing, give it a click to find out what it wants.

When an application on the Dock is open, an up-arrow (which looks like a small black pyramid) appears below its Dock icon, as shown on the right in Figure 2-5.

To discover the name of a Dock icon, just move your cursor over any item on the Dock, and the item's name appears above it (as shown in the middle of Figure 2-5). This feature is quite handy because you can't view Dock items as a list in the same the way that you can with icons that are stored in windows. And, as you can read in the section "Resizing the Dock" later in this chapter, you can resize the Dock to make the icons smaller (which does make them more difficult to see). Hovering your mouse cursor to discover the name of a teeny icon makes this feature even more useful.

Resizing the Dock

If the default size of the Dock bugs you, you can make the Dock smaller and save yourself a lot of screen real estate. This space comes in especially handy when you add your own stuff to the Dock.

To shrink or enlarge the Dock (and its icons) without opening the Dock Preferences window, drag its sizer handle. To make the sizer appear (as shown in the left margin), move your cursor over the thin line that you find on the right side of the Dock. Drag the sizer down to make the Dock smaller, holding down the mouse button until you find the size you like. The more you drag this control down, the smaller the Dock gets. To enlarge the Dock again, just drag the sizer back up. Poof! Big Dock! You can enlarge the Dock until it fills your screen from side to side.

Adding and removing Dock icons

You can customize your Dock with favorite applications, a document you update daily, or maybe a folder containing your favorite recipes — use the Dock for anything you need quick access to. The following sections tell you how to add an icon to the Dock, how to remove a Dock icon you no longer desire, as well as what kind of stuff you might want to put in your Dock.

Adding an icon to the Dock

Adding an application, file, or folder to the Dock is as easy as 1-2-3. First, open a Finder window that contains an application, file, folder, URL, or disk icon that you use frequently. Then follow these steps to add it to the Dock:

1. **Click the item you want to add to the Dock.**

   As shown in Figure 2-6, I chose the StuffIt Expander application (it's highlighted). I use StuffIt Expander constantly to decompress archives of files received in e-mail or downloaded from newsgroups on the Internet. (Find the StuffIt Expander application, if you're interested, in the Utilities folder inside your Applications folder.)

2. **Drag the icon out of the Finder window and onto the Dock.**

3. **An icon for this item now appears on the Dock.**

   Folder, disk, and URL icons must be on the right of the divider line in the Dock; Application icons must be on the left of it. Why does the Dock force these rules upon you? I suppose someone at Apple thinks this is what's best for you — who knows? — but that's the rule: apps on the left, folders, disks, and URLs on the right.

You can add several items at the same time to the Dock by selecting them all and dragging the group to the Dock. However, you can delete only one icon at a time from the Dock.

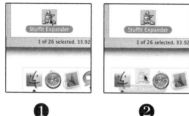 

Figure 2-6:
Drag an
icon onto
the Dock
to add it.

❶ ❷ ❸

Removing an icon from the Dock

To remove an item from the Dock, just drag its icon onto the Desktop. It disappears with a cool *poof* animation, as shown in Figure 2-7.

Figure 2-7:
To remove
an icon,
drag it off
the Dock
and
POOF —
it's gone.

By moving an icon out of the Dock, you aren't moving, deleting, or copying the item itself — you're just removing its icon from the Dock. The item is unchanged. Think of it like a library catalog card: Just because you remove the card from the card catalog doesn't mean that the book is gone from the library.

When you open an application with an icon that doesn't ordinarily appear on the Dock, its icon magically appears on the Dock until you quit that application. And when you quit, its icon magically disappears from the Dock. In other words, you see a temporary Dock icon for every program that's currently open; these temporary icons disappear when you quit the program.

If you want to keep an icon in the Dock permanently, you have two ways to tell it to stay around after you quit the program. You can Control-click (or click-and-hold) and then choose Keep in Dock from the menu that pops up, or you can drag the icon (for an application that's currently open) off and then back onto the Dock (or to a different position on the Dock) without letting go of the mouse button.

Another useful Dock menu option is Show in Finder; it opens the window containing the item and thoughtfully selects the item for you.

Last, but certainly not least, you can drag a document icon onto an application's Dock icon. If the application knows how to handle that type of document, its Dock icon will highlight and the document will open in that application. If the application can't handle that particular type of document, the Dock icon won't highlight and you can't drop the document on it.

I'm getting ahead of myself here, but if that happens to you, try opening the document this way: Select the icon and choose File⇨Open With or control-click the document icon and use the Open With menu to choose the application you want the document opened with.

What should you put in your Dock?

Put things on the Dock that you need quick access to and that you use often, or add items that aren't quickly available from menus or the sidebar. If you like using the Dock better than the Finder window sidebar, for example, add your Documents, Movies, Pictures, Music, or even your hard disk to the Dock.

I suggest adding these items to your Dock:

- ✔ **A word-processing application:** Most people use word processing software more than any other application.

- ✔ **A project folder:** You know, the folder that contains all the documents for your thesis, or the biggest project you have at work, or your massive recipe collection . . . whatever. Add that folder to the Dock and then you can access it much quicker than if you have to open several folders to find it.

Don't forget — if you *press* (click but don't let go) on a folder icon, a handy hierarchical menu of its contents appears, as shown in Figure 2-4. Better still, the same goes for disk icons. Figure 2-8 shows my hard disk's contents as a Dock menu. Give this trick a try — it's great.

- ✔ **A special utility or application:** StuffIt Expander is an essential part of my work because I receive a lot of stuffed and zipped files. You may also want to add AOL, or your favorite graphics application such as Photoshop, or the game you play every afternoon when you think the boss isn't watching.

- ✔ **Your favorite URLs:** Save links to sites that you visit every day — ones that you use in your job, your favorite Mac news sites, or your personalized page from an Internet service provider (ISP). Sure, you can make one of these pages your browser's start page or bookmark it, but the Dock lets you add one or more additional URLs.

Here's how to quickly add a URL to the Dock. Open Safari and go to the page with a URL that you want to save on the Dock. Click and drag the small icon that you find at the left of the URL in the Address bar to the right side of the dividing line in the Dock (at the arrow's head in Figure 2-9) and then release the mouse button. The icons in the Dock will slide over and make room for your URL. From now on, when you click the URL icon that you moved to your Dock, Safari opens to that page.

You can add several URL icons to the Dock, but bear in mind that the Dock and its icons shrink to accommodate added icons, thus making them harder to see. Perhaps the best idea — if you want easy access to several URLs — is to create a folder full of URLs and put that folder on the Dock. Then you can just press and hold your mouse pointer on the folder (or Control-click the folder) to pop up a menu with all your URLs.

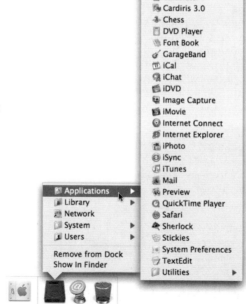

Figure 2-8: The contents of my hard disk appear in this handy menu when I press and hold (or Control-click) on its Dock icon.

Even though you can make the Dock smaller, you're still limited to one row of icons. The smaller you make the Dock, the larger the crowd of icons you can amass. You have to determine for yourself what's best for you: having lots of icons available on the Dock (even though they may be difficult to see because they're so tiny) or having less clutter but fewer icons on your Dock.

Figure 2-9:
To save a
URL to your
Dock, drag
its little icon
from the
Address bar
to the right
side of
the Dock.

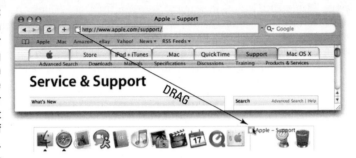

After you figure out which programs you use and don't use, it's a good idea to relieve overcrowding by removing the ones you never (or rarely) use.

Setting your Dock preferences

You can change a few things about the Dock to make it look and behave just the way you want it to. To do so, just choose Dock⇨Dock Preferences from the menu (or the *Apple menu,* meaning the menu beneath that symbol in the upper-left corner of the Finder menu bar). The System Preferences application opens, showing an active Dock pane (see Figure 2-10).

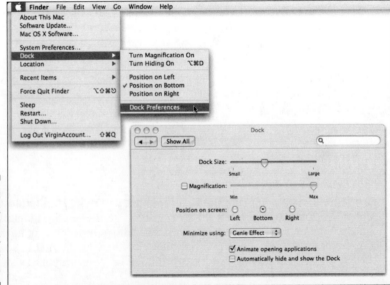

Figure 2-10:
The Dock
menu and
Dock
Preferences
window.

Now you can adjust your Dock with the following preferences:

- **Dock Size:** Note the slider bar here. Move this slider to the right (larger) or left (smaller) to adjust the size of the Dock on your Finder. As you move the slider, watch the Dock change size. (Now *there's* a fun way to spend a Saturday afternoon!)

  As you add items to the Dock, each icon — and the Dock itself — shrinks to accommodate the new ones.

- **Magnification:** This slider controls how big icons grow when you pass the arrow cursor over them. Or you can deselect this check box to turn off magnification entirely.

- **Position on Screen:** Choose from these three radio buttons to attach the Dock to the left side, the right side, or the bottom of your screen (the default). Personally, I prefer it on the right side of the screen.

- **Minimize Using:** Select, from this handy pop-up menu (PC users would call it a drop-*down* list, but what the heck, there's no gravity in a computer screen anyway), the visual effect (animation) that you see when you click a window's Minimize button (the yellow gumdrop). The Genie Effect is the default, but the Scale Effect seems a bit faster to me.

- **Animate Opening Applications:** Mac OS X animates (bounces) Dock icons when you click them to open an item. If you don't like the animation, deselect this check box, and the bouncing will cease evermore.

- **Automatically Hide and Show the Dock:** Don't like the Dock? Maybe you want to free up the screen real estate at the bottom of your monitor? Then select the Automatically Hide and Show the Dock check box; after that, the Dock displays itself only when you move the cursor (mouse) to the bottom of the screen where the dock would ordinarily appear. It's like magic! (Okay, it's like Windows that way, but I hate to admit it.)

If the Dock isn't visible, *deselect* (that is, uncheck) this Automatically Hide and Show the Dock check box to bring it back. The option remains turned off unless you change it or choose Dock➪Turn Hiding Off from the menu (or press ⌘+Option+D).

Other Icons in OS X Tiger

Icons are not just used by the Dock, of course. They're those funny little pictographs you see in Finder windows that represent things you work with on your Mac, such as programs, documents, and folders.

Don't confuse the icons you see in Finder windows with Dock icons — they're two different animals. Dock icons are like buttons — you click them once and something (a file, an application, or a folder) opens. The truth is, *Dock icons* are a special type of alias (discussed shortly); they're simply pointers to items on your hard drive. *Icons* in Finder windows, on the other hand, represent real things on your hard drive — your folders, applications, and documents. The big difference, though, is that you can select regular icons with a single click and open them with a double click; Dock icons can't be selected, and you click just once to open them.

For what it's worth, toolbar icons (in Finder windows — discussed in Chapter 4) are the same as Dock icons — they open items on your hard drive with a single (instead of a double) click.

Anyway, to avoid any confusion, from now on I'll refer to Dock icons (and toolbar icons and any other icons that open with a single click) as *buttons*, reserving the term *icons* for the little picture-thingies in Finder windows and on the Desktop.

Finder icons come in several shapes and sizes. After you've been around the Macintosh for a while, you develop a sixth sense about what an icon contains, and know just by looking at it. The three main types of icons are applications, documents, and folders.

Well, there are actually four types — aliases are an icon type in their own right. But don't worry: I show you all four icon types right now:

- ✔ **Application icons** are *programs* — the software that you use to accomplish tasks on your Mac. Your word processor is an application. So are (for example) America Online (AOL) and Adobe Photoshop. For that matter, *Halo* and *Unreal Tournament* are also applications (and great games to boot).

  Application icons come in a variety of shapes. For example, application (that is, program) icons are often square-ish. Sometimes they're diamond-shaped, rectangular, or just oddly shaped. In Figure 2-11, you can see application icons of various shapes.

- ✔ **Document icons** are files that are created by applications. A letter to your mom, which you create in AppleWorks (formerly known as ClarisWorks), is a document. So are my latest column and my Quicken data files. Document icons are almost always reminiscent of a piece of paper, as shown in Figure 2-12.

- ✔ **Folder icons** are the Mac's organizational containers. You can put icons — and the applications or documents they stand for — into folders. You can also put folders inside other folders. Folders look like . . . well, manila folders (what a concept) . . . and can contain just about any other icon.

You use folders to organize your files and applications on your hard drive. You can have as many folders as you want, so don't be afraid to create new ones. The thought behind the whole folders thing is pretty obvious — if your hard drive is a filing cabinet, folders are its drawers and folders (duh!). Figure 2-13 shows some typical folder icons.

✔ **Aliases** are wonderful — no, *fabulous* — organizational tools that Apple introduced in the days of Mac OS 7. (Although Mac OS 7 was originally called *System* 7, Apple didn't begin the Mac *OS* designation until version 7.6.) I like aliases so much, in fact, that I think they deserve their very own section. Read on for more info on this ultra-useful tool.

Figure 2-11: Application icons come in many different shapes.

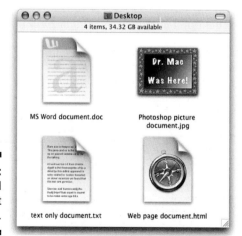

Figure 2-12: Typical document icons.

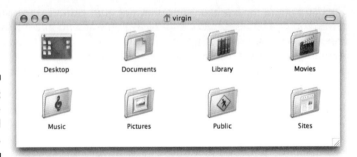

Figure 2-13:
Some run-of-the-mill folder icons.

Aliases: Greatest Thing Since Sliced Bread

An *alias* is a tiny file that automatically opens the file that it represents. Although an alias is technically an icon, it's actually an icon that opens another icon automatically. You can put aliases in convenient places, such as on the Desktop, to help you easily open programs and files that you access often.

In effect, Microsoft stole the alias feature from Apple (if you've used Windows, you may know aliases as *shortcuts*). But what else is new? And, for what it's worth, aliases usually don't break when you move or rename the original file; shortcuts do.

An alias is different from a duplicated file. For example, the Microsoft Word 2004 application uses 19.4 megabytes (MB) of disk space. A *duplicate* of Microsoft Word 2004 would give me two files, each requiring nearly 20 megabytes of space on my hard drive. An *alias* of Microsoft Word 2004, on the other hand, uses a mere 52 kilobytes (KB).

Why else do I think that aliases are so great? Well, they open any file or folder on any disk from anywhere else on any disk — which is a very good trick. But there are many other reasons I think aliases rock:

✔ **Convenience:** Aliases enable you to make items appear to be in more than one place, which on many occasions is exactly what you want to do. For example, keeping an alias of your word processor on your Desktop and another on the Dock is convenient. You may even want a third alias of it in your Documents folder for quick access. Aliases enable you to open your word processor quickly and easily without navigating into the depths of your Applications folder each time that you need it.

✔ **Flexibility and organization:** You can create aliases and store them anywhere on your hard disk to represent the same document in several different folders. This is a great help when you need to file a document that can logically be stored in any one of several files. For example: If you write a memo to Fred Smith about the Smythe Marketing Campaign to be executed in the fourth quarter, which folder does the document go in? Smith? Smythe? Marketing? Memos? 4th Quarter? Correct answer: With aliases, it can go in all the above if you like. Then you'll find the memo wherever you look, instead of guessing which folder it was filed in.

With aliases, it doesn't matter. You can put the actual file in any folder and then create aliases of the file, placing them in any other applicable folder.

✔ **Integrity:** Some programs must remain in the same folder as their supporting files and folders. Many Classic programs, for example, won't function properly unless they're in the same folder as their dictionaries, thesauruses, data files (for games), templates, and so on. Thus you can't put the icon for those programs on the Desktop without impairing their functionality. An alias lets you access a program like that from anywhere on your hard disk.

Creating aliases

When you create an alias, its icon looks the same as the icon that it represents, but the suffix *alias* is tacked onto its name and a tiny arrow called a *badge* appears in the lower-left corner of its icon. Figure 2-14 shows both an alias and its *parent* icon (that is, the icon that opens if you open the alias).

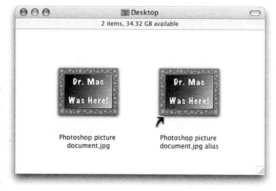

Figure 2-14:
An alias
icon (right)
and its
parent.

Dr. Mac's temporary alias theory

The Desktop is an excellent place to keep things you need most often — whether you use aliases of documents or save the actual files on the Desktop until you figure out where you want to store them. I like to keep my files as well organized as possible, so when I first create a file, I save it in its proper folder inside the Documents folder in my Home folder. If it's a document that I plan to work on for more than a day or two (such as a magazine article or book chapter), I make an alias of the document (or folder) and plop it on the Desktop. After I finish the article or chapter and submit it to an editor, I trash the alias, leaving the original file stashed away in its proper folder.

Of course, you can place that same folder in the Dock as well, so you can use the press-and-hold trick to open its subfolders. But nothing says you can't have an item appear in several places at once for maximum convenience.

Incidentally, you can use a similar technique without the aliases. Just save all your new documents on the Desktop (`yourhomefolder/ Desktop`). Later, as you finish working with each document, you can file it away in its proper folder.

To create an alias for an icon, do one of the following:

- ✔ **Click the parent icon and choose File⇨Make Alias.**
- ✔ **Click the parent icon and press ⌘+L.**
- ✔ **Click any file or folder, press and hold down the ⌘ and Option keys, and then drag the file or folder while continuing to hold down the ⌘ and Option keys.**

  Presto! An alias appears where you release the mouse button. Better still, aliases created this way don't have that pesky `alias` suffix tacked onto them.

- ✔ **Click an icon while holding down the Control key and then choose the Make Alias command from the contextual menu that appears.**

  The alias appears in the same folder as its parent. (I explore contextual menus — which are very cool — in Chapter 3.)

Deleting aliases

This is a short section because deleting an alias is such an easy chore. To delete an alias, simply drag it onto the Trash icon on the Dock. That's it! You can also Control-click it and choose Move to Trash from the contextual menu that appears, or select the icon and use the keyboard shortcut ⌘+Delete.

Deleting an alias does *not* delete the parent item. (If you want to delete the parent item, you have to go hunt it down and kill it yourself.)

Hunting down an alias' parent

Suppose you create an alias of a file, and later you want to delete both the alias and its parent file — but you can't find the parent file? What do you do? Well, you can use the Finder's Find function (try saying that three times real fast) to find it; but here are three faster ways to find the parent icon of an alias:

- ✔ Select the alias icon and choose File➪Show Original.

- ✔ Select the alias icon and use the keyboard shortcut ⌘+R.

- ✔ Control-click the alias icon and choose Show Original from the contextual menu.

Doing More with Your Icons

After checking out the different types of icons, it's time to see what you can do with and to them. In the upcoming sections, I show you how to open, rename, get rid of (again), and select icons. In a matter of moments, you'll be an icon pro!

Open sez me! Opening icons

You can open any icon in four ways. (Okay, there are *five* ways, but one of them belongs to aliases, which I discuss earlier in the section "Other Icons in OS X Tiger") Anyway, here are the ways:

- ✔ **Click the icon once to select it and then choose File➪Open.**

- ✔ **Double-click the icon by clicking it twice in rapid succession.**

    If it doesn't open, you double-clicked too slowly. You can test your mouse's sensitivity to double-click speed as well as adjust it in the Keyboard & Mouse System Preference pane.

- ✔ **Select the icon and then press either ⌘+O or ⌘+↓.**

- ✔ **Click the icon while holding down the Control key and then use the contextual menu's Open command.**

Of course, you can also open any document icon from within an application — skip ahead to Chapter 5 for more on that.

Getting rid of icons

To get rid of an icon — any icon — merely drag it to the Trash on your Dock.

Trashing an alias gets rid of only the alias, not the parent file. But trashing a document, folder, or application icon puts it in the Trash, where it will be deleted permanently the next time you empty the Trash.

Playing the icon name game: renaming icons

Icon, icon-a, bo-bicon, banana-fanna fo-ficon. Betcha can change the name of any old icon! Well, that's not entirely true. . . .

If an icon is locked (see the upcoming section "Info-mation"), busy (an application that's currently open), or you don't have the owner's permission to rename that icon (see Chapter 14 for details about permissions), you won't be able to rename it. Similarly, you should never rename certain reserved icons (such as the Library, System, and Desktop folders).

To rename an icon, you can either click the icon's name directly (don't click the icon itself because that selects the icon) or click the icon and then press Return (or Enter) on your keyboard once.

Either way, the icon's name is selected and surrounded with a box, and you can now type in a new name (as shown in Figure 2-15). In addition to selecting the name, the cursor changes from a pointer to a text-editing I-beam. An *I-beam cursor* (shown in the left margin) is the Mac's way of telling you that you can type now. At this point, if you click the I-beam cursor anywhere in the name box, you can edit the icon's original name. If you don't click the I-beam cursor in the name box but just begin typing, the icon's original name is replaced by what you type.

If you've never changed an icon's name, give it a try. And don't forget: If you click the icon itself, the icon is selected, and you won't be able to change its name. If you do accidentally select the icon, just press Return (or Enter) once to edit the name of the icon.

Figure 2-15:
Change an
icon's name
by typing
over the
old one
when it's
highlighted.

Selecting multiple icons

Sometimes you want to move or copy several items into a single folder. The process is pretty much the same as it is when you copy one file or folder (that is, you just drag the icon to where you want it and drop it there). But you first need to select all the items you want before you can drag them, en masse, to their destination. You'll find the following method a lot more convenient than selecting and copying files one at a time:

1. **To select more than one icon in a folder, do one of the following:**

   • Click once within the folder window (don't click any one icon) and drag your mouse while continuing to hold down the mouse button. You see an outline of a box around the icons while you drag, and all icons within (or touching) the box become highlighted. (See Figure 2-16.)

Navigating icons like a supergeek

In addition to the old point-and-click method of navigating icons, you can also move among icons by using the keyboard. In an active window, make sure that no icons are selected and then type the first letter of a file's name. In all views, the first icon that starts with that letter is selected. To move to the next icon alphabetically, press the Tab key. To move to the icon in reverse alphabetical order, press Shift+Tab.

If more than one icon begins with the same letter, type in more than one letter to further restrict the possible results. Suppose that you have three folders in the same window that all begin with *A: Applications, Abstracts,* and *Aunt Mary's Stuff.* To select the Applications folder, type **app**.

If no window is active, typing a letter selects the first icon on the Desktop that starts with that letter. Press the Tab key or press Shift+Tab to work your way through the icon names alphabetically forward or backward, respectively. Finally, pressing ⌘+O or ⌘+↓ opens the selected item.

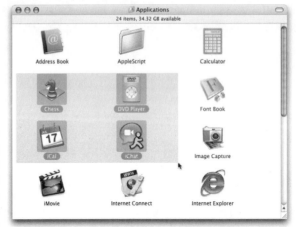

Figure 2-16:
Select more
than one
icon with
your mouse.

- Click one icon and then hold down the Shift key while you click others. As long as you hold down the Shift key, each new icon that you click is added to the selection. To deselect an icon, click it a second time while still holding down the Shift key.

- Click one icon and then hold down the Command (⌘) key while you click others. The difference between using the Shift and the ⌘ keys is that using the ⌘ key doesn't select everything between it and the first item selected when your window is in a List or Column view. In an Icon view, it really doesn't make much difference.

To deselect an icon selected in any of these three ways, click it while holding down the ⌘ key.

2. **When you select all the icons that you want, click one of them (don't click anywhere else or you deselect the icons that you just selected) and drag (or Option+drag) them to the location where you want to move (or copy) them.**

Be careful with multiple selections, especially when you drag icons to the Trash. You can easily — and accidentally — select more than one icon, so watch out that you don't accidentally put the wrong icon in the Trash by not paying close attention.

If you put something in the Trash by accident, you can almost always return it whence it came: Just invoke the magical Undo command. Choose Edit⇨ Undo or use the keyboard shortcut ⌘+Z. The accidentally trashed file will return to its original location. Usually.

Unfortunately, Undo doesn't work every time — and it only remembers the very last action that you performed when it *does* work — so don't rely on it too much.

Info-mation

Every icon has an Info window that gives you — big surprise! — information about that icon and enables you to choose which other users (if any) that you want to have the privilege of using this icon. (I discuss sharing files and privileges in detail in Chapter 14.) The Info window is also where you lock an icon so that it can't be renamed or dragged to the Trash.

To see an icon's Info window, click the icon and choose File⇨Get Info (or press ⌘+I) The Info window for that icon appears, as in Figure 2-17, which shows the Info window for the QuickTime Player icon.

Figure 2-17: A typical Info window for an application (QuickTime Player, in this case).

Documents, folders, and disks each have slightly different Info windows. In this section, I give you highlights on the type of information and options that you can find.

The gray triangles reveal what information for an icon is available in this particular Info window. Figure 2-17 shows the options for the QuickTime Player with the General section expanded. The sections that you see for most icons include the following:

Why would you want to run an app in Classic?

I once had a great USB printer (Epson Stylus Photo 750) that wasn't supported in OS X, although it worked fine in Classic. I could do most of my printing from Word and Photoshop in Classic, but every so often I needed to print a file created by some OS X-only program. I couldn't print from OS X, but I could save the file as a PDF (something almost every OS X program can do because PDF support is built into OS X's Quartz imaging architecture). Then, I used the Open in the Classic Environment feature to tell my copy of Acrobat 5 to open as a Classic application instead of a Mac OS X application, thus allowing me to print the formerly unprintable document from Classic.

✔ **General:** For information of the general kind, such as

- **Kind:** What kind of file this is — an application, document, disk, folder, and so on

- **Size:** How much disk space this file uses

- **Where:** The path to the folder that contains this file

- **Created:** The date and time that this file was created

- **Modified:** The date and time that this file was last modified (that is, saved)

- **Version:** Copyright information and the file's version number

✔ **Name & Extension:** Tells the full name, including the (possibly hidden) extension.

✔ **Color Label:** Choose or change the color label (discussed in Chapter 4) for this item.

✔ **Preview:** When you select a document icon, the menu offers a Preview option that you use to see a glimpse of what's in that document. You can also see this preview when you select a document icon in Column view — it magically appears in the rightmost column. If you select a QuickTime movie or sound, you can even play it right there in the preview pane without launching a separate application. Neat.

✔ **Languages:** Manages the language that the application uses for menus and dialogs.

This option only appears if you're using an Info window to look at certain application programs (usually the sort that contain multiple .lproj folders within their Contents/Resources folders).

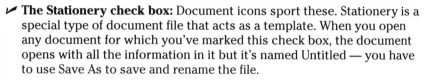

- ✔ **Ownership & Permissions:** Governs which users have access to this icon and how much access they are allowed. (See Chapter 14 for more about access privileges.)

- ✔ **Comments:** Provides a field in which you type your own comments about this icon.

- ✔ **Open in the Classic Environment check box:** This option is available for only some applications, known as *Carbon apps* — programs developed to run on both OS 9 and OS X. Selecting this check box lets you run *some* Carbon application in the Classic environment. (Don't worry if you don't know what this means — Classic is discussed in full and loving detail, but not until Chapter 12.)

- ✔ **The Locked check box:** Enabling this shows you whether you can change an icon's name or drag it to the Trash. When an application is *locked* (this check box will be marked), you can't change its name or drag it to the Trash. (I discuss the Trash earlier in this chapter.)

   Only document and folder icons can be locked; disk and application icons can't.

- ✔ **The Stationery check box:** Document icons sport these. Stationery is a special type of document file that acts as a template. When you open any document for which you've marked this check box, the document opens with all the information in it but it's named Untitled — you have to use Save As to save and rename the file.

   The Stationery document remains unchanged even after you open it; you can use it again and again to open a document with some of its content already in place.

Chapter 3

About Windows (Not the Microsoft Kind) and Menus

. . . .

In This Chapter

▶ Checking out the parts of a window

▶ Of gumdrops and windows

▶ Keeping it small with scroll bars (not to be confused with whiskey bars)

▶ Knowing your active windows from your passive windows

▶ Dealing with dealie-boppers in windows

▶ Resizing, moving, and closing windows

▶ Getting comfortable with menu basics

▶ Putting menus into context

▶ Bellying up to the menu bar

▶ Perusing the menu(s)

▶ Plus tips, tricks, hints, shortcuts, and much more

. . . .

*W*indows are and have always been an integral part of Macintosh computing. Windows in the Finder (sometimes called "on the Desktop") show you the contents of hard drive and folder icons; windows in applications do many things. The point is that windows are part of what makes your Mac a Mac; knowing how they work — and how to use them — is essential.

Like icons and windows, menus are a quintessential part of the Macintosh experience. The latter part of this chapter starts you out with a few menu basics and then moves on to the Finder menus. I provide a level of detail based on each menu item's importance; as needed, I direct you to other parts of the book for greater detail.

One last thing: The windows discussed in this chapter are Finder windows. After you get the hang of Finder windows, you have the hang of using most of the windows you ever see on your Mac.

So relax and don't worry. By the end of this chapter, you'll be ready to work with windows and menus in any application that uses them (and most applications, games excluded, do).

Anatomy of a Window

Like icons, windows are a ubiquitous part of using a Mac. The Finder appears in a window. When you open a folder, it's a window that you see. When you write a letter, the document that you're working on appears in a window, when you browse the Internet, Web pages appear in a window, and so on.

For the most part, windows are windows from program to program. You'll probably notice that some programs (Adobe Photoshop or Microsoft Word, for example) take liberties with windows by adding features (such as pop-up menus) or textual information (such as zoom percentage or file size) in the scroll-bar area of a document window.

Don't let it bug you; that extra fluff is just window dressing (pun intended). Maintaining the window metaphor, many information windows display different kinds of information in different *panes* (discrete sections).

Windows in programs running in the Classic environment look different — like Mac OS 9 windows. (I cover the Classic environment in Chapter 12.)

And so, without further ado, the following list gives you a look at the main features of a typical Finder window (as shown in Figure 3-1). I discuss these features in greater detail in later sections of this chapter.

If your windows don't look exactly like the one shown in Figure 3-1, don't be concerned. You can use what you find in this chapter (and the next) to make your Finder windows look and feel any way you like. Hang in there. Meanwhile, here's what you see:

 ✔ **Window Title:** Shows the name of the window.

 ✔ **Scroll bars:** Used for moving around a window pane.

 ✔ **Sidebar:** Where frequently-used items live.

 ✔ **Toolbar:** Buttons for frequently-used commands and actions live here.

 ✔ **Forward and Back buttons:** Take you to the next or previous folder displayed in this particular window.

If you're familiar with Web browsers, the Forward and Back buttons in the Finder work exactly the same way. The first time you open a window, neither button is active. But as you navigate from folder to folder, they remember your breadcrumb trail so you can quickly traverse backward or forward, window by window. You can even navigate this way from the keyboard, by using the shortcuts ⌘+[for Back and ⌘+] for Forward.

If you've set a Finder Preference so a folder always opens in a new window — or if you forced a folder to open in a new window (which I'll describe in a bit) — the Forward and Back buttons won't work. You have to use the modern, OS X-style window option — the one that uses a single window — or the buttons are useless.

In other words, the Forward and Back buttons remember only the other folders you've visited that appear in *that* window (the open one).

- ✔ **View buttons:** Choose from three exciting views of your window: icon, list, or column.

- ✔ **Action button:** This button is really a pop-up menu of commands you can apply to currently selected items in the Finder window.

- ✔ **Close, Minimize, and Expand (gumdrop) buttons:** Shut 'em, shrink and place them 'em in the Dock, and make 'em grow.

- ✔ **Search box:** Find items whose names contain the character string you type here.

- ✔ **Hide/Show toolbar button:** Causes your computer to melt into a puddle of molten silicon slag. Just kidding! This button actually does what its name implies — hides or shows the toolbar (and sidebar) of a window.

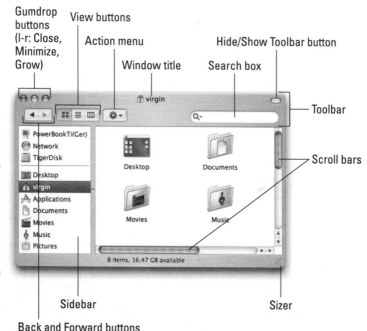

Figure 3-1:
A typical
Finder
window in
Mac OS X
10.4 Tiger.

This frosts me. If you hide the toolbar, the sidebar is also hidden, whether you like it or not. Conversely, if you want to see the toolbar, you have no choice but to also see the sidebar. So if you want to hide the toolbar and see the sidebar (or vice versa) you're $#&* out of luck. If I had my druthers, I'd hide the toolbar (which I rarely use), and keep the sidebar (which I use constantly). For some unfathomable reason, Apple doesn't allow that.

Top o' the window to ya!

Take a gander at the top of a window — any window. You see three buttons in the upper-left corner and the name of the window in the top center. These three buttons (called *gumdrop buttons* by some folks because they look like, well, gumdrops) in the upper-left corner of the window — officially known as Close, Minimize, and Zoom (some people call this button by its Mac OS 9 name, Grow) — are colored red, orange, and green (from left to right). Here's what they do:

- **Close (red):** Click this button to *close* the window.

- **Minimize (orange):** Click this button to *minimize* the window. Clicking Minimize appears to close the window, but instead of making it disappear, Minimize adds an icon for the window in the Dock. To view the window again, click the Dock icon for the window that you minimized. If the window happens to be a QuickTime movie, the movie continues to play, albeit at postage-stamp size, in its icon in the Dock. (I discuss the Dock in Chapter 2.)

- **Zoom (green):** Click this button to make the window larger or smaller, depending on its current size. If you're looking at a standard size window, clicking Zoom *usually* makes it bigger. (I say *usually* because if the window is larger than its contents, clicking this button shrinks the window to the smallest size that can completely enclose the contents without scrolling.) Click the Zoom button again to return the window to its original size.

A scroll new world

Yet another way to see more of what's in a window or pane is to scroll through it. Scroll bars appear at the bottom and right sides of any window or pane that contains more stuff — icons, text, pixels, or whatever — than you can see in the window. Figure 3-2, for example, shows two instances of the same window: Dragging the scroll bar on the right side of the front window reveals the items above Font Book and GarageBand and below Mail and Preview, which you can see in the expanded window in the background. Dragging the scroll bar on the bottom of the window reveals items to the left and right, such as iChat, iMovie, Internet Connect, and iSync.

Simply click and drag a scroll bar to move it either up or down or side to side. And yes, the scroll bars also look a bit gumdrop-like. As best as I can tell, Steve Jobs (Apple's charismatic CEO) has a thing for gumdrops.

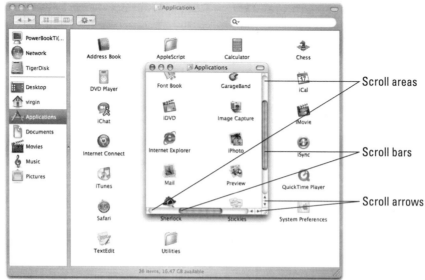

Figure 3-2: The same window twice; in the front window, you use the scroll bars to see the hidden icons.

Scroll areas

Scroll bars

Scroll arrows

You can scroll in the following four ways:

✔ **Click a scroll bar and drag.** The content of the window scrolls proportionally to how far you drag the scroll bar.

✔ **Click in the scroll bar area but not on the scroll bar itself.** The window scrolls either one page up (if you click above the scroll bar) or down (if you click below the scroll bar). If the scroll-bar area is white (that is, it doesn't have a blue scroll bar showing), you have no items to scroll to — which means the window already contains everything visible. You can change a setting in your General System Preference pane (discussed in Chapter 13) to cause the window to scroll proportionally to where you click.

For what it's worth, the Page Up and Page Down keys function the same as clicking the grayish scroll-bar area (the vertical scroll bar only) in the Finder and many applications. But these keys don't work in every program; don't become too dependent on them. Also, if you've purchased a mouse, trackball, or other pointing device with a scroll wheel, you can scroll vertically in the active (front) window with the scroll wheel, or press and hold the Shift key to scroll horizontally.

✓ **Click a scroll arrow at the top or bottom of a scroll area.** By default, both arrows appear at the bottom of the scroll bar. The window scrolls a little; press and hold a scroll arrow, and the window scrolls a lot. Click the up-pointing arrow to scroll toward the beginning and the down-pointing arrow to scroll toward the end.

If you have your General System Preferences set to have the scroll arrows together rather than at top and bottom, they'll be at the bottom and right of the scroll areas, as shown in Figure 3-2. If you don't, you'll see one arrow at each end of the scroll area.

✓ **Use the keyboard.** In the Finder, first click an icon in the window and then use the arrow keys to move up, down, left, or right. Using an arrow key selects the next icon in the direction it indicates — and automatically scrolls the window, if necessary. In other programs, you may or may not be able to use the keyboard to scroll. The Page Up and Page Down keys work in most programs, but many programs don't use the arrow keys for scrolling their windows. The best advice I can give you is to try it — either it'll work or it won't.

In the Finder, you can also press the Tab key on the keyboard to select the next icon in the active window alphabetically and press Shift+Tab to select the previous icon alphabetically.

(Hyper) Active windows

To work within a window, the window must be *active.* The active window is always the frontmost window, and inactive windows always appear behind the active window. Only one window can be active at a time. To make a window active, click it anywhere — in the middle, on the title bar, or on a scroll bar — it doesn't matter where, with one proviso: You can't click the red, orange, or green gumdrop buttons or the clear hide/show button of an inactive window to activate it.

When you hover your mouse pointer *over* the red, orange, or green gumdrop buttons of an inactive window — but don't click your mouse button — the gumdrops light up, enabling you to close, minimize, or expand an inactive window without first making it active.

Look at Figure 3-3 for an example of an active window (the Applications window) in front of an inactive window (the Utilities window).

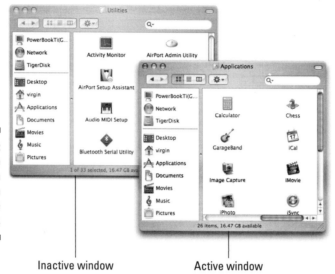

Figure 3-3:
An active window in front of an inactive window.

Inactive window   Active window

The following is a list of the major visual cues that distinguish active from inactive windows:

✔ **The active window's title bar:** The Close, Minimize, and Zoom buttons — the red, orange, and green ones — are, well, red, orange, and green. The inactive windows' buttons are not.

This is a nice visual cue — colored items are active and gray ones are inactive. Better still, if you move your mouse over an inactive window's gumdrop buttons, they light up in their usual colors so you can close, minimize, or expand an inactive window without first making it active. Neat!

✔ **Other buttons and scroll bars in an active window look different:** They're bright. In an inactive window, these features are grayed out and more subdued.

✔ **Active windows have bigger and darker drop shadows:** They grab your attention more than those of inactive windows.

Dialog Dealie-Boppers

Dialogs are special windows that pop up over the active window. You generally see them when you select a menu item that ends in an ellipsis (. . .).

Dialogs can contain a number of standard Macintosh features (I call them *dealie-boppers*), such as radio buttons, pop-up menus, text-entry boxes, and check boxes. You see these features again and again in dialogs. Take a moment to look at each of these dealie-boppers in Figure 3-4.

Pop-up menu

Check box (unchecked)   Text Entry box

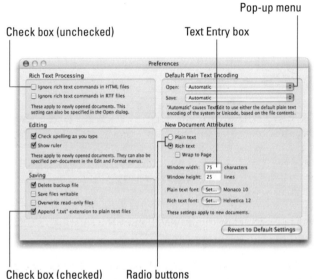

Figure 3-4: This window offers most dealie-boppers you're ever likely to encounter.

Check box (checked)   Radio buttons

✔ **Radio buttons:** *Radio buttons* are so named because, like the buttons on your car radio (if you have a very old car), only one at a time can be active (when they're active, they appear to be pushed in, just like the old radio buttons). Radio buttons always appear in a group of two or more; when you select one, all the others are automatically deselected. Eggheads call this setup *mutually exclusive.* Take a look at Figure 3-4 for an example of radio buttons.

As shown in Figure 3-4, the second radio button (Rich Text) is selected. If you were to click the radio button above it for Plain Text, you would deactivate (deselect) Rich Text. Got it? Good. Moving right along . . . .

Here's a nifty and undocumented shortcut: You can usually select check boxes and radio buttons by clicking their names (instead of the buttons or boxes). Didn't know that, did ya?

✔ **Pop-up menus:** These menus are appropriately named because that's what they do — they pop up when you click them. You can always tell a pop-up menu — it appears in a slightly rounded rectangle and has a double-ended arrow symbol (or, a pair of back-to-back triangles if you like) on the right. For an example, check out Figure 3-4 (the Open and Save pop-up menus both read *Automatic*).

Have you figured out yet what radio buttons and pop-up menus have in common? *Hint:* They both enable you to make a single selection from a group of options. (Well, okay, that was more of an answer than a hint.)

✔ **Text-entry boxes:** In text-entry boxes (sometimes called *fields*), you type in text (including numbers) from the keyboard. When you see one or more text-entry boxes sporting a selected radio button, you can only make an entry when that radio button is selected. In Figure 3-4 (for example), the Window Width and Window Height options are both text-entry boxes.

✔ **Check boxes:** The last dealie-bopper that you see frequently is the check box. You use check boxes to choose items that are not mutually exclusive. In a group of check boxes, you can select or deselect each one individually. Check boxes are selected when they contain a check mark, and they are deselected when they're empty. Unlike radio buttons, which force you to choose one (and only one) item, check boxes are independent. Each one can be either selected or deselected. In Figure 3-4, you can see several check boxes, four of which are selected and five of which are not.

Some applications have what they call *tri-state* check boxes (and no, we're not talking geography here). These special check boxes are empty when everything selected doesn't have this feature applied, sport an **x** when everything does, and sport a – when *some* selected items have the feature and some don't. This type of check box is often used for the Custom Install screen of Mac OS X installers.

Working with Windows

In this section, I give you a closer look at windows themselves: how you move them, size them, and use them. And although Mac OS X windows are similar to windows you've used in other versions of Mac OS, you'll find some new wrinkles.

If you're relatively new to the Mac, you may want to read this section while sitting at your computer, trying the techniques as you read them. You may find it easier to remember something that you read if you actually do it. If you've been using your Mac for a while, you probably figured out how windows work by now.

Resizing windows

If you want to see more (or less) of what's in a window, use the sizer in the extreme lower-right corner of a window. (Refer to Figure 3-1 to see the sizer; it's in the lower-right corner and has little diagonal grippy lines on it). Just drag the sizer downward and/or to the right to make a window larger. Or drag it upward and/or to the left to make a window smaller. In other words, after you grab the sizer, you can make a window whatever size you like.

Resizing window panes

Display windows, like those in the Finder, frequently consist of multiple panes. In the metal-looking strip between two panes you'll often encounter what looks, at first glance, like a speck of dirt on your monitor. On closer inspection, you'll see a tiny knob (as in Figure 3-1, between the Sidebar and the actual contents of the window to the right of it).

When your mouse is over that knob, the cursor changes to a vertical bar (or it could be horizontal if the panes are one above the other) with little arrows pointing out of both sides.

When you see this cursor, you can click and drag anywhere in the strip that divides the Sidebar from the rest of the window. Doing so resizes the two panes relative to each other (one will get larger and one smaller). And double-clicking this knob usually expands the more important pane to full-size and hides the other pane completely. Usually.

Moving windows

To move a window, click anywhere in a window's title bar (or anywhere in the metallic part of a display window, except on a knob) and drag the window to wherever you want it. The window moves wherever you move the mouse, stopping dead in its tracks when you release the mouse button.

Shutting yo' windows

Now that I've gone on and on about windows, maybe I should tell you how to close them. You can close an active window in one of three ways (the last two require the window to be active, by the way):

Hunting the seldom-seen Close All command

If you're like me, by the end of the day your Desktop is cluttered with open windows — sometimes a dozen or more. Wouldn't you love to be able to close them all at once with a single Close All command? But you don't see a Close All command in any of the menus, do you?

Well, even though Apple (in its infinite wisdom) has hidden this useful command from mere mortals, you can make it come out and play by doing one of the following:

✔ Hold down the Option key and click any window's red gumdrop Close button.

✔ Hold down the Option key and choose File⇨ Close All. (The Close All command usually reads Close Window but becomes Close All when you hold down the Option key. Release the Option key, and it changes back to Close Window.)

✔ Press ⌘+Option+W.

✔ **Click the red Close button in the upper-left corner of the title bar.**

✔ **Choose File ⇨ Close Window from the Finder menu.**

✔ **Press ⌘+W.**

Hold down Option (and occasionally Control, ⌘, or come combination of the three) and pull down menus in both the Finder and in your favorite application programs. It doesn't always reveal anything interesting in the menu, but sometimes it does.

And that should just about do it for windows. Next up: menus . . .

Menu Basics

Mac menus are often referred to as *pull-down menus*. To check out the Mac OS X menus, click the Finder button in the Dock to activate the Finder and then look at the top of your screen. From left to right you see the Apple menu, the Finder menu, and six other menus that I discuss throughout this chapter, as shown in Figure 3-5. To use an OS X menu, you click its name to make the menu appear and then pull (drag) down to select a menu item. Piece of cake!

Ever since Mac OS 8, menus stay down after you click their names. They stay down until you either select an item or click outside the menu's boundaries.

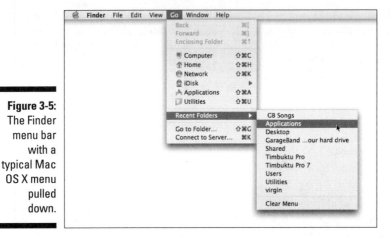

Figure 3-5:
The Finder
menu bar
with a
typical Mac
OS X menu
pulled
down.

Before you start working with OS X menus, you really, really should know this about menus in general: *They can change unexpectedly.* Why? Well, the menus you see in the menu bar at the top of the screen always reflect the program that's active at the time. When you switch from the Finder to a particular program — or from one program to another — the menus change immediately to match whatever you switched to.

For example, when the Finder is active, the menu bar looks like Figure 3-5. But if you launch TextEdit, the menu bar changes to what you see in Figure 3-6.

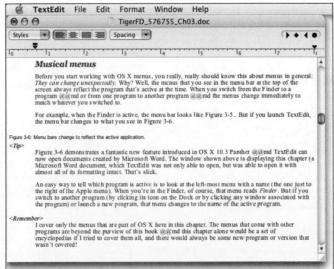

Figure 3-6:
Menu bars
change to
reflect the
active
application.

Figure 3-6 demonstrates a fantastic feature introduced in OS X 10.3 Panther — TextEdit can now open documents created by Microsoft Word. The window shown above is displaying this chapter, a Microsoft Word document that TextEdit was not only able to open, but was able to open with almost all of its formatting intact. That's slick.

An easy way to tell which program is active is to look at the leftmost menu with a name (the one just to the right of the Apple menu). When you're in the Finder, of course, that menu reads *Finder*. But if you switch to another program (by clicking its icon on the Dock or by clicking any window associated with the program) or launch a new program, that menu changes to the name of the active program.

I cover only the menus that are part of OS X here in this chapter. The menus that come with other programs are beyond the purview of this book — this chapter alone would be a set of encyclopedias if I tried to cover them all, and there would always be some new program or version that wasn't covered!

Contextual menus: They're sooo sensitive

Contextual menus are, as the name implies, context sensitive; they list commands that apply only to the item that is currently selected. Contextual menus may be available in windows, on icons, and most places on the Desktop. To use them, you hold down the Control key and click — what we Mac users like to call a *Control+click*. Figure 3-7 shows the contextual menu that appears when you Control+click a document icon.

Figure 3-7:
Only relevant items appear in a contextual menu.

Actions appear in contextual menus only if they make sense for the item that you Control+click. For example, if you Control+click inside a window but you don't click any icon, the contextual menu contains actions that you perform on a window. By contrast, if you Control+click an icon inside a window, you see a contextual menu for that icon. In a similar way, a contextual menu for a document differs from that of a window.

Don't believe me? Control+click the Desktop (that is, click somewhere that's not in any window and not on any icon). The contextual menu that appears contains only items that apply to the Desktop, and no item that pertains to a document. Don't believe me? Compare the Desktop contextual menu shown in Figure 3-8 with the document contextual menu shown in Figure 3-7.

Figure 3-8:
The Desktop's contextual menu differs from a document's contextual menu.

That's why they call 'em *contextual!* They stick to the immediate context.

Contextual menus are also available in many applications. Open your favorite app and try Control+clicking to find out whether they're there. In most cases, using a contextual menu is a quick way to avoid going to the menu bar to choose a command. In some programs, such as AppleWorks 6, iMovie, iTunes, and many more, contextual menus are the only way to access certain commands.

To make the Finder-related contextual menus available to users who didn't have the foresight to purchase this book, Apple added the Actions button to the toolbar in the previous version of OS X (10.3 Panther). So these days, people who don't know about Control+clicking (or have only one free hand) can access their contextual menus by clicking the Actions button and displaying the contextual menu; you, on the other hand, gentle reader, know how to get at these commands without having to run your mouse all the way up to the toolbar.

I'm a big fan of multi-button mice, and contextual menus are a huge reason for this preference. Just about the first thing I do when I get a new Mac is replace the standard mouse (pretty as it is) with a multi-button mouse. When you have a mouse (or trackball) with at least two buttons, OS X knows that clicking the right button is the same as Control+clicking. Now, I only have to use one hand to access these little beauties.

Get in the habit of Control+clicking (or right-clicking if your mouse has more than one button) items. Before you know it, using contextual menus will become second nature to you.

Disabled options

Menu items that appear in black on a menu are currently available. Menu items not currently available are grayed out, meaning they're disabled for the time being. You can't select a disabled menu item.

In Figure 3-9, the File menu on the left is pulled down while nothing is selected in the Finder; this is why many of the menu items are disabled (in gray). These items are disabled because an item (such as a window or icon) must be selected in order for you to use one of these menu items. For example, the Show Original command is grayed out because it works only if the selected item is an alias. In the picture on the right, I selected a document before I pulled down the menu; notice that many of the formerly disabled commands are enabled when an icon is selected.

Figure 3-9: File menu with nothing selected (left) and with a document selected (right); the disabled items are grayed out.

Submenus

Some menu items have more menus attached to them, and these are called *submenus* — menus that are subordinate to a menu item. You can tell whether a menu item has a submenu if it has a black triangle to the right of its name.

To use a submenu, click a menu name once (to drop the menu down) and then slide your cursor down to any item with a black triangle. When the item is highlighted, move your mouse to the right just slightly. The submenu should pop out of the original menu's item. Figure 3-5 shows an example: the Recent Folders submenu opens underneath the Go menu. If you were to release the mouse button while doing exactly what is pictured, a Finder window would pop open, showing you a Finder window displaying your Applications folder.

The pop-up menus that you see when you click-and-hold (or Control+click) a Dock icon can also have submenus. In fact, if you were to put your Home folder in the Dock, you could access any file in it — or in its subfolders — via the menu and its submenus, as shown in Figure 3-10.

Figure 3-10:
Drag your
Home folder
into the
Dock and
enjoy the
conve-
nience of
submenus.

Submenus used to be called *hierarchical* menus, but that's a mouthful. For a while, people liked to call them *pull-right* menus. But these days, just about everyone refers to them as submenus. If you ever hear folks talk about hierarchical menus or pull-rights, they're talking about submenus.

Keyboard shortcut commands

Most menu items, or at least the most common ones, have *keyboard shortcuts* to help you quickly navigate your Mac without having to haggle so much with the mouse. Using these key combinations activates menu items without using the mouse; to use them you press the Command (⌘) key and then press another key (or keys) without releasing the ⌘ key. Memorize the shortcuts that you use often.

Some people refer to the Command key as the *Apple key*. That's because on many keyboards, that key has both the pretzel-like Command-key symbol (⌘) *and* an Apple logo (⌘) on it. To avoid confusion, I'll always refer to ⌘ as the Command key.

Here are five things to know that will give you a handle on keyboard shortcuts:

✔ **Keyboard shortcuts are shown in menus.** For example, Figure 3-5 shows that the keyboard shortcut for the Find command appears on the menu after the word *Find*: ⌘+F. Any menu item with one of these pretzel-symbol-letter combinations after its name can be executed with that keyboard shortcut. Just press the ⌘ key and the letter shown in the menu — *N* for New Finder Window, *F* for Find, and so on — and the appropriate command executes.

✔ **Capital letters don't mean that you have to press Shift as part of the shortcut.** Although the letters next to the ⌘ symbol in the Finder menus are indeed capitals, they just identify the letters; you don't have to press the Shift key to use the keyboard shortcut. For example, if you see ⌘+P, just hold down the ⌘ key and then press *P*. Some programs have keyboard combinations that require the use of ⌘ *and* the Shift key, but those programs tell you so by calling the key combination something like ⇧+⌘+ S or ⇧+⌘+ O. A very few (usually older) programs indicate when you need to use the Shift key by using the word *Shift* rather than the ⇧ symbol.

Of course, there's an exception to every rule, and one of them is Mac Help, which does demand the ⇧ key in its shortcut, but you'll get that whole sordid story in a few pages.

✔ **Recognize the funky-looking Option key symbol.** You'll see one other symbol sometimes used in keyboard shortcuts: It represents the Option key (sometimes abbreviated in keyboard shortcuts as *Opt* and, on some keyboards, also labeled *Alt*). Check it out next to the Hide Others command, shown in Figure 3-11.

What this freakish symbol means in the Finder menu item (Hide Others in Figure 3-11) is that if you press both the ⌘ and Option keys *and hold them down* as you press the H key, all applications other than the Finder will be hidden.

✔ **Okay, there was more than one more symbol.** Occasionally you'll see a *caret* (^) used as the abbreviation for the Control key, as shown in Figure 3-12. It points up; think *uppercase*.

Figure 3-11: Some keyboard shortcuts, such as Hide Others, use the Option key in combination with the Command key.

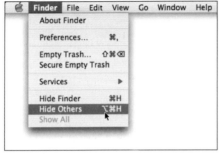

Figure 3-12: The ^ means "Control key."

✔ **If it makes sense, it's probably a shortcut.** Most keyboard shortcuts have a mnemonic relationship to their names. For example, here are some of the more basic keyboard shortcuts:

Command	Mnemonic Keyboard Shortcut
New Finder Window	⌘+N
New Folder	⌘+Shift+N
Open	⌘+O

Get Info	⌘+I
Select All	⌘+A
Copy	⌘+C
Duplicate	⌘+D

It's elliptical

Another feature of Mac menus is the ellipsis after some menu-item names. *Ellipses,* in case your English teacher forgot to mention them, are the three little dots (...) that appear in place of missing text. They basically mean that you can reach more options by clicking the menu item.

Those three little dots aren't separate, though — they make up one character. If you want to type an ellipsis, you can do so (in most fonts) by holding down the Option key and pressing the semicolon (colon) key.

When you see an ellipsis after a menu item, choosing that item displays a dialog or sheet, in which you can make further choices. (I discuss dialogs and sheets in Chapter 5.) Refer to Figure 3-11 to see that the Preferences command has an ellipsis. If you choose Preferences, the Finder Preferences window opens.

Choosing a menu item with an ellipsis never actually makes anything happen other than to open a dialog (whether in the form of a box or a sheet); from there, you make further choices and then click a button. This button is usu-ally called OK or Cancel, but occasionally — as in the Finder Preferences dialog — you use the red Close button/gumdrop in the upper-left corner of the window to dismiss the dialog.

Underneath the Apple Menu Tree

The Macintosh interface has sported an *Apple* () *menu* since time immemo-rial (well, the 1980s anyway). So when the Mac OS X Public Beta appeared without an Apple menu, Mac users everywhere crawled out of the woodwork to express their outrage. The bruised Apple ultimately relented, and now OS X has an menu, as did every version of Mac OS before it.

Alas, you can't customize the OS X Apple Menu the way you used to under OS 9.

Location, location, location

I'm getting a little bit ahead of myself, but because you're probably wondering, a *location* reflects all the settings made in the Network System Preferences pane. They're mostly useful to PowerBook and iBook users, who often have different network configurations (locations) for different places where they may need to use their Macs — such as the office (to connect to an Ethernet network), home (to connect to a Digital Subscriber Line [DSL] or cable connection), and out of town (to connect using an internal modem). Each configuration (for office, home, and out of town) corresponds to a location, and you can switch from one location to another quickly and painlessly by using this menu item. Got it? If not, you will after you read Chapter 9.

If you miss customizing your Apple menu, try Fruit Menu from Unsanity (www.unsanity.com), a fabulous shareware offering that provides all the functionality of the OS 9 menu and is reasonably priced at $10.

You won't find any programs available from the new OS X menu — no Calculator, no Scrapbook, no programs at all (other than System Preferences and the ones in your Recent Items submenu). Instead, the menu provides a set of useful commands, described here, that are always available no matter what program is active.

From top to bottom, the Apple menu's items are

- ✔ **About This Mac:** Choose this item to see what version of Mac OS X you're running, what kind of Mac and processor you're using, and how much memory your Mac has. The window that appears also sports a Get Info button that will launch Apple System Profiler; there you can find out more than you'll probably ever want or need to know about your Mac's hardware and software.

  If you click the version number in this window, it changes to the *build number* (Apple's internal tracking number for versions). Click the build number in this window, and it changes to the serial number of your Mac. Finally, click the serial number of your Mac in this window, and it changes to the version number again. This interesting effect is shown in Figure 3-13. Any or all of this information may come in handy for troubleshooting, repair, upgrades, or who knows what else. At least now you know where to find it.

- ✔ **Software Update:** If you're connected to the Internet, choose this item to have your Mac check with the mothership (Apple) to see whether any updates are available for OS X or its included applications (or even Apple-branded peripheral devices, such as the iPod).

Figure 3-13:
Click the
version,
build, or
serial
number
to cycle
through
these three
variations
of About
This Mac.

- **Mac OS X Software:** This launches your Web browser and takes you to the Apple Web site.

- **System Preferences:** Choose this item to open the System Preferences window (which I discuss in great detail in Chapter 13).

- **Dock (submenu):** This lets you mess with, well, the Dock! Scour Chapter 2 for more info on the Dock.

- **Location (submenu):** This enables you to switch network configurations quickly. I describe locations and network configurations in Chapter 9.

- **Recent Items (submenu):** Your Mac keeps track of the applications and documents that you've recently used. Expand this menu item to choose one of them. You can set the maximum number of applications and documents that Recent Items tracks in your General System Preference pane.

- **Force Quit:** When a program misbehaves — freezes or otherwise becomes recalcitrant — this is the command for you. Choosing this brings up the Force Quit Applications dialog, from which you choose the application that you want to quit (as shown in Figure 3-14).

   This command is so handy that it has a keyboard shortcut: ⌘+Option+ powerbutton. It also has an alternate keyboard shortcut, ⌘+Shift+Esc, which is not on the menu but is displayed on the Force Quit Applications window (lower-left part of Figure 3-8).

   Unlike earlier versions of Mac OS, you don't need to reboot to continue working after you force a program to quit in OS X. If a program ever freaks out on you, Force Quit can almost certainly put it out of its misery and allow you to continue using your Mac.

- **Sleep:** This puts your Mac into its low-powered sleep mode. I talk more about sleep in Chapter 13. (Yawn!)

Figure 3-14:
Use
Force Quit
Applications
to exit
a badly
behaved
program.

✔ **Restart:** Choose this to reboot your Mac, which is essentially the same as shutting down your machine and then turning it back on.

✔ **Shut Down:** Use this to turn off your Mac safely.

✔ **Log Out:** Because OS X is a multiuser operating system, you can have multiple users at one Mac. This command enables you to switch users without restarting or shutting down.

Logging out means that the current user, as identified by username and password, is leaving the scene. The next person to use the Mac (even if it's you) has to enter a username and password to regain entry. All this sharing stuff can be found in Chapter 14.

The Restart, Shut Down, and Log Out options have ellipses next to them and will display an Are You Sure dialog. If you don't want to have to bother with the dialog, press the Option key before selecting one of the options from the menu; the ellipses disappear and the dialog won't intrude.

Your Constant Companion: The Application Menu

The very first menu on the Mac OS X menu bar is the *Application menu* — so named because it includes commands you use to control the way lots of things work in the current application. But it's really much more than a command center for the application.

When you have an application open, the Application menu name changes to the name of that application, and the commands available change — but just a little bit. (I discuss this unusual phenomenon in the section "Menu Basics,"

earlier in this chapter.) What makes this cool is that you have access to some standard Application menu items even when you're running an application such as AppleWorks or Safari. (I have more to say about that as I work my way through the Application menu.)

The following list is an overview of the main items in the Application menu, which is called the Finder menu when the Finder is the active application. It's not too long, but it's packed with useful goodies, such as

✔ **About Finder:** Choose this to find out which version of the Finder is running on your Mac.

Okay, so this menu item isn't particularly useful — or at least not for very long. But when a different application is running, the About Finder item becomes About `application_name` and usually gives information about the program's version number, the developers (the company and the people), and any other tidbits that those developers decide to throw in. Sometimes these tidbits are useful, sometimes they're interesting, and sometimes they're both.

✔ **Preferences:** Use choices here to control how the Desktop looks and acts. Choosing Preference opens the Finder Preferences window, which has four panes: General, Labels, Sidebar, and Advanced. All panes are shown in Figure 3-15.

• In the **General pane,** select the Show These Items on the Desktop check boxes to choose whether icons for hard drives, CDs, DVDs, and other types of disks and servers appear on the Desktop. OS X selects all three options by default (which mimics earlier versions of Mac OS). But if you don't want disk icons cluttering your beautiful Desktop, you have the option of deselecting (clearing) them. If they're deselected, you can still work with CDs, DVDs, and other types of disks. You just have to open a Finder window and click the one you want from the top portion of the Sidebar.

• You can also choose whether opening a new Finder window displays your Home directory, the Computer window, or some other directory. (Home is the default.)

• The Always Open Folders in a New Window check box makes OS X work the same way as Mac OS 9.

Try it the OS X way — with windows opening "in place" so that you avoid window clutter. Press ⌘ before double-clicking to force a folder to open in a new window. I've learned to love this new way, although I hated it at first. Now, between this feature and the Column view, I rarely need more than two or three windows on-screen, and I get by most of the time with just a single window in Column view.

Figure 3-15:
Set Finder
preferences
here.

- Selecting the Open new windows in Column View check box tells the Finder that you want each window to be in Column view when you double-click or (⌘ double-click) to open it. The default behavior is to use whichever view type the folder was last displaying.

- The **Labels pane** lets you rename the colored labels that appear in the File menu. The default names are the same as their color, but you can change them to anything you like, as shown in Figure 3-15.

- The **Sidebar pane** lets you choose which items are displayed in the Sidebar, as shown in Figure 3-15. Check the check box to display the item; uncheck the checkbox to not display it.

- Finally, in the **Advanced pane,** the Show Warning before Emptying the Trash check box (on by default) allows you to turn off the nagging dialog telling you how many items are in the Trash and asking whether you really want to delete them.

- Finally, selecting the Always Show File Extensions check box tells the Finder to display the little three-, four-, or more-character filename suffixes (like .doc in summary.doc) that make your Mac's file lists look more like those of a Windows user. The Finder hides those from you by default, but if you want to be able to search for files by their extension (Using File⇨Find or ⌘+F), you need to turn this on.

✓ **Empty Trash:** Deletes all items in the Trash from your hard drive — period. I talked about the Trash in Chapter 2.

I've said it before and I'll say it again: Use this command with a modicum of caution. After a file is trashed and the Trash is emptied, it's gone. (Okay, maybe Norton Utilities can bring it back, but don't bet the farm on it.)

✓ **Secure Empty Trash:** Choosing this option makes the chance of recovery by even the most ardent hacker or expensive disk recovery tool difficult to virtually impossible. Now, the portion of the disk that held the files you're deleting will be overwritten 1, 7, or 35 times (your choice in the submenu) with randomly generated gibberish.

✓ **Services:** One of the really cool features of OS X applications is the accessibility of Services. You can select an e-mail address and create a mail message addressed to that individual, spell-check a document or selection even if the program didn't come with a spell-checker, or calculate exchange rates on currency. Unfortunately, many applications still don't support Services.

Carbon is an Apple API (Application Program Interface): programming technology that allows software developers to make applications originally created for OS 9 run in OS X with a minimum of modification. Some (but not all) Carbon applications run under both OS 9 and OS X.

Programs written exclusively for OS X that use Apple's latest generation of development tools are called Cocoa applications. Cocoa apps support OS X features such as Services automatically, unless the developer goes out of his or her way to disable them (see iPhoto for an example).

From your perspective, there's little or no difference between Carbon and Cocoa apps. Some Carbon apps are awesome; some Cocoa programs stink. It's not about the underlying development environment or APIs used.

But I digress yet again. Cocoa and Carbon are far beyond the scope of this book, but at least I snuck in the extremely abridged version.

✓ **Hide Finder (⌘+H):** Use this command when you've got Finder windows open and they're distracting you. Choosing it makes the Finder inactive (another currently running program becomes active) and hides any open Finder windows. To make the Finder visible again, either choose Show All from the Finder menu (or whatever it's called in the active application — the command should still be there) or click the Finder button (shown in the margin here) on the Dock.

Spring-loaded folders have sprung (again)

Spring-loaded folders and windows let you drag items onto closed folders or disks and have them spring open. It's harder to describe than to do, so try it a few times. Open Finder Preferences, mark the Spring-loaded Folders and Windows check box, and then follow these steps:

1. Select any icon (except a disk icon).

2. Drag it onto a folder or disk icon (but don't release the mouse button).

3. Press the spacebar (or just wait a few seconds depending on where you've set the Delay slider).

The window of the folder or disk that you dragged onto springs open. If that's the original icon's final destination, release the mouse button now. Or, if you want to drill down deeper into the folder hierarchy, don't release the mouse button and drag the icon onto any folder or disk icon. *Its* window will spring open. And so on.

Spring-loaded folders clean up after themselves, too. When you release the mouse button, regardless of how many windows you've traversed, all windows except the original (if there was one; if you dragged an icon from the Desktop, there wouldn't be) and the destination folder spring shut again, leaving your screen clean and uncluttered. Spring-loaded folders work in all three Finder window views and also with folder or disk icons in the Sidebar. Neat! If you're like me, you'll end up using spring-loaded folders a lot.

The advantage to hiding the Finder — rather than closing or minimizing all your windows to get a clean screen — is that you don't have to open them all again when you're ready to get the windows back. Instead, just choose Show All or click the Finder button in the Dock.

✔ **Hide Others (Option+⌘+H):** This command hides all windows associated with all running programs except the active program. It appears in most application's Application menus and is good for hiding distractions so you can focus on one thing — the unhidden application.

✔ **Show All:** Use this as the antidote to both of the Hide commands. Choose this, and nothing is hidden anymore.

File Management and More: Meet the File Menu

The File menu contains many commands that you use to manipulate your files and folders. I discuss file management in Chapter 6, but here I give you the lowdown on the actual Finder File menu itself.

You'll use these commands frequently, so it would behoove you to memorize their keyboard shortcuts.

- ✔ **New Finder Window (⌘+N):** Opens a new Finder window.

- ✔ **New Folder (⌘+Shift+N):** Creates a new, untitled folder in the active window. If no window is active, it creates a new, untitled folder on the Desktop.

- ✔ **Open (⌘+O):** Opens the selected item, be it icon, window, or folder.

- ✔ **Open With:** Lets you open the selected document with an application other than that document's default application. For example, in Figure 3-16, I'm about to open a graphic file. The default application for this document happens to be Apple's multipurpose document viewer, Preview.

  If I double-click this document, it would open in the default application, Preview. But that's not what I want. I want it to open it in QuickTime Player so I can copy and paste it into a movie I'm making. This menu item tells the Finder to do just that.

  This command is inactive if the selected icon isn't a document.

  Using this menu item from the Contextual menu (Control+click the document icon) or even the Finder toolbar's Action popup button is often easier than it is to reach all the way up to the menu bar to invoke it, as shown in Figure 3-17. With my two-button mouse (as described earlier), it's just right-click-and-drag 'em in one quick motion.

  If you hold down the Option key before you click the File menu, the Open With command changes to Always Open With, as shown in Figure 3-18, which enables you to change the default application for this document permanently.

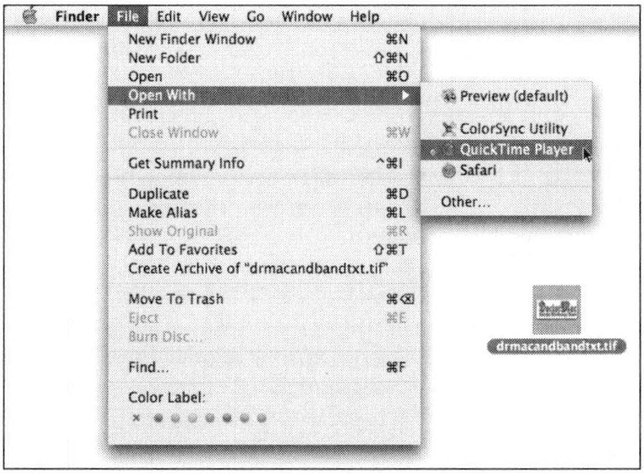

Figure 3-16:
Open a
document
with an
application
other than
its default.

Figure 3-17:
I prefer the contextual version of this particular menu item.

Figure 3-18:
Hold down the Option key before you pull down the File menu to change Open With to Always Open With.

This Option key trick also works on the contextual menu version of this command — just hold down the Option key after you Control-click the document.

✔ **Close Window (⌘+W):** Closes the active window. If no windows are open or if none are selected, the Close Window command is grayed out and can't be chosen.

Most menu commands are intuitive. So how did Apple come up with ⌘+W as a shortcut for Close Window? You think Apple would assign the letter *C*, for *C*lose. However, ⌘+C is the shortcut for Copy.

If you also press Option, the Close Window command changes to Close All. This very useful command enables you to close all open Finder windows. But it only shows up when you press the Option key; otherwise, it remains hidden.

✔ **Get Info (⌘+I):** Opens an Info window for the selected icon. (I told you about the Info window in Chapter 2.)

If you hold down Option, the Get Info command changes to Show Inspector. The Inspector window is almost identical to a Get Info window, but it displays information for whatever icon is currently selected in the Finder. If you click a different icon, the Inspector window updates to show you information about that item. A Get Info window, on the other hand, is associated with exactly one icon or a set of selected icons — you can have multiple Get Info windows on screen simultaneously but there's always only one Inspector window. Got it? If not, play with your Get Info and Inspector windows until you do.

It's good to have choices; sometimes one is more convenient to use for a particular task than the other, and sometimes you use them both.

✔ **Duplicate (⌘+D):** Makes a copy of the selected icon, adds the word *copy* to its name, and then places the copy in the same window as the original icon. You can use the Duplicate command on any icon except a disk icon.

You can't duplicate an entire disk onto itself. But you can copy an entire disk (call it Disk 1) to any other disk (call it Disk 2), as long as Disk 2 has enough space available. Just hold down Option and drag Disk 1 onto Disk 2's icon. The contents of Disk 1 will be copied to Disk 2 and will appear in a folder named Disk 1.

✔ **Make Alias (⌘+L):** Creates an alias for the selected icon in the same folder as the selected icon (or on the Desktop if the selected icon is on the Desktop). I covered aliases in detail in Chapter 2.

✔ **Show Original (⌘+R):** Displays the folder that contains the parent icon. Suppose that you make and use an alias, you put it on your Desktop or in your Favorites folder, and everything's peachy. But now you want to delete or move the original file or folder as part of a little spring-cleaning. Where is that original? You've been using the alias so long that you can't remember. To find it, click the alias and then choose File➪Show Original or use the keyboard shortcut, ⌘+R. Quick as a flash, the folder that contains the parent icon appears so you can delete, copy, move, or do anything you like with the parent icon.

This command, of course, is available only when an alias icon is selected.

✔ **Add to Sidebar (⌘+T):** Adds the selected item to the Sidebar. You can now reach the item by clicking it in any Finder window's Sidebar.

✔ **Create Archive:** Creates a compressed .zip file out of your selection. The compressed file will be smaller than the original, sometimes by quite a bit.

If you're going to send a file or files as an e-mail enclosure, creating an archive of the file(s) first and sending the archive instead of the original will save you time sending the file and save the recipient time downloading it.

✔ **Move to Trash (⌘+Delete):** Moves the selected icon to the Trash.

The icon (that is, the item that the icon represents) that you move to the Trash is not deleted from your hard drive until you choose the Empty Trash or Secure Empty Trash command from the Finder menu, the Trash pop-up menu, the Finder window's Action pop-up menu, or the contextual menu.

✔ **Eject (⌘+E):** Ejects the selected removable disk (such as a CD, DVD, floppy, or Zip).

✔ **Burn Disc:** Burns data to a CD or DVD. If you have a compatible CD-RW or DVD-R drive and you've prepared the media, choosing this command tells the Finder to finish the job and actually burn the data to the CD or DVD. I cover burning CDs and DVDs in Chapter 7.

✔ **Find (⌘+F):** Finds a file or folder on your hard drive. Use the File⇨Find command when you can't remember where you put it in a file or folder. This command kicks some butt; I'll discuss it in detail in Chapter 6.

✔ **Color Label:** Lets you apply a colored label to any icon. You select the icon and then choose a color with this menu item.

The Color Label item also appears on the Contextual (Control+Click) Menu; it's often easier to use it instead of the File menu.

The Edit Menu (Which Shoulda Been Called the Clipboard Menu)

In contrast to the File menu, which has commands that mostly deal with file management and are exclusive to the Finder window, the Edit menu's commands and functions are available in almost every Macintosh program ever made.

Because almost every program has an Edit menu and because almost every program uses the same keyboard shortcuts on its Edit menu, it behooves you to know the Edit menu keyboard shortcuts by heart, even if you remember no others.

With Mac OS X version 10.1, Apple added one of the few features that people really like about Windows — using the Copy and Paste commands to copy files from one location to another. Before that, Copy and Paste only worked with selected text; you couldn't use Copy and Paste with icons at all.

Comprehending the Clipboard

The *Clipboard* is a holding area for the last thing that you cut or copied. That copied item can be text, a picture, a portion of a picture, an object in a drawing program, a column of numbers in a spreadsheet, or just about anything that can be selected. In other words, the Clipboard is the Mac's temporary storage area.

The Clipboard commands in the Edit menu are enabled only when they can actually be used. If the currently selected item can be cut or copied, the Cut and Copy commands in the Edit menu are enabled. If the selected item can't be cut or copied, the commands are unavailable and are dimmed (gray). And when nothing is selected, the Cut, Copy, Paste, and Clear commands are also dimmed.

Copying or cutting to the Clipboard

To cut or copy something to the Clipboard, select the item and then choose Cut or Copy from the Edit menu or use the keyboard shortcuts ⌘+X (cut) or ⌘+C (copy). Choosing Cut *deletes* the selected item and puts it on the Clipboard; choosing Copy *copies* the selected item to the clipboard but does not delete the selected item.

You can cut an icon's name but you can't cut the icon itself; you may only copy an icon.

To achieve the effect of cutting an icon, select the icon, Copy it to the Clipboard, move the original icon to the Trash, and Paste the icon in its new location.

As a storage area, the Clipboard's contents are temporary. *Very* temporary. When you cut or copy an item, that item remains on the Clipboard only until you cut or copy something else. When you do cut or copy something else, the new item replaces the Clipboard's contents and in turn remains on the Clipboard until you cut or copy something else. And so it goes.

Of course, whatever's on the Clipboard heads straight for oblivion if you crash, lose power, log out, or shut your Mac down, so don't count on it too heavily or for too long.

Pasting from the Clipboard

To place the item that's on the Clipboard someplace new, click where you want the item to go and then paste what you've copied or cut (choose Edit⇨ Paste or use the keyboard shortcut ⌘+V). Pasting does *not* remove the item from the Clipboard; the item remains there until you cut or copy another item.

Pasting doesn't purge the contents of the Clipboard. In fact, an item stays on the Clipboard until you cut, copy, clear, crash (these used to be the four Cs of Macintosh computing, but Mac OS X almost never crashes), restart, shut down, or log out. This means that you can paste the same item over and over and over again, which can come in pretty handy at times.

Almost all programs have an Edit menu and use the Macintosh Clipboard, which means you can usually cut or copy something from a document in one program and paste it into a document in another program.

Usually.

Checking out the main Edit menu items

The previous sections give you probably 75 percent of what you need to know about the Edit menu. Still, because I get paid to be thorough and because the Finder's Edit menu has a few commands that aren't Clipboard-related, in this section, I go through the Edit menu's commands one by one.

- ✔ **Undo/Redo (⌘+Z):** This command undoes the last thing you did. For example, if you change the name of a folder and then choose this command, the name of the folder reverts back to what it was before you changed it. The Undo or Redo command is followed by the name of the action you're about to undo or redo.

The Undo command toggles (that is, switches back and forth) between the new and old states as long as you don't do anything else. For example, if you rename a file from *Do Me* to *Undo Me* and then choose Edit⇨ Undo, the file name reverts to *Do Me.* If you pull down the Edit menu now, the Undo command reads Redo instead of Undo. Select Redo, and the name of the file changes back to *Undo Me.* You can continue to Undo and Redo until you click somewhere else.

Don't forget about this command because it can be a lifesaver. Almost every program has an Undo command. Now for the bad news: The Undo command is ephemeral, like the Clipboard: You can only use Undo to reverse your last action. As soon as you do something else — even just clicking a lousy icon — you lose the ability to undo the original action. At least, this is true in the Finder. Some programs, such as Microsoft Word, BBEdit, iMovie, and Adobe Illustrator, allow multiple Undo operations.

Here's a cool feature introduced in Mac OS X 10.3 Panther — the Undo command works with certain actions that it never worked with before, such as moving icons. That's way cool because sometimes you drag an icon somewhere and drop it accidentally. Finding it used to be a hassle; now you can just undo the move. Kewl beans.

As you find out more about your Mac and OS X, you'll no doubt discover actions that you can't undo. Still, Undo is a great command when available, and I urge you to get in the habit of trying it often.

✔ **Cut (⌘+X):** This command removes the selected item and places it on the Clipboard. You can then paste the item from the Clipboard to another document, text box, or other valid destination. For more info on Cut and the Clipboard, see the earlier section "Copying or cutting to the Clipboard."

✔ **Copy (⌘+C):** This command makes a copy of a selected item and places it on the Clipboard. However, the original is not removed like it is when you cut something. For more info on Copy and the Clipboard, see the earlier section "Copying or cutting to the Clipboard."

✔ **Paste (⌘+V):** This command places the contents of the Clipboard at the place you last clicked. For more info on Paste and the Clipboard, see the earlier section "Pasting from the Clipboard."

✔ **Select All (⌘+A):** This command selects all icons in the active window. Or, if no window is active, using Select All selects every icon on the Desktop. If a window is active, choosing Select All selects every icon in the window, regardless of whether you can see them onscreen.

✔ **Show Clipboard:** This command summons the Clipboard window, which lists the type of item (such as text, picture, or sound) on the Clipboard and a message letting you know whether the item on the Clipboard can be displayed.

✔ **Special Characters:** This command opens the Character Palette, where you can choose special characters such as mathematical symbols, arrows, ornaments, stars, accented Latin characters, and so on. To insert a character into your document at the insertion point, simply click it and then click the Insert button.

A View from a Window: The View Menu

The View menu controls what the icons and windows look like, how icons and windows are arranged and sorted, and the look of your windows. The View menu affects the icons in the active window; if no window is active, it affects the icons on the Desktop.

The following list gives you a brief description of each of the menu items on the View menu:

- **As Icons (⌘+1):** Using Icon view is the traditional Macintosh view — the one most closely associated with the Macintosh experience. In my humble opinion, however, this view is one of the two least useful views; those big icons take up far too much valuable screen real estate. (I discuss Icon view in Chapter 4.)

- **As List (⌘+2):** In List view, you can copy or move items from different folders with a single motion without opening multiple windows. In either Icon view or Columns view, on the other hand, moving files from two or more different folders can require opening several windows and two separate drags or the use of Copy and Paste introduced in version 10.1.

- **As Columns (⌘+3):** This changes the active window to Columns view. Choosing Columns view is a new way (added in Mac OS X) to view your files in a Finder window where the folders on your computer are displayed in a column at the left of the Finder window's Browser pane and the contents of those folders are displayed in columns to the right. See Chapter 4 for more info on Columns view.

- **Clean Up:** Choose this to align icons to an invisible grid; you use it to keep your windows and Desktop neat and tidy. (If you like this invisible grid, don't forget that you can turn it on or off for the Desktop and individual windows by using View Options.) Clean Up is available only in Icon view or when no windows are active. If no windows are active, the command instead cleans up your Desktop. (To deactivate all open windows, just click anywhere on the Desktop.)

If you're like me, you've taken great pains to place icons carefully in specific places on your Desktop. Cleaning up your Desktop destroys all your beautiful work and moves all your perfectly arranged icons. And alas, cleaning up your Desktop is not something you can undo.

- **Arrange:** This rearranges the icons in the active window in your choice of six different ways: alphabetical order (by Name); modification date (by Date Modified); creation date (by Date Created); Size; Kind; or Label. Like Clean Up, it's only available for windows viewed as icons, and it's not undo-able.

- **Hide/Show Toolbar (⌘+Option+T):** This shows or hides the buttons on the toolbar of the active window. Suppose that you want to see more files and fewer buttons. Because the buttons on this toolbar are also available from the Go menu (see the next section "Going Places"), and the Action button's popup menu is just whatever contextual menu goes with your current selection, you're safe in hiding them. Just choose Hide Toolbar to make the toolbar go away or Show Toolbar to bring it back. (As I detail in Chapter 5, the gray oval button in the upper-right corner of every Finder window does the same thing.) The only thing you lose is the Search box, and you can use Find for that if you want.

What they don't tell you ahead of time (but I will) is that hiding the toolbar also hides the Sidebar. As I mentioned previously in one of my rants, I find this quite annoying because I use the Sidebar a lot, but don't use the toolbar nearly as often (there are keyboard equivalents for all of them).

When the toolbar is hidden, opening a folder opens a *new* Finder window rather than reusing the current one (which is what happens when the toolbar is showing unless you've changed this preference in Finder Preferences or are using Column view). Go to Chapter 4 for more about the toolbar in Finder windows.

✔ **Customize Toolbar:** This one is way cool — use it to design your own Finder window toolbar. Find out more about this nifty feature in Chapter 4.

✔ **Hide/Show Status Bar:** Shows or hides the status bar for Finder windows, at the bottom of the window. The status bar tells you how many items are in each window and, if any are selected, how many you've selected out of the total, and how much space is available on the hard drive containing this window.

✔ **Show View Options (⌘+J):** Here's where you can soup up the way any window looks and behaves. You can do this either globally (so that all windows use the same view when opened) or on a window-by-window basis. I discuss Show View Options more in Chapter 4.

Going Places: Checking Out Go Menu Items

The Go menu is chock-full of shortcuts. The items on this menu take you to places on your Mac — many of the same places that you can go with the Finder window toolbar — and a few other places.

The following list gives you a brief look at the items on the Go menu.

See the next section for info on some menu items that aren't listed here, such as Computer, Home, iDisk, and Favorites.

✔ **Back (⌘+[):** Use this menu option to return to the last Finder window that you had open. It's equivalent to the Back button in the Finder toolbar, in case you have the toolbar hidden.

Think of this command as a breadcrumb trail that moves backward through every folder you open. For example, suppose that you open seven folders to get to the destination folder that you desire — call them folders 1, 2, 3, 4, 5, 6, and 7. Each time that you select the Back command, the previous folder appears — 6, 5, 4, 3, 2, and 1.

✔ **Forward (⌘+]):** This is the opposite of using the Back command, moving you forward through every folder you open. Picking up from the previous example, suppose that you've moved back to folder 1. Each time you select the Forward command, you move forward through those folders — 2, 3, 4, 5, 6, and 7. If you haven't gone back, you can't go forward.

✔ **Enclosing Folder (⌘+up arrow {↑}):** This command tells the Finder window to display the folder where the currently selected item is located.

✔ **Computer (⌘+Shift+C):** This command tells the Finder window to display the Computer level, showing Network and all of your disks.

✔ **Home (⌘+Shift+H):** Use this command to have the Finder window display your Home directory (which is named with your short name).

✔ **Network (⌘+Shift+K):** This command displays whatever is accessible on your network in the Finder window.

✔ **iDisk:** Use this submenu to mount your iDisk (⌘+Shift+I), another user's iDisk, or another user's iDisk Public Folder.

✔ **Applications (⌘+Shift+A):** This command positions the Finder window to your Applications directory, the usual storehouse for all the programs that came with your Mac (and the most likely place that the programs you install will be placed).

✔ **Utilities (⌘+Shift+U):** This command gets you to the Utilities folder inside the Applications folder in one fell swoop. The Utilities folder is the repository of such useful items as Disk Utility (which lets you erase, format, verify, and repair disks) and Disk Copy (which you use to create and mount disk-image files).

✔ **Recent Folders:** Use this submenu to quickly go back to a folder that you recently visited. Every time you open a folder, Mac OS X creates an alias to it and stores it in the Recent Folders folder. You can open any of these aliases from the Recent Folders command in the Go menu.

✔ **Go to Folder (⌘+Shift+G):** This summons the Go to Folder dialog, as shown in Figure 3-19. Look at your Desktop. Maybe it's cluttered with lots of windows, or maybe it's completely empty. Either way, suppose you're several clicks away from a folder that you want to open. If you know the path from your hard drive to that folder, you can type the path to the folder that you want in the Go to the Folder text box (separating each folder name with a forward slash [/]) and then click Go to move (relatively) quickly to the folder that you need.

The first character you type must also be a forward slash, as shown in Figure 3-19, unless you're going to a subdirectory of the current window.

Figure 3-19:
Go to a
folder by
entering its
path.

This particular window is clairvoyant; it tries to guess which folder you mean by the first letter or two that you type. For example, in Figure 3-19, I typed the letter **A** and paused, and the window guessed that I wanted *Applications;* then I pressed the right-arrow key to accept the guess and typed a **U**, and the window guessed the rest *(tilities)* and filled it in for me. (The final letters I *didn't* type are highlighted in Figure 3-19).

✔ **Connect to Server (⌘+K):** If your Mac is connected to a network or to the Internet, use this command to reach these remote resources.

Window Dressing

Again with the windows! I already spent plenty of pages giving you the scoop on how to work with windows. But wait; there's more . . . the commands on the Window menu provide you with tools that you can use to manage your windows. Here is a brief look at each of the menu items on the Window menu.

✔ **Minimize Window (⌘+M):** Use this command to unclutter your Desktop. It's the same as clicking the orange gumdrop.

With a Finder window selected (the command will be unavailable — grayed out — if you don't have an active Finder window), using the Minimize Window command makes the window disappear, as it were: The file or folder is still open, but it's not active, and you don't see it on your screen. You do see, however, an icon representing it in the Dock. (Read all about the Dock in Chapter 2.)

✔ **Bring All to Front:** In previous versions of Mac OS, when you clicked a window belonging to an application, *all* that application's windows came to the front. That is, windows moved within layers and as layers. Under OS X, windows interleave. For example, you could have a Finder window, a Word window, a Photoshop window, a Word window, and another Finder window in a front-to-back order. Choosing Bring All to Front enables you to have all the Finder windows move to the front of those belonging to other applications (while keeping their own relative ordering). What you get is an emulation of the layering to which Mac (and Windows) users are accustomed.

If you want to bring the all windows belonging to the Finder (or any other program, for that matter) to the front at once you can also click the application's Dock icon.

If you hold down the Option key when you pull down the Window menu, the Minimize Window changes to the Minimize All Windows, and the Bring All to Front command changes to the useful Arrange in Front, which arranges all your Desktop windows neatly — starting in the upper-left corner of the Desktop, as shown in Figure 3-20.

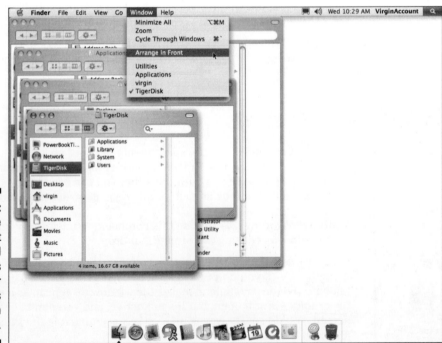

Figure 3-20:
The Arrange in Front command stacks up your windows neatly in the corner.

✔ **Other items:** The remaining items on the Window menu are the names of all currently open Finder windows. Click a window's name to bring it to the front.

The names of windows that you minimize (the ones with icons appearing on the Dock) remain on the Window menu. You can view the window by choosing its name from the Window menu.

Not Just a Beatles Movie: Help and the Help Menu

One of the best features about all Macs since System 7.*x* is the system's excellent built-in help. And Mac OS X doesn't cheat you on that legacy: This system has online help in abundance. When you have a question about how to do something, the Mac Help Center is the first place you should visit (after this book, of course).

The sole item in the Help menu — Mac Help (⌘+?) — opens the Mac Help window, as shown in Figure 3-21.

Figure 3-21: Mac Help is nothing if not helpful.

The one exception to the rule I mention earlier in this chapter — that you don't have to press Shift for capital letters in a keyboard shortcut on a menu — is the keyboard shortcut for Help. This shortcut appears on the Help menu as ⌘+?, and you do have to hold down the Shift key to type the question mark. In fact, if you press ⌘+/ (the Command key and a front slash, which is what you get when you type a lowercase question mark), nothing happens. This result is different from what you'd get from earlier versions of Mac OS.

In other words, the shortcut for Help *should be* ⌘+Shift+/ even though the menu says ⌘+?. Got it? If you're wondering why this is, Apple says it's because you're going to be asking questions, and the question mark is a great device for remembering that. It's the same way for other non-alphabetic keys used in shortcuts. Personally, I think it's lame — it should work one way or the other all the time.

To use Mac Help, simply type a word or phrase into the text field at the top right and then press Enter or Return. In a few seconds, your Mac provides you with one or more articles to read, which (theoretically) are related your question. Usually. For example, if you type **menus** and press Return, you get more than 50 different help articles, as shown in Figure 3-22.

Figure 3-22:
You got questions? Mac's got answers.

More menus 4 U

If you like the menus you've seen so far, have I got a treat for you: Mac OS X Tiger includes 23 additional special-purpose menus, known as Menu Extras, that you can install if you like. Some, including Sound, Displays, Battery, and others, can be enabled from the appropriate System Preferences pane (more on this in Chapter 13). But the easiest way is to open the Menu Extras folder (/System/Library/CoreServices/Menu Extras) and double-click each Menu Extra you want to install.

Here are the contents of the Menu Extras folder:

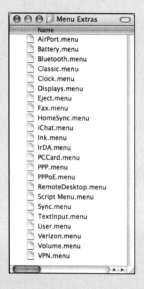

And here are a handful of Menu Extras installed in the menu bar:

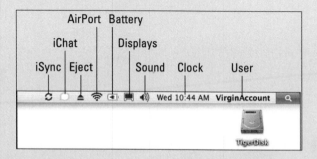

If you install a Menu Extra and later decide you don't need or want it in your menu bar, hold down the ⌘ key and drag it off the menu bar; it'll disappear with a satisfying "poof."

Although you don't have to be connected to the Internet to use Mac Help, you do need an Internet connection to get the most out of it. That's because OS X installs only certain help articles on your hard drive. If you ask a question that those articles don't answer, Mac Help will connect to Apple's Web site and download the answer (assuming that you have an active Internet connection). These answers are the "results from product support," denoted by a plus sign and underlined text, as shown in the lower part of the window in Figure 3-22. Click one and Help Viewer retrieves the text over the Internet. While this can sometimes be inconvenient, it's also quite smart. This way, the help system can be updated at any time by Apple without requiring any action from you.

Furthermore, after you've asked a question and Mac Help has grabbed the answer from the Apple Web site, the answer remains on your hard drive forever. If you ask for it again (even in a later date), your computer won't have to download it from the Apple Web site again.

Part II
Rounding Out Your Basic Training

In this part . . .

*P*eruse the chapters in this part to discover how to perform important hands-on tasks. But don't get all worked up — this stuff is easy. In fact, I think of this part as "The Lazy Person's How-To Guide."

I start by showing you more about the all-important Finder, which is followed by a pair of all-important skills: saving and opening files. Then you discover the joys of removable media — a good thing to know! Next is a short discourse on managing your files without tearing your hair out. I finish with what is perhaps the most important information in this entire book — information about backing up your valuable data.

It might sound imposing but I assure you this part will be (mostly) painless.

Chapter 4

Newfangled Finder

*B*elieve it or not, all the stuff on your Mac can fit in one window — the Finder window. In this window, you can double-click your way to your favorite application, your documents, or out onto the Internet. In fact, the Finder is the place you are when you haven't yet gone any place at all. The Finder window appears on the Desktop when you start up your Mac, and it's always available. And if you close the Finder, you can get it back easily. Even if you're an old hand with Mac OS, I show you how to get the most from the OS X Finder in this chapter.

The Finder is, among other things, a window. A very talented window, but a window just the same. (For the lowdown on windows in general, see Chapter 3.)

Getting to Know the Finder

A Finder window is a handy friend. And the Finder is indeed a window (or multiple windows) in OS X. Use the Finder to navigate through files, folders, and applications on your hard drive — or to connect to other Macs and Internet servers — right from your Desktop.

Figure 4-1 shows a typical Finder window, with all the standard features highlighted.

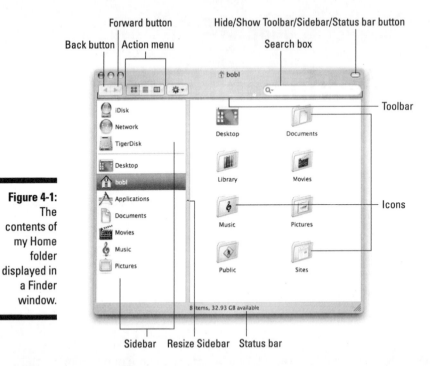

Forward button

Hide/Show Toolbar/Sidebar/Status bar button

Back button | Action menu

Search box

Toolbar

Icons

Figure 4-1:
The
contents of
my Home
folder
displayed in
a Finder
window.

Sidebar   Resize Sidebar   Status bar

Hey, I know you!

If you're an experienced Mac user, you know the Finder well. Every version of Mac OS before Max OS X has included a Finder, and its appearance has been pretty much the same since the Mac was introduced in 1984. What's new in the Mac OS X Finder is that you can use a single window instead of multiple windows if you like. Imagine using a single window to display just about everything stored on all your hard drives and removable disks. Instead of opening a new window for each folder or disk, the Mac OS X Finder can display everything in the same window, shifting your view of items as you click or select them with buttons in the window.

If you liked it the old way and prefer multiple Finder windows onscreen, you can tell your

Mac to give you what you want temporarily or permanently. To open a folder or disk in a new window just this once, merely hold down the ⌘ key when you double-click the folder or disk and it will open in a new window. To make that the default behavior for your Finder, set your Finder Preferences (in the Finder menu) to open a new window when you double-click a folder.

Note: If you've hidden the toolbar by clicking a Finder window's Hide/Show Toolbar button, new windows open automatically when you open a folder — you don't have to hold down the ⌘ key at all.

This can be quite disconcerting. All of a sudden Finder windows behave differently as a result of your doing something totally unrelated — hiding the Toolbar.

One last thing: If you want to use the new one-window approach on a window with its toolbar hidden — or if you've set your Finder Preferences to open folders in a new window —

just hold down the Option key when you double-click a folder or disk. It closes the current window and opens the new window as if you had never hidden the toolbar or changed the Finder preference setting.

Belly Up to the Bar (s):
The Toolbar and Sidebar

Right below the title bar, you find the Finder window toolbar (refer to Figure 4-1). On it are tools and buttons that let you navigate quickly and act upon selected icons. To activate a toolbar button, click it once.

You say you don't want to see the toolbar at the top of the window? Okay! Just choose View⇨Hide Toolbar or click the little gray jelly bean-looking thing in the upper-right corner of every Finder window, and it's gone. (If only life were always so easy!)

Alas, hiding the Toolbar also hides the useful Sidebar and Status Bar. If only you could choose to hide them independently. . . .

If you've customized your toolbar, as you discover later in this chapter, it won't look exactly like this. But here's the lowdown on the toolbar's default buttons, from left to right:

✔ **Forward and Back buttons:** Clicking the Forward and Back buttons displays the folders that you've viewed in this window in sequential order. If you've used a Web browser, it's a lot like that.

The keyboard shortcuts ⌘+[for Back and ⌘+] for Forward are more useful (in my opinion) than using the buttons. (For more on this nifty navigation device, see the "Hither and yon: The Forward and Back buttons" section later in this chapter.)

✔ **View buttons:** The three view buttons change the way that the window displays its contents. Stay tuned for an entire section on views coming up in just a few pages.

✔ **Action:** Click this button to see a popup menu of all the context-sensitive actions you can perform upon selected icons, as shown in Figure 4-2.

Finding the Finder

If you don't see a Finder window on the Desktop when your Mac finishes the start-up process, you probably closed it the last time that the Mac was on. So how do you find the Finder window again?

✔ Click the Finder icon in the Dock. (It's the one with a smiley blue Mac face on it.)

✔ Choose File➪New Finder window (or use the keyboard shortcut ⌘+N), and a Finder window appears. New Finder windows always open up showing your Home directory. In other words, they open up labeled YourShortName, the same as if you chose Go➪Home or clicked the Home button in the Sidebar.

Note: In Finder Preferences, you can change what is displayed when a New Finder window opens — to your Home, Computer, Documents folder, or any other folder you choose.

You'll probably open a lot of new windows, so consider memorizing this keyboard shortcut: ⌘+N. This shortcut is good to know because most software programs use the ⌘+N shortcut to create a new document. If your memory is bad, use this mnemonic device: N is for New.

Figure 4-2: Clicking the Action button displays a menu of actions you can perform on the selected icon or icons in the Finder window.

✔ **Search:** The toolbar's Search box is a nifty way to search for files. Just type a word or even just a few letters and after a few seconds, the window will fill with a list of files that match, as shown in Figure 4-3.

Figure 4-3:
When the toolbar's Search box isn't good enough, use the Find command instead.

The File⇨Find command (shortcut: ⌘+F), which used to open its own unique search window, opens a special Finder window (as shown in Figure 4-3). The cursor appears promptly (so to speak) in the Search box so you can begin typing your search string immediately.

When you use this technique, you have a choice of where to search — Servers, Computer (selected in Figure 4-3), Home, or Others — and then choose additional criteria (such as the Kind of file, last date the file was opened, modification date, creation date, keywords, label, file contents, or size). To add a criterion, click the + button on the right side of the window; to save a search for reuse in the future, click the Save button on the right side of the window.

Navigating the Finder: Up, Down, and Backwards

In addition to the Sidebar described previously and some good old-fashioned double-clicking, the Mac OS X Finder window offers additional navigation aids — the current folder drop-down menu and the Back and Forward buttons.

Like a roadmap: The current folder drop-down menu

In the center of the window's title bar is the name of the folder that you're viewing in this window — the highlighted folder. To see a roadmap to this folder from the top level, ⌘+click and hold on the folder's name (Desktop) in the title bar, as shown in Figure 4-4.

Figure 4-4:
Traverse
folders
from this
convenient
drop-down
menu.

A drop-down menu appears with the current folder (Desktop) at the top.

Select any folder in the menu, and it becomes the highlighted folder in the current window; release the mouse button and that folder's contents are displayed.

Put another way, in Figure 4-4, the contents of the Desktop folder are displayed (actually, they would be displayed if there were any, but there aren't). If I released the mouse button, the contents of the highlighted folder (bobl) would appear.

Use this pop-up menu to move from your current folder to the bottom folder, which represents your computer (PowerBook TiGer in Figure 4-4). Now click the Back button. Hey, you're right back where you were before you touched that pop-up menu.

If you like this feature a lot, use the Customize Toolbar command (in the View menu) to add a Path button to your toolbar. It displays the menu of folders previously described without having to hold down the ⌘ key.

To remove an item from the Toolbar, simply hold down the ⌘ key and drag it out of the Toolbar. When you release the mouse button, the item will disappear with a satisfying poof. This technique also works for removing items from the Dock or Sidebar, but you don't have to press the ⌘ key. Just drag them out onto the desktop and *poof!*

Hither and yon: The Forward and Back buttons

Suppose you're fiddling around in a Finder window, opening stuff, and maybe even looking for a particular file. You realize that the item you want is in the folder you just left. D'oh! What to do? Click the Back button — yes, just like the one on a Web browser. The Back button (shown on the left in the margin) is the left-pointing arrow at the left end of the Finder window toolbar. If you want to move to the last folder you were at, just click the Back button, and there you are! If you use a Web browser (and who doesn't these days?), you're probably a pro at this already.

Here's an example of how the Back button works. Say you're in your Home folder, you click the Favorites button, and then a split-second later you realize that you actually need something in the Home folder. Just a quick click of the Back button and poof! You're back Home.

As for the Forward button, well, it moves you the opposite direction through folders that you've visited in this window.

Play around with them both — you'll find them invaluable. And don't forget even more invaluable keyboard shortcuts — ⌘+[and ⌘+] for Forward and Back, respectively.

Customize Your Finder Windows

You have three ways to view a window — Column view, Icon view, and List view. Some people like columns, some like icons, and others love lists. To each her own. Play with the three Finder views to see which one works best for you. For what it's worth, I usually prefer Column view with a dash of List view thrown in when I need a folder's contents sorted by creation date or size.

The following sections give you a look at each view.

Column view

The Column view is my favorite way to display windows in the Finder.

To display a window in the Column view, click the Column view button in the toolbar (as shown in the margin), choose View➪As Columns from the Finder's menu bar, or use the keyboard shortcut ⌘+3.

You can have as many columns in a Column view window as your screen can handle. Just use the window sizer (also known as the resize control) in the lower-right corner to enlarge your window horizontally so new columns have room to open. Or click the green Zoom (also known as Maximize) gumdrop to expand the window to its maximum width instantly.

You can use the little grabber handles at the bottom of a column to resize the column widths. When you drag this handle left or right, the column to its left resizes; if you hold down the Option key when you drag, *all* the columns resize at the same time. Furthermore, if you double-click one of these little handles, the column to its left expands to the width of the widest item it contains. And if you Option-double-click any handle, all the columns expand to the width of the widest item at the same time.

See what a Finder window displayed in Column view looks like in Figure 4-5.

Figure 4-5:
A Finder
window in
Column
view.

Here's how it works: When I click the Tiger Disk icon in the Sidebar, its contents appear in the column to the right. When I click the Applications folder in this column, its contents appear in the second column. When I click the Utilities folder in the second column, its contents appear in the third column. When I click the Java folder in the third column, its contents appear in the fourth column. Finally, when I click Java Web Start in the fourth column, a big icon plus some information about this file appears (it's an application, 1.3 MB in size, created on 10/5/04, and so on).

This rightmost column displays information about the highlighted item to its left, but only if that item is not a folder or disk. (If it were, its contents would be in this column, right?) That's the preview column. For most items, the picture is an enlarged view of the file's icon, as shown in Figure 4-5. But if that item is a graphic file (even a PDF) saved in a format that QuickTime can interpret (most graphic file formats), a preview picture appears instead of an icon, as shown in Figure 4-6. If you don't like having the Preview displayed, you can choose View⇨Show View Options and turn off Show Preview Column.

Figure 4-6: The preview of a graphic file is a picture instead of an icon.

Column view is a darn handy way to quickly look through a lot of folders at once, and is especially useful when those folders are filled with graphics files.

Icon view

Icon view is a free-form view that allows you to move your icons around within a window to your heart's content. Check out the Finder window in Figure 4-1 to see what Icon view looks like.

To display a window in the Icon view, click the Icon view button in the toolbar (as shown in the margin), choose View➪As Icons from the Finder's menu bar, or use the keyboard shortcut ⌘+1.

List view

Finally, I come to the view that I loved and used most in Mac OS 9 (but use much less often since the advent of the Column view): the List view (as shown in Figure 4-7). The main reason why I liked it so much was the little triangles to the left of each folder, known as *disclosure triangles,* which let you see the contents of a folder without actually opening the folder. It also allows you to select items from multiple folders at once.

Icon view: The ol' stick-in-the-mud view

In all fairness, I must say that many perfectly happy Macintosh users love Icon view and refuse to even consider anything else. Fine. But as the number of files on your hard drive increases (as it does for every Mac user), screen real estate becomes more and more valuable. In my humble opinion, the only real advantages that the Icon view has over the Column or List views is the capability to arrange the icons anywhere you like within the window, and to put a background picture or color behind your icons. Big deal.

I offer this solution as a compromise: If you still want to see your files and folders in Icon view, make them smaller so that more of them fit in the same space on-screen.

To change the size of a window's icons, choose View⇨Show View Options (or press ⌘+J). In

the View Options window that appears, click the This Window Only radio button. Drag the Icon Size slider that you find there to the left. This makes the icons in the active window smaller. Conversely, you could make 'em all bigger by dragging the Icon Size slider to the right. Bigger icons make me crazy, but if you like them that way, your Mac can accommodate you.

If you want to make the icons in *every* window bigger or smaller, click the All Windows radio button in the View Options window and drag the Icon Size slider right or left. This affects all windows displayed in Icon view. (Read more on the View Options window coming up in a page or two. . . .)

Note: If you like Icon view, consider purchasing a larger monitor — I hear that monitors now come in a 30-inch size.

To disclose a folder's contents you merely click on the triangle to its left; when you do, its contents are disclosed. In Figure 4-7, the Logs and CrashReporter folders are disclosed.

 To display a window in List view, click the List view button in the toolbar (as shown in the margin), choose View⇨As List from the Finder's menu bar, or use the keyboard shortcut ⌘+2.

Now look at the little triangle at the right edge of the selected column; it's the Name column in Figure 4-7). If this little arrow points up, the items in the corresponding column sort in descending order; if you click the header (Name) once, the arrow now points down and the items are listed in the opposite (ascending) order, as shown in Figure 4-8. This behavior is true for all columns in List-view windows.

 To change the order in which columns appear in a window, press and hold on a column's name and then drag it to the left or right until it's where you want it. Release the mouse button, and the column moves.

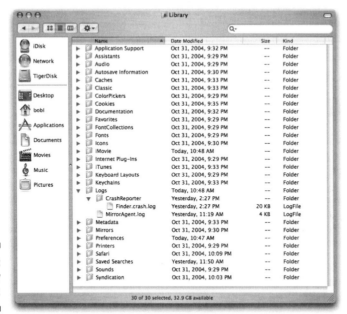

Figure 4-7:
A window
in List view.

Figure 4-8:
Sort items in
descending
order in List
view . . .

The exception to this (isn't there always an exception?) is that the Name column always appears first in List view windows; all other columns can be moved about at will. And, in fact, you can even hide and show columns other than Name if you like, as you'll see in the *Showing those View Options*

On Using View Options

The Finder is outrageously handy. It not only gives you convenient access to multiple windows, but also offers ways to tweak what you see till you get what works best for you.

To customize the way Finder windows look, you use the View Options window. When you choose View⇨Show View Options from the Finder menu bar (or use the keyboard shortcut ⌘+J), you see the View Options window, as shown in Figure 4-9.

Figure 4-9:
Set the appearance of Finder windows here.

Start by selecting the All Windows radio button at the top of the View Options window. Now, whatever choices you set in this window affect *all* Finder windows for which you haven't specified explicit options (which you do with the This Window Only radio button, which I get to in a moment).

First decide whether you want to modify the Icon, List, or Column view by displaying the window in that view. Here's the deal:

 ✔ If you choose Icon view, your options apply to all windows in Icon view

 ✔ If you choose List view, your choices apply to all windows in List view.

✔ Because there are no This Window Only choices for Column view, your choices in View Options for Column view always apply to all Column view windows.

The choice that you make determines what options you see in the View Options window. The following sections describe your choices.

Icon view options

So you just can't kick that icon habit, eh? Okay . . . here's how to make global settings so all your windows use the Icon view. (If this concept excites you, you *really* need to get out of the house more!)

In the window, select the All Windows radio button. Now you can set how big you want your icons, how to arrange them in windows, and whether you want to insert a picture as a background for your folder windows (yup, *all* folders) or make the background color something other than white.

The following list describes the View Options that you see after you choose Icon view:

✔ **Icon Size:** Use the Icon Size slider to make icons larger or smaller. To save valuable screen-real-estate space, I recommend keeping your icons small. The largest icon size is nothing short of huge.

Have a Finder window open in which icons are visible as you move the slider, so you can monitor the icons' size as they shrink or grow, depending on how far you move the slider.

✔ **Text Size:** What it says . . . the size of the icon's name. Just choose the point size that you want from the popup menu here.

✔ **Label Position:** Select either the Bottom or the Right radio button here to set where the icon's name appears — below it or to its right.

✔ **Icon Arrangement:** Okay, it doesn't label this group of check boxes, but icon arrangement is what they do. Here you specify whether those icons should be penned up or free-range with these check boxes:

- **Snap to Grid:** Creates nice, straight lines of icons.

- **Show Item Info:** Adds a line of text below the icon's name with info about the file (or folder).

- **Show Icon Preview:** Got me. Nobody I know has figured this one out yet. It doesn't seem to do anything. If you know what it does, please let me know.

- **Keep Arranged By:** Lets you specify the sort order for your icons from the pop-up menu below. Your choices are Name, Date Modified, Date Created, Size, and Kind.

✔ **Background:** From this list of radio buttons, you can pick a color or pic-
    ture for your windows or opt for none at all (white, the default). Look at
    Figure 4-10 to see what a folder looks like with a picture in its back-
    ground. I'm not sure that windows should have pictures in their back-
    grounds, but if you like them, this is how it's done.

    Whatever you choose — insert a picture, choose a color, or neither —
    appears in each of your windows if you've chosen the All Windows radio
    button in the View Options window.

Figure 4-10:
All windows
now have
this faux-
rock-band
logo as their
background.

List view options

Suppose you prefer List view (instead of Icon view) and want to set global
options for viewing your items this way. With your Finder window in List
view, choose View➪Show View Options from the Finder menu bar, and then
select the All Windows radio button from the View Options window that
appears. In Figure 4-11, you see a cluster of check boxes beneath the Show
Columns heading. (These are the ones I was talking about a few paragraphs
ago.) Check the ones you want to appear in all your List view windows.

Most of the options here tell Mac OS X which fields to display or hide. The
choices depend on what information you want displayed, such as

  ✔ Date modified
  ✔ Date created
  ✔ Size
  ✔ Kind

　　✔ Version

　　✔ Comments

　　✔ Labels

Figure 4-11:
Choose
which fields
to display in
List view.

Select the ones you want to see, and then decide whether you like the view you selected. You can always change your selections later if you find you aren't using a particular field.

The first three — modification date, creation date, and size — can be useful if you want to sort the items by something other than name.

Here are two more options that may prove useful. Near the bottom of this window are these two check boxes:

　　✔ **Use Relative Dates:** Select this check box, and Mac OS X intelligently substitutes relative word equivalents — such as *yesterday* or *today* — for numerical dates.

　　　When you set your clock back a day and look at files that you updated that day before setting your clock back, the relative date reads *tomorrow*. (Curious but true.)

　　✔ **Calculate All Sizes:** Selecting this check box instructs Mac OS X to (yup) calculate all sizes. Select this view to see how much stuff is in each folder when you look at it in List view. The items (including folders) in the active window are sorted in descending order from biggest to smallest when you sort by size.

　　　If you don't select the Calculate All Sizes check box, items other than folders are sorted by size, with all folders — regardless of their size — appearing at the bottom of the list (or top, if the sort order is ascending).

Being really finicky and choosing your views window by window

Perhaps choosing a global look for your Finder windows is just too big of a commitment for you, or you have a setup that you like but need a special view for a particular window. Here's how to adjust your window view settings individually.

1. **Open the window that you want to set up.**

2. **Choose View⊃Show View Options from the menu bar.**

3. **Select the This Window Only radio button in the View Options window.**

4. **Choose View⊃As List or View⊃As Icons to get the view that you want to set.**

The options are conveniently the same as the global options that I describe earlier, so have at it and make this special window look just the way you like it.

Near the top of the View Options dialog, you find the Icon Size radio buttons. Select from these two radio buttons to choose between small and large icons in your List views. For my money, I think the smallest ones make windows appear noticeably faster — and they definitely allow more items to be shown. (Your mileage may vary.)

One more thing: Spring-loaded folders were resurrected in OS X version 10.2 Jaguar. They work in all the views and with icons in the toolbar.

If you were among the millions who requested that Apple bring them back, I'm happy to report that Apple did and that OS X's spring-loaded folders are better than ever. I'll show you why they're so cool in Chapter 6.

Making It Your Very Own Finder: Introducing Finder Preferences

Another way to customize your Finder to choose Finder⊃Finder Preferences (or use the keyboard shortcut, ⌘+comma). The Finder Preferences window has four panes — General, Labels, Sidebar, and Advanced — as shown in Figure 4-12.

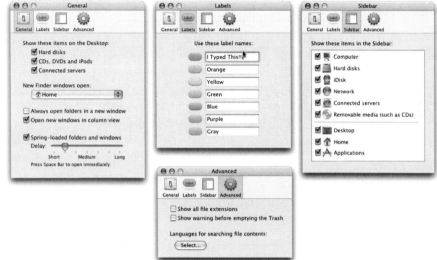

Figure 4-12:
The four
panes of
the Finder
Preferences
window.

Using the General pane

The General pane starts off with a series of Show These Items on the Desktop check boxes, which let you hide or show hard disks, CDs, DVDs, iPods, and connected servers on your desktop.

If a check box contains a check mark, the associated item appears on your desktop. If the check box is empty, click it once to make a check mark appear. If a check box already contains a check mark, you can click it once to make the check mark disappear.

Here's a quick rundown of the items that show up in the General pane:

✓ **New Finder Window Opens:** This menu lets you choose what folder appears (when you create a new window in the Finder using File➪ New Window or the shortcut ⌘+N.)

Other: If you don't like the choices the menu offers — Home, Documents, or your computer, hard disk, or iDisk — choose this bottom item in the menu instead. It'll let you choose any folder you like for new Finder windows.

- ✔ **Always Open Folders in a New Window:** This check box does exactly what its name implies, as discussed earlier in this chapter.

- ✔ **Open New Windows in Column View:** This check box also does exactly what its name implies — it causes your new windows to open in Column view, instead of whichever view you last used with that folder or disk.

- ✔ **Spring-Loaded Folders and Windows:** This check box turns spring-loaded folders on and off, whereas the Delay slider below it governs how long a spring-loaded folder takes to spring open.

    Spring-loaded folders are very useful; I recommend turning them on and using them as often as possible. To see how they work, turn them on now and drag any icon onto a folder or disk icon BUT DO NOT RELEASE THE MOUSE BUTTON. The folder icon inverts to let you know you're in the right place, and shortly thereafter (how shortly depends upon your Delay slider setting), the folder pops open right under your cursor.

To accelerate the process of popping open a folder — regardless of your Delay slider setting — press the spacebar after the folder (or disk) icon inverts.

Using the Labels pane

Did you know that you can label files? You can. Select a file or folder (or several files and folders), pull down the File menu, and move the cursor over the color dot that represents the label you want to assign to the file or folder. Release the mouse button and the file takes on the hue of its label.

The Labels tab in Finder Preferences lets you change the names of those labels. Just select the existing name (Red, Orange, and so on) and type a new one.

Using the Sidebar pane

The Sidebar pane (also called the Sidebar tab) offers check boxes to hide or show items in the Sidebar. In Figure 4-12, I've got everything it offers checked, so all the items you see — Computer, Hard disks, iDisk, Network, Connected servers, CDs, Desktop, Home, and Applications — appear in the Sidebar of my Finder windows.

There's an even easier way to add icons to the Sidebar — drag them onto the lower part of it and then release the mouse button. The icon isn't moved from its actual location, but you can now access its contents by clicking it in the Sidebar rather than opening a bunch of folders to get to it.

Using the Advanced pane

The Advanced tab offers a check box to Show All File Extensions. When it's checked, all your document files will display a three- or four-letter extension such as .doc, .jpeg, .mp3, and so on. Uncheck the check box and the extensions are hidden.

The second check box, Show Warning before Emptying the Trash, lets you turn off the annoying trash warning — the one that asks if you're SURE you want to empty the Trash — whenever you empty the Trash.

Last but not least, if you click the Select button below Languages for Searching File Contents, a window appears, showing check boxes for languages you might want to use when you search the contents of your files. Any language with a check mark gets indexed and searched; those without check marks are not.

The fewer languages you choose, the faster the indexing occurs — and the less disk space those indexes consume. Unless you need them, I suggest you uncheck all but one or two.

The choices you make here affect the File➪Find (⌘+F) search mechanism, as well as the Spotlight search mechanism in the upper-right corner of the menu bar. (You can find more info on Spotlight in Chapter 11.) Another nifty factoid: If you deselect all the languages here, you effectively turn off indexing.

Customizing the Finder with Folder Actions

Apple has this really cool technology called AppleScript. It's been around since System 7 was released and hasn't ever really gotten the respect it deserves. AppleScript lets you program repetitive tasks so you don't have to go through all the steps yourself every time you want to perform the task.

Almost a decade later (Mac OS 8.5), Apple introduced Folder Actions, a way to attach these AppleScripts to a folder so an appropriate script would run whenever the folder was opened, closed, moved, had an item placed in it, or had an item removed.

Having an AppleScript run when items are added to a closed folder sounds like a great tool for drop-box-style folders to me — how about you? For example, you could have Mail launch and send a notification to your project leader or project team whenever a new file was added to the folder.

The first thing to do is create or obtain AppleScripts to perform the tasks you want done. Programming AppleScript is beyond the purview of this book — in fact, a book teaching you all about programming AppleScript is the size of this book alone — it's *AppleScript For Dummies,* Second Edition, by Tom Trinko (Wiley). Closer to hand, you can find ready-to-go scripts for Folder Actions on your hard drive at

```
Library/Scripts/Folder Action Scripts
```

and even more at Apple's Web site in the AppleScript pages (`www.apple.com/applescript`).

After you've enabled Folder Actions, you can Control+click the folder's icon again and choose a new item from the contextual menu, Attach a Folder Action. This opens a Choose a File dialog (really an Open dialog, which I tell you about in Chapter 5) where you can select your Folder Action script. The dialog conveniently defaults to the Folder Action Scripts folder mentioned previously. Select the script, click Choose, and you're set to go.

If you want to know more about writing Folder Action scripts, check out `www.apple.com/applescript/folder_actions`.

Chapter 5

Mastering the Save Sheet and the Open Dialog

In This Chapter

▶ Saving your document

▶ Discovering the differences between Save and Save As

▶ Mastering the Open dialog

▶ Discerning the subtle differences between the Open dialog and Save sheets

▶ Knowing what the Open dialog doesn't show you

*T*his could be the most important chapter in this book. If you don't understand how to open and save files using the Open dialog and Save sheets, you'll have a heck of a time getting the hang of your Mac. Ask any long-time Mac user — the old lament is pretty common: "Well, I saved the file and now I don't know where it went." It happens all the time with new users; if they don't master these essential techniques, they often become confused about where files are located on their hard drive.

This chapter is the cure-all for your Save, Save As, and Open woes. Hang with me and pay attention; everything will soon become crystal-clear. And keep saying to yourself, "The Save sheets and the Open dialog are just another way of looking at the Finder," as I explain in this chapter.

 You work with Open dialogs and Save sheets within applications. You only see them after you launch your favorite application and open or save a file. (For more on launching applications, read through Chapter 2 on icons; for more on creating and opening documents, see the documentation for the program that you're using.)

Saving Your Document Before It's Too Late

You can create as many documents as you want, using one program or dozens of 'em, but all is lost if you don't save the files to a storage device like your hard drive or other disk. When you *save* a file, you're committing a copy to a disk — whether a disk mounted on your Desktop, one available over a network, or on a removable medium such as a Zip or floppy disk, CD-R, CD-RW, DVD-R, or DVD-RW.

In this section, I show you how to save your masterpieces. Prevent unnecessary pain in your life by developing good saving habits. I recommend you save your work

- ✔ Every few minutes
- ✔ Before you switch to another program
- ✔ Before you print a document
- ✔ Before you stand up

Hiding your stuff under the right rock

If you've used previous versions of Mac OS, the rules about where to store things were a lot looser. Storing everything within your Documents folder wasn't at all important. But Mac OS X arranges its system files, applications, and other stuff a bit differently from the way the older versions did.

I *strongly* advise you to store all your document files and the folders that contain them in the Documents folder within your Home folder or your Home folder's Movies folder, Music folder, or Pictures folder if that's where the application (such as iMovie) recommends. Files that you place outside the Documents folder are very likely to get lost while you navigate through a maze of aliases and folders that belong to (and make sense to) particular programs or parts of the system software — and not to you as a user.

An exception to this rule is to place files you need to share with other users in the Shared folder, inside the Users folder in which your Home folder resides.

If other people besides you use your Mac (and they changed privilege settings to give you access to their directories — see Chapter 14), you could even save a file in another user's folder by accident, in which case you'd probably *never* find it again.

So, trust me when I say that the Documents folder in your Home folder is the right place to start, not only because it's easy to remember, but also because it's only a menu command (Go⇨Home) or keyboard shortcut (⌘+Shift+H) away, wherever you're working on your Mac.

If you don't heed this advice and the program that you're using crashes while switching programs, printing, or sitting idle (which, not coincidentally, are the three most likely times for a crash), you lose everything that you did since your last save. The fact that a program crash doesn't bring down the entire system (as it did under Mac OS 9) is small consolation when you've lost everything you've typed since the last time you saved . . .

The keyboard shortcut for Save in almost every program I know is ⌘+S. Memorize it. See it in your dreams. Train your finger muscles to do it unconsciously. Use it (the keyboard shortcut) or lose it (your unsaved work).

Checking out the Save sheet

When you choose to save a file for the first time (by choosing File⇨Save or pressing ⌘+S), a Save sheet appears in front of the window that you're saving, as shown in Figure 5-1 — we'll call this a Basic sheet. You can choose any folder or volume listed in a Finder window's Sidebar by clicking a Basic sheet's Where pop-up menu and taking your pick — or you can expand the sheet (as shown in Figure 5-2), and navigate folders just as you would in the Finder: by opening them to see their contents.

Before you can navigate the columns in a Save sheet, you need to click the downward-pointing disclosure triangle to expand the sheet. It's to the right of the Save As text field in Figure 5-1 and my pointer is hovering over it, about to click.

So, the disclosure triangle toggles between the basic and expanded Save sheets. If yours is small (as shown in Figure 5-1) and you want it expanded, click the disclosure triangle; the result of doing so is shown in Figure 5-2.

The Save sheet offers both Column or List views. In Column view, you click an item on the left to see its contents on the right, just as you do in a Finder window. List view offers no disclosure triangles (as you see in Finder windows), so you double-click folders to open them and see their contents.

In an Expanded sheet, the pop-up menu shows a path from the currently selected folder; it's similar to the menu you see when you Command+click a Finder window's title but with Recent Places grafted onto its bottom.

You can also use the Forward and Back buttons or the Sidebar, both only available in an expanded Save dialog, to conveniently navigate your disk.

Choose between Column and List view in Save sheets by clicking the List or Column view buttons which look like their counterparts in Finder windows (they're between the pop-up menu and the Forward and Back buttons in Figure 5-2).

Figure 5-1:
Basic Save
sheets can
look like
this.

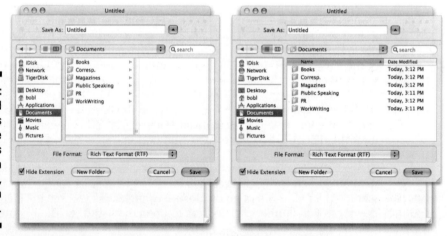

Figure 5-2:
Expanded
Save sheets
can look like
this or this
(Column
view on left,
List view on
right).

Like the List or Column view in a Finder window, you can enlarge the Save sheet to see more. Just drag the lower-right corner of the sheet down or to the right. Then, when you click items in the current right column of the Save sheet (note that you must have the columns showing before you can have any columns to deal with here), their contents appear in a new, third column.

After you've saved a file for the first time, choosing File➪Save or pressing ⌘+S doesn't bring up a Save sheet anymore. It just saves the file again without any further intervention on your part. Get in the habit of pressing ⌘+S often. It can't hurt and just may save your bacon someday.

In Figures 5-1 and 5-2, you see, respectively, the Save sheet for the TextEdit program, default and expanded. In programs other than TextEdit or when you open a Plain Text document in TextEdit, the Save sheet may contain additional options, fewer options, or different options, and therefore may look slightly different. Don't worry. The Save sheet always *works* the same, no matter what options there are.

In Mac OS X, you can move the window and attached Save sheet (just as you can any window) by dragging the window's title bar. Just click the title bar and then hold down the mouse button while you drag the window wherever you desire. The Save sheet moves right along with the window. (Unlike the Save dialog in earlier versions of Mac OS, a Save sheet isn't "modal," which means it doesn't prevent you from using other programs or windows when it's on-screen.)

Wherefore art thou, Where pop-up menu?

Take some time and get to know the Where pop-up menu. It's a great navigation aid, but a bit confusing for new users. With it, you can quickly move to a location on your hard drive and open or save a file stored there. Consider the Where pop-up menu a shortcut menu to all the items in a Finder window's Sidebar.

The Where pop-up menu in the Basic view looks a lot like the pop-up menu that appeared at the top of the Open/Save dialogs in earlier versions of Mac OS. But instead of tracing the folder path (as it did in versions of yore, and as it still does in the Expanded view), the Where pop-up menu lists one or more places where you may save your files (Documents, Home) as well as other folders where you have opened or saved files recently. Note the correlation between the items in the Where menu on the unexpanded Save sheet on the right and the items in the Sidebar of the expanded Save sheet on the left in Figure 5-3.

Figure 5-3: Notice how its contents change depending upon whether you're using the Expanded view (left) or Basic view (right).

After you've chosen a folder from the Where menu, you can still navigate to other folders by using the Sidebar or the List or Column browser if you're using the Expanded view.

With all of these ways to navigate to your target folder — the mouse, the Where menu, the Sidebar, the browsers, and the arrow keys — you should always be able to get to your target folder (for saving the document) with just a few clicks or keystrokes.

In this section, I run down the parts of the Where pop-up menu. In the process, I show you why it's best to store your files in certain places on your Mac. Finally, I show you how to use the Where menu to quickly reach your favorite folders.

The Where menu is *contextual* — it displays different folders based on which view you're in, whether Basic or Expanded. If you haven't expanded the Save sheet, the Where pop-up menu displays your currently active directory at the top (Documents in Figure 5-3), followed by your available computers and volumes (iDisk, Network, and TigerDisk in Figure 5-3), followed by folders in your Sidebar in Finder windows (Desktop, bobl, Applications, Documents, Movies, Music, and Pictures in Figure 5-3), followed by folders or disks you've used recently (none are showing in Figure 5-3).

When you expand the Save sheet, the pop-up is no longer labeled "Where." And it now displays the hierarchy from the current folder to the Computer level, just like ⌘+clicking a window's name in the Finder.

Saving to the active folder

In an expanded Save sheet, the name at the top in the Where pop-up menu is the name of the active item (be it a folder, a drive, or the Desktop). In Figure 5-4, the active folder is Folder 2.

A file saved into Folder 2 appears in the column where you see Folder 3 in Figure 5-4.

Think of the active item in a Save sheet as akin to the active window on the Desktop. That's where your file is saved by default if you click the Save button without changing the destination folder at all. This concept is important. In other words, if the Documents folder is the active item (as it is in both Figures 5-1 and 5-2), your document is saved in the Documents folder when you click the Save button. If Folder 2 is the active item (as it is in Figure 5-4), your document is saved in Folder 2 when you click the Save button.

In Figure 5-4, if I clicked Folder 3 before I clicked the Save button, the menu would have changed to say Folder 3, and the file would be saved in Folder 3 instead of Folder 2.

And so on.

Figure 5-4:
Saving a file
into Folder 2.

The best places to save

Here's a quick rundown of the folders that appear by default in your Sidebar
and Where menu (in unexpanded Save sheets):

- ✔ **Documents:** Located within your Home folder, the Documents folder is
  the best place to store your files (in my humble opinion). You can organize stuff inside your Documents folder by creating subfolders with
  meaningful names. For example, in my Documents folder, you'd find subfolders named Fonts that start with the letter V, Agrapha Icon Sets,
  NonCom, and so on.

- ✔ **Desktop:** A good place to save files you're going to be using in the
  short term.

  The Desktop is not a great place for long-term storage of files and folders. If the Desktop becomes overcrowded, you'll have trouble finding
  files (and a big pile of icons isn't a pretty sight on-screen).

- ✔ **Home:** All users have their own Home folder that contains all their stuff —
  their documents, their preferences, their applications — everything that
  belongs to them. You can save documents to your Home folder, which is
  named for you (the example is called bobl in all of this chapter's figures).
  To save files here, choose Home from the Where menu, or click the
  Home folder (bobl) in the Sidebar, and then click the Save button.

I don't, however, recommend saving most of your stuff to your Home folder. It quickly gets overcrowded and unmanageable. I find it easier to organize and find files in the Documents folder, away from the Library, Pictures, Music, and other folders that live in Home already.

✔ **Applications:** This is where OS X likes to find your application programs.

Do not save documents here! The only reason that it appears in the Sidebar and the Where pop-up menu is that you use it frequently to find an application to launch.

✔ **Movies, Music, and Pictures:** The Movies, Music, and Pictures folders appear in the Sidebar by default and are good locations for saving iMovies, songs, and photos or scans, respectively.

If you can't find the folder you want to save your document into, type its name into the search box, click the Computer, Home, or current folder button, and the Save sheet will show you items that match what you typed.

Here's a handy shortcut for naming files in the Save sheet. Click a grayed-out file name in the file list and it becomes the name of the file you're saving, as shown in Figure 5-5.

Figure 5-5:
Before (left)
and after
(right)
clicking a
grayed-out
file's name
in a Save
sheet.

Be careful using this shortcut — unless you change the name that appears in the Save As field before you click the Save button, you could overwrite the existing file with the file you're about to save — which may or may not be what you want to do. Luckily, Mac OS X looks out for you and you'll see a warning like the one shown in Figure 5-6 if you're about to overwrite a file. So give it some thought before you blithely click the Replace button or press the Enter or Return key.

Figure 5-6:
If I don't change the file's name now, I'll replace an existing file with the one I'm saving.

Even with the proviso just stated, this can be a handy shortcut as long as you remember to alter the name of the file you're saving (so as not to accidentally overwrite an existing file).

So, in Figure 5-6, I'd select the date in the Save As field (09.28.04), delete it, and type today's date, which would not only avoid overwriting any files in this folder, it would also make the file's name more descriptive.

Getting active with the Save As field

When a Save sheet appears for the first time, the Save As field is active and displays the name of the document. The document name (often Untitled) is selected; when you begin typing, the name disappears and is replaced by the name you type.

If you press the Tab key while the Save As field is active, it becomes inactive, and the Search box becomes active. Press Tab again and the Sidebar becomes active. Press the Tab key one more time and the file list box (more accurately known as the detail pane — the part with the list view or columns in it) becomes active. That's because the file list box, the Search box, the Sidebar, and the Save As field are all mutually exclusive. Only one can be active at any time.

Look at Figure 5-7. In the top-left picture, the Save As field is active; in the top-right picture, the Search box is active; in the bottom-left picture, the Sidebar is active; and in the bottom-right picture, the file list box is active.

You can always tell which item is active by the thin blue or gray border around it.

Active (has border)   Active (has border)

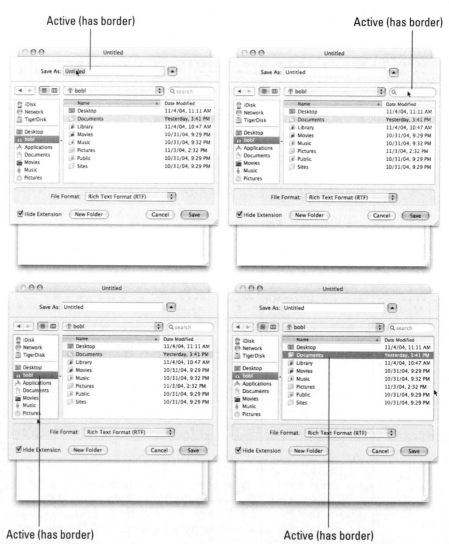

Figure 5-7: Check the borders to tell active fields from inactive fields.

Active (has border)   Active (has border)

When you want to switch to a different folder to save a file, click the folder in the Sidebar (if you're using Column view) or click anywhere in the file list box (Column or List view) to make the file list active.

The Save As field, the Search box, the Sidebar, *or* the file list box is active at any given time; no two can ever be active at the same time.

The following lists are some things to help you get a hold on this whole active/inactive silliness:

✔ Look for the thin border that shows you which part of the Save sheet is active as indicated in Figure 5-7.

✔ If you type while the file list box is active, the list scrolls and selects the folder that most closely matches the letter(s) that you type. It's a little strange because you won't see what you type: You'll be typing blind, so to speak. Go ahead and give it a try. For example, typing the letters **mu** in the file list box of Figure 5-7 selects the Music folder.

✔ If you type while the Sidebar is active, nothing happens. You can, however, use the up- and down-arrow keys to move around in the Sidebar.

✔ When the file list is active, the letters that you type don't appear in the Save As field. If you want to type a file name, you have to activate the Save As field again (by clicking in it or using the Tab key) before you can type in it.

✔ Regardless of which box or field is active at the time, when you press the Tab key on your keyboard, the next in sequence becomes active. So if the Save As field is active, it becomes inactive when you press Tab, and the Search box becomes active. Tab again and the Sidebar becomes active. Tab again, and the file list box becomes active. Press Tab again, and the Save As field becomes active again.

✔ Pressing Shift reverses the order. Press Shift-Tab and the active item moves from the Save As field to the file list box to the Sidebar to the Search box and back to the Save As field again.

If you don't feel like pressing the Tab key, you can achieve the same effect by clicking the file list box, the Sidebar, or the Save As field to make it active. Try it yourself and notice again how visual cues let you know which is active. When the file list is active, it displays a border; when the Save As field or the Sidebar is active, the file list has no border, and the active field displays a border — which means you can edit it or navigate it.

Putting your finger on the button

Most Save sheets contain the following three buttons (New Folder, Cancel, Save), and many offer a Hide Extension check box (refer to Figure 5-2). I describe them all briefly in the following list:

✔ **New Folder:** The New Folder button is a nice touch, but is present only in an expanded Save sheet. Click this button, and you create a new folder inside the active folder. You first get the opportunity to name the folder; then you can save your document there.

The keyboard shortcut for New Folder is Ô+ N.

I've never seen this shortcut documented in Mac Help (or anywhere else, for that matter). So it may well be a *Mac OS X Tiger For Dummies* exclusive.

✔ **Cancel:** Clicking this button dismisses the Save sheet without saving anything anywhere. In other words, the Cancel button returns things to the way they were before you displayed the Save sheet.

The keyboard shortcut for Cancel is ⌘+. (⌘+ a period). Pressing the Esc key usually (but not always) does the same thing. This shortcut is a good command to memorize because it cancels almost all dialogs, and it also cancels lots of other things. If a program is dragging — your spreadsheet is calculating or your database is sorting or your graphics program is rotating, for example, and it's taking too long — try pressing either Esc or ⌘+. (period). (They work — usually.)

✔ **Save:** Click this button to save the file to the active folder.

But wait! What if the Save button is grayed out? This happens when the Save As field is blank; typing even one character will activate the Save button again.

Make sure that the folder you want to save your document in is showing in the (Where) pop-up menu. If you're not sure and you click the Save button, *you* could be the next one to say, "Well, I saved the file and now I don't know where it went."

✔ **Hide extension:** Marking this check box turns off the display of file name extensions, such as `.rtf`, `.pdf`, or `.txt`, in Save sheets.

Looks like Save, acts like Save — why's it called Save As?

The Save As command — which you can find in the File menu of almost every program ever made (at least those that create documents) — lets you resave a file that has already been saved by giving it a different name.

Why would you want to do that? Here's a good (albeit kind of rude) example:

Suppose you have two cousins, Kate and Zelda. You write Kate a long, chatty letter and save this document with the name `Letter to Kate`. At some point afterward, you decide you want to send this same letter to Zelda, too, but you want to change a few things. So you change the part about your date last night (Zelda isn't as liberated as Kate) and replace all references to Kevin (Kate's husband) with Zeke (Zelda's husband). (Aren't computers grand?)

So you make all these changes to `Letter to Kate`, but you haven't saved this document yet. And although the document on your screen is actually a letter to Zelda, its file name is still `Letter to Kate`. Think of what would happen if you were to save it now without using the Save As feature: `Letter to Kate` reflects the changes that you just made (the stuff in the letter meant for Kate is blown away, replaced by the stuff that you write to Zelda). Thus, the file name `Letter to Kate` is inaccurate. Even worse, you would no longer have a copy of the letter you sent to Kate!

The solution? Just use Save As to rename this file `Letter to Zelda` by choosing File➪Save As. A Save sheet appears, in which you can type a different file name in the Save As field. You can also navigate to another folder, if you like, and save the newly named version of the file there.

Now you have two distinct files: `Letter to Kate` and `Letter to Zelda`. Both contain the stuff they should but both started life from the same file. *That's* what Save As is for.

An even better idea is to choose Save As just before you begin modifying the document and give it the new name. That way, when you're done with your changes, you don't have to remember to choose Save As — you can just perform your habitual Save. It also protects you from accidentally saving part of the Letter to Zelda without changing its name first (which you're likely to do if you're following my advice to save often). So when you decide you're going to reuse a document, Save As *before* you begin working on it, just to be safe.

Open Sez Me

If you've read the earlier parts of this chapter, you probably already know how to use the Open dialog — you just don't yet *know* that you know. Open dialogs are so much like Save sheets that it's scary. To summon an Open dialog, launch your favorite program and choose File➪Open (or use the keyboard shortcut ⌘+O, which works in 98 percent of all programs ever made).

Check out a typical Open dialog in Figure 5-8.

If I were to click the Open button in Figure 5-8, the file *Dr. Mac 11.15.04.doc* would open in TextEdit, the program I'm using.

If you can't find the folder in which you want to save your document, type the folder's name into the Search box, and then click (a) the Computer button to search everywhere, (b) the Home button to search only in your Home folder, or (c) the current folder button to search the active folder. You don't even have to press Enter or Return; the Save sheet updates itself to show you only items that match the characters as you've typed them.

Figure 5-8:
The Open
dialog in all
its glory.

Knowing the differences between Open dialogs and Save sheets

After you master navigating the Save sheet, you should have smooth sailing when you use an Open dialog. They work the same except for a few minor differences:

✔ **No Save As field:** A Save As field isn't needed in an Open dialog. Why would it be? You're looking for items to open, not naming items you're saving. Ergo, since you're not saving or naming a file here, you don't need the Save As field.

✔ **No Where pop-up menu:** In the Open dialog, you find the path pop-up menu instead. Why? Because you're opening a file *From* a certain folder, rather than telling your Mac *Where* to save it. The path menu has the same basic job as the path menu in an expanded Save sheet, and you see the same folders in it.

✔ **No Expand button:** You always have to be able to select a file, so the file list pane (and the Sidebar) are omnipresent. I mean, if the Open dialog weren't expanded, where would you select the file to open?

✔ **No New Folder button:** Why? Well, you can't open something that you haven't yet created, right? You don't need to create new folders when you're opening a file, basically.

You may notice a couple of other differences between the Save sheet and the Open dialog. At the bottom of the Open dialog (refer to Figure 5-8), note the Plain Text Encoding popup menu and the Ignore Rich Text Commands check box. These are specific to TextEdit and have to do with the format that TextEdit uses to save text files. Don't worry about these for now. Just remember that many applications add special items to their Open dialogs and Save sheets that help you to select formats and other options specific to those programs.

Navigate through the Open dialog just as you would a Save sheet. Don't forget the mantra, "The Open dialog and the Save sheet are just another way of looking at the Finder."

Knowing what the Open dialog doesn't show you . . .

When you use a program's Open dialog, only files that the program knows how to open appear enabled (in a bold font) in the file list. In other words, the program filters out the files it can't open, so you barely see them in the Open dialog. This method of selectively displaying certain items in Open dialogs is a feature of most applications. Therefore, when you're using TextEdit, its Open dialog dims all your spreadsheet files (that's because TextEdit can only open text, Rich Text, Microsoft Word, and some picture files). Pretty neat, eh?

Some programs — such as AppleWorks, Microsoft Word, and Adobe Photoshop — have a Show or Format menu in their Open dialogs. This menu lets you specify the type(s) of files you want to see in the Open dialog. You can usually open a file that appears dimmed by choosing All Documents in the Show or Format menu (in those applications with Open dialogs that offer such a menu).

Chapter 6

File Management without Tearing Your Hair Out

*I*n other parts of this book, you can discover the basics about windows and icons and menus. Here, you begin a never-ending quest to discover the fastest, easiest, and most trouble-free way to manage the files on your Mac. And, along the way, you'll discover what some of the special folders (most notably the multiple Library folders) in Mac OS X are all about.

I've been wrangling with Macintosh files and folders for more than 20 years now, and I've learned a lot about what works and what doesn't — *for me.*

And although Mac OS X is very different from earlier versions of Mac OS, the fundamentals of organizing files and folders haven't changed that much. So this chapter spares you at least part of my 15-year learning curve.

One thing I stress throughout this chapter is that what works for one user may not work for another. So I encourage you to develop your own personal style. I don't preach (much) about the "right" way to organize your files. After you've read this chapter, you'll have all the ammunition that you need to organize your files into a Mac environment designed by you, for you.

I won't pretend to be able to organize your Mac for you. Organizing your files is as personal as your taste in music; you develop your own style with the

Mac. This section simply gives you some food for thought — some ideas about how I do it, and some suggestions that should make organization easier for you, regardless of how you choose to do it yourself.

Working with Files and Folders

Before I go any farther, a closer look at files and folders is in order — the difference between a file and a folder, how you can arrange and move files and folders around, and how to nest folders. Then you can concentrate on becoming a savvier — and better organized — Mac OS X user.

Then, after I discuss *your* files and folders, I offer more about the folders that Mac OS X creates (and requires). By the end of this chapter, you'll not only know all about *your* files and folders, you'll also know about the files and folders that Mac OS X creates when you install it — and what they do.

Files versus folders

When I speak of a *file*, I'm talking about what's connected to any icon except a folder or disk icon. A file can be a document, an application, an alias of a file or application, a dictionary, a font, or any other icon that *isn't* a folder or disk. The main distinction is that you can't put something *into* most file icons.

The exceptions are icons that represent Mac OS X packages. A *package* is an icon that acts like a file but isn't. Examples of icons that are really packages include most installers and applications as well as "documents" saved by some programs (such as Keynote). When you open an icon that represents a package the usual way (double-click, File⇨Open, ⌘+O, and so on), the program or document opens. To see the contents of an icon that represents a package, you have to Control+click it and look for the Show Package Contents item in the menu. If it's there, that icon is a package and you can see the files and folders it contains by choosing Show Package Contents; if you don't see a Show Package Contents item in the contextual menu, the icon represents a file, not a package.

When I talk about *folders*, I'm talking about things that work like manila folders. Their icons look like folders; they can contain files or other folders (*subfolders*). You can put any icon — any file or folder — into a folder.

Here's an exception: If you put a disk icon into a folder, you get an alias to the disk (as I explain in Chapter 2) unless you hold down the Option key. Remember that you can't put a disk icon into a folder on itself. In other words, you can only copy a disk icon to a different disk. Put another way, you can never copy a disk icon into a folder that resides on that disk.

Finally, *disks* are (in Desktop terms, anyway) nothing more than big folders. A disk icon is, for all intents and purposes, the same as a folder icon. (Look in the margin to see a typical folder icon.)

 File icons can look like practically anything. If the icon doesn't look like a folder or one of the numerous disk icons, you can be pretty sure it's a file.

Creating new folders

So you think Apple has already given you enough folders? Can't imagine why you'd need more? Think of creating new folders the same way you'd think of labeling a new folder at work for a specific project. New folders help you keep your files organized, enabling you to reorganize them just the way you want. Creating folders is really quite simple.

To create a new folder, just follow these steps:

1. **Decide which window you want the new folder to appear in, and then make sure that window is active.**

   If you want to create a new folder right on the Desktop, make sure *no* windows are active.

   You can make a window active by clicking it, and you can make the Desktop active if you have windows on-screen by clicking the Desktop itself.

2. **Choose File⇨New Folder (or press ⌘+Shift+N).**

   A new, untitled folder appears in the active window with its name box already highlighted, ready for you to type a new name for it.

3. **Type a name for your folder.**

   If you accidentally click anywhere before you type a name for the folder, the name box will no longer be highlighted. To highlight it again, select the icon (single-click it) and then press Return (or Enter) once. Now you can type its new name.

   Name your folders with relevant names. Folders with nebulous titles like *sfdghb* or *Stuff* — or, worst of all, *Untitled* — won't make it any easier to find something six months from now.

    For maximum compatibility with other users and other operating systems, avoid using punctuation marks in file and folder names. Periods, slashes, backslashes, and colons, in particular, can be reserved for use by other operating systems. Although Tiger will let you use almost any character except a period (as the first character) or a colon (anywhere in the name), it's a good idea to avoid using any punctuation marks in your folder or file names.

While we're on the subject, it's not a good idea to use characters you have to hold down the Option key to type in file or folder names. I'm talking about ones like: (tm) (Option+2), (r) (Option+r) ¢ (Option+4) or even (c) (Option+g). So get in the habit of not using those in file names, either.

For files you might share with users of non-Macintosh computers, here's the rule for maximum compatibility: No punctuation and no Option-key characters in the file name.

Navigating Nested Folders

Folders within other folders are often called *nested folders*. To get a feel for the way nested folders work in Mac OS X, check out Figure 6-1. You can see the following from the figure:

- ✔ Folder 1 is one level deep.
- ✔ Folder 2 is inside Folder 1, which is one level deeper than Folder 1, or two levels deep.
- ✔ Folder 3 is inside Folder 2 and is three levels deep.
- ✔ The files inside Folder 3 are four levels deep.

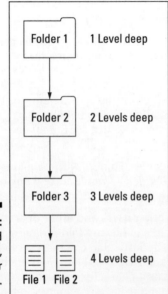

Figure 6-1:
Nested folders, going four levels deep.

If the previous list makes sense to you, you're golden. What's important here is that you are able to visualize the path to Folder 3. That is, to get to files inside Folder 3, you open Folder 1 and then open Folder 2 to be able to open Folder 3. Understanding this concept is important to understanding the relationships between files and folders. Keep reviewing this section and eventually the concept will click — you'll slap yourself in the head and say, "Now I get it!"

Moving files and folders

You can move files and folders around within a window to your heart's content as long as that window is set to the Icon view. Just click and drag any icon to its new location in the window.

Some people spend hours arranging icons in a window so that they're just so. But because using Icon view wastes so much screen space, I avoid using icons in a window.

You can't move icons around in a window that's viewed as a list or as columns, which makes total sense when you think about it. (Well, you can move them to put them in a different folder in List or Column view, but that's not moving them around, really.)

As you may expect from Apple, the King of Having Lots of Ways to Do Anything, you have choices for how you move one file of folder into another folder. You can use these techniques to move any icon — folder, document, alias, or program icon — into folders or onto other disks.

> ✔ **Drag an icon onto a folder icon:** Drag the icon for one folder (or file) onto the icon for another folder (or disk) and then release when the second folder is highlighted (see Figure 6-2). The first folder is now inside the second folder. Put another way, the first folder is now a subfolder of the second folder.
>
> This technique works regardless of whether the second folder's window is open.

Figure 6-2:
Placing one folder into another.

✔ **Drag an icon into an open folder's window:** Drag the icon for one folder (or file) into the open window for a second folder (or disk), as shown in Figure 6-3.

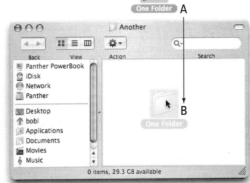

Figure 6-3:
You can also move a file or folder by dragging it into the open window of another folder.

If you try to move an item from one disk to another disk, it's only copied — not moved. If you want to *move* a file or folder from one disk to another, you have to trash the original manually after the copying is complete unless you use the following tip.

If you hold down the ⌘ key when you drag an icon from one disk to another, it's moved instead of copied, and the original is deleted automatically. The little Copying Files window even changes to read *Moving* Files. Nice touch, eh?

Copying files or folders

What if you want to *copy* an icon from one place to another, leaving the icon in its original location and creating an identical copy in the destination window? No problem — all it takes is the addition of the Option key.

If you're wondering why anyone would ever want to do that, trust me: Someday you will. Suppose (for example) you have a file called Long Letter to Mom in a folder called Old Correspondence. You figure that Mom has forgotten that letter by now, and you want to send it again. But before you do, you want to change the date and delete the reference to Clarence, her pit bull, who passed away last year. So now you need to put a copy of Long Letter to Mom in your Current Correspondence folder. This technique yields the same result as making a copy of a file by using Save As, which I describe in Chapter 5.

When you copy a file, it's wise to change the name of the copied file. Having more than one file on your hard drive with the same exact name is not a good idea, even if the files are in different folders. Trust me, having 10 files called Expense Report or 15 files named Doctor Mac Direct Invoice can be confusing, no matter how well organized your folder structure is. Add distinguishing words or dates to file and folder names so they're named something more explicit, such as Expense Report 10-03 or Doctor Mac Direct Invoice 4-4-05.

You have four ways to copy a file or folder, as follows:

✔ **Drag an icon from one folder icon onto another folder icon while holding down the Option key.**

Drag the icon for one folder onto the icon for another folder and then release when the second folder is highlighted (refer to Figure 6-2). This technique works regardless of whether the second folder's window is open.

When you copy something by dragging and dropping it with the Option key held down, the mouse pointer changes to include a little plus sign (+) next to the arrow, as shown in the margin. Neat!

✔ **Drag an icon into an open window for another folder while holding down the Option key.**

Drag the icon for the file or folder that you want to copy into the open window for a second folder (or removable media, such as a floppy disk) — refer to Figure 6-3.

✔ **Copy an icon and paste it into another folder's window.**

Introduced to the Mac with the OS X 10.1 release, you can now click an icon, choose Edit⇨Copy (or press ⌘+C), click where you want the icon to go, and then choose Edit⇨Paste (or press ⌘+V) — it's done.

✔ **Choose File⇨Duplicate or Control+click the file or folder that you want to duplicate, and then select Duplicate from the contextual menu that appears.**

For more about the Duplicate command, check out Chapter 3.

You can have lots of files with the same name *on the same disk* (although, as I mentioned earlier, it's probably not a good idea). But your Mac won't let you have more than one file with the same name *in the same folder.*

Everything I've discussed so far in this chapter works at least as well for windows that use the List or Column views as it does for windows using the Icon view. In other words, I used the Icon view in the previous examples only because it's the best view for pictures to show you what's going on. For what it's worth, I find moving and copying files easiest in windows that use the List or Column views.

Opening files with drag-and-drop

Macintosh *drag-and-drop* is usually all about dragging text and graphics from one place to another. But there's another angle to drag-and-drop — one that has to do with files and icons. I tell you the real deal in this section.

You can open a document by dragging its icon onto that of the proper application. For example, you can open a document created with Microsoft Word by dragging the document icon onto the Microsoft Word application's icon. The Word icon will highlight, and the document will launch. Of course, it's usually easier to just double-click a document's icon to open it; the proper application opens automatically when you do — or at least it does most of the time. Which reminds me . . .

If you try to open a file and Mac OS X can't find a program to open the file, Mac OS X prompts you with an alert window, as shown in Figure 6-4. You can either click Cancel (and abort the attempt to open the file) or pick another application to open.

Figure 6-4:
Oops! Mac OS X helps you find the correct application.

There is no default application specified to open the document "OSXFD4eCh06".

Cancel   Choose Application...

Of course, you can click the Choose Application button and pick another program from a regular Open File dialog (see Chapter 5 for details). If you click the Choose Application button, a dialog appears (conveniently opened to your Applications folder, and shown in Figure 6-5). Applications that Mac OS X doesn't think can be used to open the file are dimmed. For a wider choice of applications, choose to view All Applications instead of Recommended Applications from the Enable pop-up menu.

Here is a better way: Use drag-and-drop to open a file using a program other than the one that would *ordinarily* launch when you open the document. To do so, just drag the file onto the application's icon (or alias icon or Dock icon), and presto — the file opens in the application.

If the icon doesn't highlight and you release the mouse button anyway, the document will end up in the same folder as the application with the icon that didn't highlight. If that happens, just choose Edit⇨Undo (or press ⌘+Z), and the mislaid document magically returns to where it was before you dropped it. Just remember — don't do anything else after you drop the file, or Undo may not work. If Undo doesn't work, you must move the file back to its original location by hand.

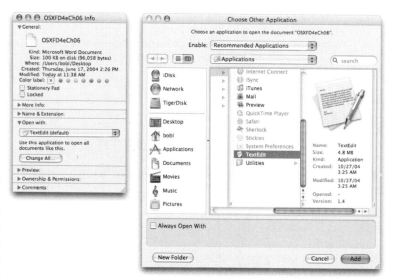

Figure 6-5:
Choose an
application
to open
a file.

You can't open every file with every program. For example, if you try to open an MP3 (music) file with Microsoft Excel (a spreadsheet), it just won't work — you'll get an error message or a screen full of gibberish. Sometimes you just have to keep trying until you find the right program; other times, you won't have a program capable of opening the file.

Only applications that *might* be able to open the file will highlight when you drag the document on them. That doesn't mean the document will be usable, just that the application *can* open it. Suffice to say that Mac OS X is smart enough to figure out which applications on your hard drive can open what documents — and to offer you a choice.

You're usually best off clicking the Choose Application button and sticking to the Recommended Applications choice in the Choose Application dialog. But if that doesn't work for you, at least you now know another way — drag the file onto an application's icon and see what happens.

I don't know if you noticed, but in Figure 6-5, Mac OS X is recommending I use TextEdit to open a document I created in Microsoft Word. That's right — the free word processor that comes with Mac OS X can open Microsoft Word files, and it can modify and save them again, too. Why does this make me rave and marvel? Because now, even if you don't own a copy of Microsoft Word, you can open documents created by others using Microsoft Word, edit, and resave them, all without having to buy your own copy of Microsoft Word.

Don't get me wrong — I use Word more than any other program, and I have no qualms. But for those of you who don't need a full-featured, professional-quality, relatively expensive writing environment, the freebie (TextEdit) may very well be all the word processor you'll ever need.

There is one last technique that works great when you want to open a document with a program other than its default. For example, if I were to double-click an MP3 file, the file will open in iTunes. But I frequently want to listen to MP3 files using QuickTime Player (so they're not added to my iTunes music library). Dragging the MP3 file onto QuickTime Player's Dock icon solves this conundrum quickly and easily.

Assigning an application to a document or document type

I don't know about you, but people send me files all the time that were created by applications I don't use . . . or at least that I don't use for that document type. Mac OS X lets you specify the application in which you want to open a document in the future when you double-click it. More than that, you can specify that you want all documents of that type to open with the specified application. "Where is this magic bullet hidden?" you ask. Right there in the file's Show Info window.

Suppose, for example, that you want all graphic files that default to opening in Preview JPEG to open with GraphicConverter (one of my favorite pieces of OS X-savvy shareware) instead. Just click one of these files in the Finder and then choose File⇨Get Info (⌘+I). Then, in the Info window, click the gray triangle to disclose the Open With pane, as shown in Figure 6-6.

Figure 6-6:
Select an application to open this document.

A pop-up menu lets you choose from the applications that Mac OS X believes will open this document type. In Figure 6-6, I'm choosing GraphicConverter.

Now, GraphicConverter will open when you double-click this particular document — but if you click the Change All button at the bottom of the window (as I've done in Figure 6-7), you make GraphicConverter the default application for all .jpg documents owned by Preview.

Figure 6-7: Make the selected application the default for this document type by clicking the Change All button.

Organizing your stuff with subfolders

As I mention earlier in this chapter, you can put folders inside other folders to organize your icons. I call a folder that's inside another folder a *subfolder.*

You can create subfolders according to whatever system makes sense to you — but why reinvent the wheel? Here are some organizational topic ideas and naming examples for subfolders:

- **By type of document:** Word-Processing Documents, Spreadsheet Documents, Graphics Documents
- **By date:** Documents May–June, Documents Spring '03
- **By content:** Memos, Outgoing Letters, Expense Reports
- **By project:** Project X, Project Y, Project Z

When you notice your folders swelling and starting to get messy (that is, filling up with tons of files), subdivide them again by using a combination of these methods that makes sense to you. For example, suppose you start by subdividing your Documents folder into multiple subfolders. Later, when those folders begin to get full, you may subdivide them even further, as shown in Figure 6-8.

Figure 6-8: Before (left) and after (right) organizing the Books and Finance folders with subfolders.

My point (yes, I do have one!): Allow your folder structure to be organic, growing as you need it to grow. Let it happen. Don't let any one folder get so full that it's a hassle to deal with. Create new subfolders when things start to get crowded.

 If you want to monkey around with some subfolders yourself, a good place to start is the Documents folder — it's inside your Home folder (that is, it's a *subfolder* of your Home folder).

 If you use a particular folder a great deal, make an alias of it and then move the alias from the Documents folder to the Dock, your Home folder, your Desktop(for more info on aliases, see Chapter 2) to make the folder easier to access. Or drag the folder (or its alias) to the Sidebar where it's always available, even in Open dialogs and Save sheets. For example, if you write a lot of letters, you could keep an alias to your Correspondence folder in your Home folder, in the Dock, or on your Desktop for quick access. (By the way, there's no reason you can't have a folder appear in all three places if you like. That's what aliases are all about, aren't they?)

 If you put the Documents folder in the Dock, you can click and hold on it (or Control+click) to reveal its subfolders, as shown in Figure 6-9.

Spring-loaded folders

Spring-loaded folders were resurrected in Mac OS X version 10.2 Jaguar, and they work in all views and with all folder or disk icons in the Sidebar. Because

TECHNICAL STUFF

Creating subfolders . . . or not

How full is too full? When should you begin creating subfolders in a folder? That's impossible to say, but having too many items in a folder can be a nightmare, as can having too many subfolders with just one or two files in them. My guideline is this: If you find more than 15 or 20 files in a single folder, begin thinking about ways to subdivide it.

On the other hand, some of my bigger subfolders contain things that I don't often access. For example, my Bob's Correspondence 1992 folder contains more than 200 files. But because I want to keep this folder on my hard drive in case I do need to find something there — even though I don't use it very often — its overcrowded condition doesn't bother me. (Your mileage may vary.)

Here are some tips to help you decide whether to use subfolders or just leave well enough alone:

- ✔ **Don't create subfolders until you need them.** In other words, don't create a bunch of empty folders because you think you may need them someday. Wait to create new folders until you need them; that way, you avoid opening an empty folder when you're looking for something else — a complete waste of time.

- ✔ **Let your work style decide the file structure.** When you first start working with your Mac, you may want to save everything in your Documents folder for a week or two (or a month or two, depending on how many new documents that you save each day). When a decent-sized group of documents has accumulated in the Documents folder, consider taking a look at them and creating logical subfolders for them.

you just got the short course on folders and subfolders and various ways to organize your stuff, you're ready for your introduction to one of my favorite ways to get around my disks, folders, and subfolders.

Figure 6-9:
It's super-convenient to have your Documents folder in the Dock.

Here's how they work: Select any icon except a disk icon and drag it onto any folder or disk icon — but don't release the mouse button. The folder or disk icon will highlight to indicate that it's selected. I call this *hovering* because you're doing just that — hovering the cursor over a folder or disk icon without releasing the button.

In a second or two, the highlighted folder or disk will flash twice and then spring open, right under the cursor. Then some more handy operations are possible:

✔ You can continue to traverse your folder structure this way until you release the mouse button. When you do, the icon you've been dragging will be dropped into the active folder at the time. That window will remain open — but all the windows you traversed will close.

✔ You can toggle spring-loaded folders on or off in the Finder's Preference window. There's also a setting for how long the Finder waits before it springs the folders open. If you're impatient, you can spring a folder open instantly by pressing the spacebar as you hover your mouse over the folder.

✔ If you want to cancel a spring-loaded folder, drag the cursor away from the folder icon or outside the boundaries of the sprung window — the folder will pop shut.

After you get used to spring-loaded folders, you'll wonder how you ever got along without them. They work in all three window views, and they work with icons in the Sidebar. Give 'em a try and you'll be hooked.

Getting Up to Speed with the Mac OS X Folder Structure

In addition to your personal files and folders, your Mac OS X system has its own folder structure. These folders contain the system software that runs the Mac, as well as folders that include system preferences, fonts, and other files used by everyone with access to this Mac. These shared files include applications, programs, utilities, and other software.

Also, each person who uses the Mac has his or her own set of folders — these contain documents, preferences, and other information used by only that person. If you're the sole person who accesses your Mac, you have only one user. Regardless, the folder structure that Mac OS X uses is the same, whether you have one user or ten.

I realize that a lot of people don't share their Macs with others. And if you're one of these folks, you may wonder why I keep mentioning sharing and multiple users and the like. Well, Mac OS X is based on the UNIX operating system — a multiuser operating system found on high-end servers and workstations that are often shared by several people. Mac OS X has both the benefit of this arrangement and a bit of the confusion caused when a single user (could it be you?) fires up a computer that could be set up for several people. That's why Mac OS X folders are organized the way they are — with different hierarchies for each user and for the computer as a whole.

All these files are stored in a nested folder structure that's a bit tricky to understand at first. This structure makes more sense after you spend a little time with it and learn some basic concepts.

In this section, I walk you through these different folder structures one by one, starting with the place where you'll spend most of your time — your Home folder.

The Mac OS X folder structure in depth

I start with the Computer folder, which is the top level of the folder hierarchy. The Computer folder shows all the storage devices (hard drives, CD- or DVD-ROM, Zip disk, and so forth) that are currently connected to your Mac. Figure 6-10 shows a hard disk and a Network icon, with which you can access servers or shared Macs on your network. (Don't quite know what file sharing is all about? Read Chapter 14 for the whole scoop on sharing files with other Macs and sharing your Mac with other users.

The computer name, Tiger TiBook in Figure 6-10, can be changed in the Sharing System Preference pane.

Figure 6-10:
Contents
of the
Computer
folder.

To find the Computer folder, use the keyboard shortcut ⌘+Shift+C or click its icon in the Sidebar of any Finder window.

You may have more or fewer icons in your Computer folder than the two that you see in Figure 6-10 (depending upon how many disks that you have mounted), but I'm going to drill down on the one that holds your Mac OS X stuff. In Figure 6-10, that hard drive is called *TigerDisk* — of course, I have no idea what yours is called; if you haven't changed it, it's probably called *Macintosh HD*. Double-click that icon to open it.

Inside your boot-disk icon (the one with OS X installed on it; the one called *TigerDisk* in Figure 6-10) is everything on that disk. You should see at least four folders (unless you've added some — if you installed the Developer Tools CD, for example, or an OS 9 System Folder, you'll have more). I'll go through each of them for you.

Applications

The Applications folder, located at the root level of your boot drive (the one with OS X installed on it), is accessible with a click of the Application icon on the Sidebar, from the Go menu, or by using the keyboard shortcut ⌘+Shift+A. In this folder, you find applications that Apple includes with Mac OS X. All users of a given Mac have access to the items in this Applications folder.

Library

The Library folder at the root level of your Mac OS X hard drive is like a public library — it stores items that everyone with access to this Mac can use. You'll find two different library folders on your hard drive — the one at the root level of your OS X disk and another in your Home folder.

Okay, I wasn't entirely truthful but only for your own good: There's actually a third Library folder inside the System folder, which I discuss in a page or two. But for now, heed this warning: **Leave this folder alone** — don't move, remove, or rename it or do anything within it. It's the nerve center of your Mac. In other words, you should never have to touch this third Library folder.

Think of the Library folder inside your Home folder like a library in your own house (have you ever actually been in a house with its own library?) and the one at root level as a public library. I talk more about these Library folders in the upcoming sections.

You find a bunch of folders inside the Library folder at root level (the public Library folder). Most of them contain files that you never need to open, move, or delete.

By and large, the Library subfolder that gets the most use is the Fonts folder, which houses all the fonts installed on the Mac. Fonts can be available in one of two ways:

- ✔ **To everyone who uses the Mac:** If that's the case, they're stored here in the Fonts folder.

- ✔ **To a single user:** In this case, you look for the fonts in the user's Library folder (that familiar subfolder of the Home folder).

I discuss fonts more in Chapter 10. Meanwhile, some other subfolders that you may use or add to are the iMovie and iTunes folders (where you put plug-ins for those programs), the Scripts folder (which houses AppleScripts accessible to all users), and Desktop Pictures (where you can place pictures to be used as Desktop backgrounds).

Leave the "public" Library folder pretty much alone unless you're using the Fonts folder or know what you're adding to one of the other folders. Don't remove, rename, or move any files or folders. Mac OS X uses these items and is very picky about where they're kept and how they're named.

Note: Under most circumstances, you won't actually add or remove items from folders in this Library yourself. Software installers usually do the heavy lifting for you by placing all their little pieces into appropriate Library folders. You shouldn't need to touch this Library often, if ever. That said, knowing what these folders are — and who can access their contents — may come in handy down the road a piece.

If you want to add something to a Library, it's usually best to add it to your Home/Library.

Mac OS 9

If you have Mac OS 9.2.2 installed on the same disk as OS X, this folder contains your Mac OS 9.2.2 System folder (which the Classic environment requires) as well as the System Disk program (which enables you to choose to boot your Mac from Mac OS 9.2.2 or OS X).

You can read more about Classic in Chapter 12.

System

The System folder includes the files that Mac OS X needs to start up and keep working. **Leave this folder alone** — don't move, remove, or rename it or anything within it. It's a part of the nerve center of your Mac.

If you've used any previous version of Mac OS, you should notice two things:

✔ The System folder doesn't include the same items or the same arrangement of files and folders.

✔ This folder is now simply called System rather than System Folder.

Also gone are the System file and Finder file that have been around since the first Mac. Located here instead is the slew of files that make up the Mac OS X system.

Users

When you open the Users folder, you see a folder for each person who uses the Mac as well as the Shared folder.

The Shared folder that you see in the Users folder allows everyone who uses the Mac to use the files stored there. If you want other people who use your Mac to have access to a file or folder, this is the place to stash it.

In the next section, I drill down from the Home folder `bob1` to see what's inside. When the user `bob1` logs onto this Mac, his Home folder (`bob1`) appears whenever he either clicks the `bob1` Home icon in the Sidebar, chooses Go⇨Home, or uses the keyboard shortcut ⌘+Shift+H.

Enough with the big-picture folder structure! Read on as I dig into how to work with the folders and files in Mac OS X.

There's no place like Home

Your Home folder is the most important folder to you as a user — or at least the one where you'll probably spend most of your time — but it's only part of Mac's higher-level folder structure. I walk you through this configuration so that you understand where your Home folder fits in and so that you'll be able to find applications and other items shared by everyone who uses your Mac. It's kind of complicated, especially if you're an old-time Mac user who's used to arranging things pretty much the way you want. Take heart, though: After you get the hang of the new way of arranging things, it makes sense.

I strongly recommend that you store all files you create or work with in a subfolder within your Home folder. The advantage of using the Documents folder to hold your documents is that it's easy to find, and many programs use it as the default folder when you open or save a file.

When you open your Home folder, you see a Finder window with your username in the title bar. Seeing your username in the Finder window's title bar tells you that you're in your Home folder. Every user has a Home folder named after his or her short username (as specified in the Accounts System Preference pane). In Figure 6-11, you can see that my Home folder is named `bob1` — the short name I used when I first set up my Mac.

Your Home folder has several folders inside it created by Mac OS X. You can create more if you like — in fact, every folder that you *ever* create (at least every one you create on this particular disk or volume) should be within your Home folder. I explain this necessity as I describe the other main folders on your hard drive.

Figure 6-11:
My Home
folder.

Your Home folder contains eight folders by default. The following four are the most important ones:

- ✔ **Desktop:** If you put items (files, folders, applications, or aliases) on the Desktop, they appear on the Desktop. The files themselves, however, are actually stored in this folder.

- ✔ **Documents:** This is the place to put all the documents (letters, spreadsheets, recipes, and novels) that you create.

- ✔ **Library:** Preferences (files containing the settings you create in System Preferences and other places) are stored in the Library folder, along with fonts (ones that are only available to you, as described previously in this chapter), and other stuff to be used by you and only you.

- ✔ **Public:** If you share your Mac, you can't work inside other users' folders. But you can share files with others by storing them in the Public folder of your Home folder. (Read more about Public folders in Chapter 14.)

Following are a few more tidbits to keep in mind as you dig around your Home folder:

- ✔ If you decide you don't want an item on the Desktop anymore, delete it by dragging its icon from the Desktop folder to the Trash or by dragging its icon from the Desktop itself to the Trash. Both techniques yield the same effect — the file is in the Trash, where it remains until you empty the Trash.

- ✔ In previous versions of Mac OS, there was no Desktop folder. Items stored on the Desktop appeared on the Desktop, and that same Desktop was seen and used by everyone that used this Mac. In Mac OS X, each user has his or her own Desktop, and the items there are stored in the user's Desktop folder.

✔ The other four folders that you may see in your Home folder are Movies, Music, Pictures, and Sites. All these folders except Sites are empty until you (or a program like iTunes or iPhoto, which create files inside these folders automatically the first time you launch them) put something in them; Sites contains a few files that your Mac needs if you enable Web Sharing (in the Sharing System Preferences pane, as I describe in Chapter 14).

Your Library card

The Library subfolder of your Home folder is the repository of everything that Mac OS X needs to customize your Mac to your tastes. You won't spend much time (if any) adding things to the Library folder or moving them around within it, but it's a good idea for you to know what's in there. In the "Library" section earlier in this chapter, I discuss the Library folder that's used to specify preferences for the Mac as a whole. But *this* Library folder is all about you and your stuff.

Be cautious with the Library folder because OS X is very persnickety about how its folders and files are organized. As I discuss in the "Library" section earlier in the chapter, you can add and remove items safely from most Library folders, but *leave the folders themselves alone.* If you remove or rename the wrong folder, you could render OS X inoperable. It's like the old joke about the guy who said to the doctor, "It hurts when I do that," and the doctor replies, "Then don't do that."

To find the Library folder, click the Home icon in the Sidebar of any Finder window and then open the Library folder. You should see several folders there. The exact number of folders in the Library folder depends on the software that you install on your Mac — for example, if you have an e-mail account, you should see a folder called Addresses (if you don't have an e-mail account, it won't be there). Some of the more important standard folders in the Library folder include the following:

✔ **Documentation:** Where some applications store their Help files. Others store theirs in the main (root-level) public Library folder.

✔ **Fonts:** This folder is empty unless you install your own fonts here. The fonts that come with Mac OS X aren't stored here but rather in the Library folder at root level for everyone who uses this Mac. I discuss this earlier in this chapter in the "Library" section. If you want to install fonts that only you have access to, put them in the Fonts folder of *your* Library folder.

To install a font, drag its icon to the folder in which you want to keep the font. It will only be available when you're logged in; other users won't be able to use a font stored here. To install a font that's available to anyone who uses this Mac, drag it into the Fonts folder in the public Library folder, the one at root level that you see when you open your hard disk's icon.

If your Mac is set up for multiple users, only users with Administrator (admin) privileges can put stuff into the public Library folder. (For more information on admin privileges, check out Chapter 14.)

✔ **Preferences:** The files here hold the information about whichever things you customize in Mac OS X. Whenever you change a system or application preference, that info is saved to a file in the Preferences folder.

Don't mess with the Preferences folder! You should never need to open or use this folder unless something bad happens — for example, you suspect that a particular preference file has become corrupted (that is, damaged). My advice is to just forget about this folder and let it do its job.

Finding Your Stuff, Fast

Even if you follow every single bit of advice provided in this chapter, there will come a time when you won't be able to find a file or folder although you know for certain it's right there on your hard disk. Somewhere. Fortunately, Tiger includes a fabulous new technology called Spotlight that can help you find almost anything on any mounted disk in seconds. Spotlight can

✔ Search for files

✔ Search for folders

✔ Search for text inside documents

✔ Search for files and folders by their metadata (for example, creation date, modification date, kind, size, and so on)

Spotlight finds what you're looking for and then organizes its results logically, all in the blink of an eye (on most Macs).

Spotlight is both a technology and a feature. The technology is pervasive throughout Tiger, and is the underlying power behind the search boxes in many Apple applications and utilities such as Mail, Address Book, System Preferences, Finder, and others. You can also use it right from the Spotlight menu, the little magnifying glass on the right side of the menu bar. And, you can reuse Spotlight searches in the future by turning them into Smart Folders.

Finding files and folders has never been faster or easier than it is in Tiger. So in this section, I look at the three separate but related ways Spotlight helps you find files, folders, and even text inside document files — the Search box in Finder windows, the Spotlight menu, and Smart Folders.

The Search box in Finder windows

NEW IN TIGER

If you used previous versions of Mac OS X, you may think you know how the Search box in the toolbar of Finder windows works. But you don't. Even though it looks almost the same as before, it is a Search box on major-league steroids. With its power provided by Spotlight, this is definitely not your father's Search box.

So what's new and different? Glad you asked. First, notice that the window changes completely as soon as you type a single character into the Search box, as shown in Figure 6-12.

Figure 6-12:
The Search box looks the same as it did previous versions of Mac OS X (top) until you type a character or word into it (bottom).

TIP

If you choose File⇨Find or type its keyboard shortcut (⌘+F), you'll see the same thing shown in the bottom window of Figure 6-12.

Notice that the list is sorted into categories and each category can be expanded and collapsed by clicking the little disclosure triangle to the left of its name. At the top of the results list are buttons to select where you want to search — Servers, Computer (selected in the bottom window in Figure 6-12), Home, and Others.

Or, if the folder or volume you wish to search isn't Servers, Computer, or Home, click the Others button and a sheet drops down, allowing you to choose specific folders or volumes for the search, as shown in Figure 6-13.

Figure 6-13:
Click the +
button or
drag and
drop folders
or volumes
here to
search only
those
folders or
volumes.

For more information on a file or folder, merely click the little "i" at the right side of it and information about the file or folder appears, as shown in Figure 6-14. If the file is a graphic, video, or audio file, you'll also see (or hear) a preview of it, as shown in Figure 6-14.

Figure 6-14:
Click the
little "i" to
learn more
about the
selected file
or folder.

After you search, you can open any item in the list by double-clicking it.

Last but not least, if you want to know where a file or folder resides on your hard disk, look at the very bottom row of the window, where you'll see the path to that file (bob1/Music/Smell The Glove XIII, Brown to Blue.mp3 in Figure 6-14).

So there you have it — fast searches made easy in the Finder. But there are many ways to access the power of Spotlight and the Search box in the tool-bar of Finder windows is merely one of them.

Spotlight

Another way to search for files and folders is to use the Spotlight menu itself — the aqua magnifying glass icon on the far right in your menu bar. Click the icon to open Spotlight's Search box, and then type a character, word, or series of words in the search box to find an item, as shown in Figure 6-15.

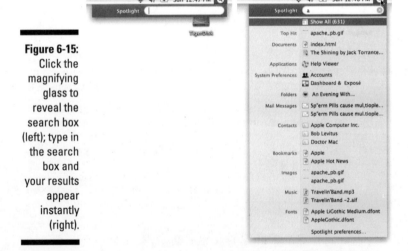

Figure 6-15: Click the magnifying glass to reveal the search box (left); type in the search box and your results appear instantly (right).

Another way to open the Spotlight search box is with its keyboard shortcut, which is ⌘+Space by default.

You can change this shortcut to whatever you like in the Spotlight System Preference pane, which I discuss in Chapter 13.

Spotlight is more than just a menu, though. You can also use the Spotlight Window to create and perform more sophisticated searches, as shown in Figure 6-16.

Figure 6-16:
Use the
Spotlight
Window if
you prefer
additional
control over
how search
results are
presented.

You can access this window two ways:

✔ Click the Show All item in the Spotlight menu (the first item in the list in Figure 6-15), or use its keyboard shortcut (⌘+Option+Space by default).

You can change this shortcut to whatever you like in the Spotlight System Preference pane, discussed in Chapter 13.

✔ In the Spotlight Window, use the column on the right to fine-tune your search. You can select the way categories are grouped (by kind, date, people, or a flat list with no categories); how items within each group are sorted (by name, date, kind, or people); when the item was last used (any date, today, since yesterday, this week, this month, this year); and where (Computer, Home, TigerDisk).

When you click an item in this column, the results update to reflect your choice immediately. The point is, you should use these items whenever a search results in a huge number of files. For example, click any of the When items to narrow the date range for your search, or click Group by Kind if you know you're searching for a particular type of file (a .doc file, a PDF file, and so on).

Regardless of which method you choose to invoke it — the Search box in a Finder window, the Spotlight Search box in the menu bar, or the Spotlight window — Spotlight saves you time and effort.

Smart Folders

Now, as Steve Jobs is fond of saying near the end of his annual keynote addresses, "There is one more thing." Those things are called Smart Folders, and they let you save a search to reuse in the future.

Smart Folders are updated continuously, so they always find all the files on your computer that match the search criteria. The difference here is that all those files will appear in one convenient Smart folder. So, for example, you can create a Smart Folder that contains all the Microsoft Word files on your system that you've opened in the past week. Or create a Smart Folder that displays graphics files, but only ones bigger (or smaller) than a specified file size.

The possibilities are endless. And because Smart Folders use alias-like technology to display items, the actual files reside in only one location — the folder where you originally put them. In other words, Smart Folders don't gather files in a separate place, they gather aliases of files, leaving the originals right were you stashed them. Neat!

Also, because Spotlight is built deep into the bowels of the Mac OS X file system and kernel, Smart Folders are always current, even if you've added or deleted files since you created the Smart Folder.

Smart Folders are so useful Apple provides five different ways to create one:

✔ Choose File➪New Smart Folder.

✔ Use the keyboard shortcut ⌘+Option+N.

✔ Choose File➪Find.

✔ Use the keyboard shortcut ⌘+F.

✔ Type at least one character into the Search box in a Finder window.

Once you've done any of the above, refine the criteria for your search by clicking the + button to add a criteria or the – button to delete one. When you're satisfied and ready to turn your criteria into a Smart Folder, click the Save button below the Search box. A sheet drops down so that you can save it wherever you like, as shown in Figure 6-17.

If you want to add the Smart Folder to the Sidebar, check the Add to Sidebar check box.

After you create your Smart Folder, you can move it anywhere on any hard disk and then use it like any other folder. If you want to change the criteria for a Smart Folder, open it and click the Edit button as shown in Figure 6-18. When you're finished editing criteria, click the Save button to resave the folder with its new criteria. You may be asked if you want to replace the previous Smart Folder of the same name; you (usually) do.

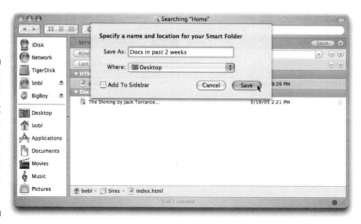

Figure 6-17:
A Save sheet appears when you click the Save button below the Search box.

Figure 6-18:
Open a Smart Folder and click the Edit button (top) to change criteria for this Smart Folder.

Smart Folders will save you a lot of time and effort, so if you haven't played with them much (or at all) yet, be sure and give 'em a try.

Chapter 7

Haggling with Removable Media

. . . .

In This Chapter

▶ Initializing and erasing your disks

▶ Using PC-formatted disks

▶ Creating your own CDs and DVDs

▶ Ejecting disks

. . . .

*1*n this chapter, I show you disk basics: how to format them; how to format them so that our Windows-using brethren (and sisteren) can use them; how to eject them; how to copy or move files between disks; and much more. Onward!

Now, some of you may be thinking, "My Mac doesn't even have a floppy drive. Why should I read a whole chapter about disks?" Well, I'll tell ya. This chapter offers lots of info that applies to every Mac user — including folder management and moving or copying files to and from disks other than your internal hard drive. I also show you how to work with other types of removable magnetic media (such as Zip and Jaz drives), as well as optical media such as CD-R, CD-RW, DVD-R, DVD-RW, and DVD-RAM — all of which many Mac users deal with regularly. If you have a recently minted Mac, for example, you probably have an internal Combo drive (plays DVDs and plays and burns CDs) or Apple SuperDrive (CD + DVD player/burner). Or you may have added an external USB flash drive, floppy disk drive, Zip, Jaz, or iMation SuperDisk drive which can read both standard 1.4MB floppies and 120MB iMation SuperDisks (not to be confused with Apple's DVD-burning drive, which they call "SuperDrive").

The bottom line is that removable-media drives allow you to easily copy files for friends, regardless of whether they use a Mac or a PC, and to move your files between home and work. And, as you'll see in Chapter 8, they allow you to protect your valuable data by backing up your hard disk to another type of media for safekeeping.

Comprehending Disks

You should think of the disk icons that appear on the Desktop (and/or in the Places sidebar of Finder windows) as if they were folders. That's because your Mac sees disks as nothing *but* giant folders. When you double-click them, their contents appear in the Finder window, just like a folder. You can drag stuff in and out of a disk's window, and you can manipulate the disk's window in all the usual ways, just like a folder. In fact, for all intents and purposes, disks are folders.

The only exception to the disks-are-folders rule that I can think of is that you can't use the Duplicate keyboard shortcut (⌘+D) on a disk, although you can use it on a folder.

Some Disks Need to be Formatted First

Brand-new disks sometimes need to be *formatted* — prepared to receive Macintosh files — before they can be used.

When you pop in an unformatted disk, your Mac will usually pop up a dialog that asks what you want to do with the disk. One option is usually to *format* (or *initialize*) the disk — that is, to get it ready to record data. If you choose to format the disk, the Disk Utility program launches itself so you can format the disk from the Erase tab.

Is that a disk or a disc?

So how do you spell this critter, anyway? Sometimes you see it spelled d-i-s-*k*; other times you see it spelled d-i-s-*c*. If you're wondering what's up with that, here's the skinny. In the good old days, the only kind of computer disk was a disk with a *k*: floppy disk, hard disk, Bernoulli disk, and so on. Then one day, the compact disc (you know, a CD) was invented. And the people who invented it chose to spell it with a *c* instead of a *k*, probably because it's round like a *disc*us (think track and field). From that time on, both spellings have been used more or less interchangeably.

Now some people will tell you that magnetic media (floppy, hard, Zip, Jaz, Orb, and so on) are called *disks* (spelled with a *k*). And that optical media — that is, discs that are read with a laser (such as CD-ROMs, audio CDs, DVDs, and CD-RWs) — are called *discs* (spelled with a *c*). Maybe that's true, but the two terms have been used pretty much interchangeably for so long that you can't depend on the last letter to tell you whether a disk is magnetic or optical.

The bottom line is that I'm going to compromise and use the *disk* spelling throughout this chapter. If you're offended that I call CD-ROMs, audio CDs, DVDs, CD-RWs, and such *disks* instead of *discs*, I'm sorry.

My editors made me do it.

If you ever need to format or initialize a blank disk and don't see the dialog, all you have to do is open Disk Utility manually (it's in your Applications/ Utilities folder) and use its Erase tab to format the disk.

Moving and Copying Disk Icons

Moving a file icon from one on-screen disk to another works the same as moving an icon from one folder to another, with one notable exception: When you move a file from one disk to another, you automatically make a copy of it, leaving the original untouched and unmoved. If you want to move a file completely from one disk to another, you have to delete that leftover original by dragging it to the Trash or by holding down the ⌘ key when you drag it.

Copying the entire contents of any disk or volume (floppy, CD, DVD, or external hard drive among others) to a new destination works a little differently. To do this, click the disk's icon and then, while holding down the Option key, drag the disk icon onto any folder or disk icon or any open Finder window.

If you don't hold down the Option key when you drag a disk icon to another destination, it creates an *alias* of the disk (that is, a link back to the original) instead of a copy of its contents. As you might expect, the alias will be worthless after you eject the disk.

When the copy is completed, a folder bearing the same name as the copied disk appears in the destination folder or disk. The new folder contains each and every file that was on the disk of the same name.

Surprise: Your PC Disks Work, Too!

One of the most excellent features of Mac OS X (if you have friends unfortunate enough not to own Macs and you want to share files with them) is that it reads both Mac- and PC-formatted CDs and DVDs without any user intervention. *PC disks* are formatted for use with personal computers (PCs) that run Windows. If a friend has a Windows computer, you can read disks he or she has created by just sticking them in your disk drive. Your unfortunate friend, on the other hand, can't do doodly-squat with your Mac-formatted disks — yet another reason why Macs are better.

Although PC-formatted disks will work in your Mac, the *files* on them may or may not. If the files are documents, one of your Mac programs can probably open them. If the files are Windows programs (these often sport the `.exe` suffix, which stands for *executable*), your Mac won't be able to do anything with 'em without additional software designed to run Windows programs.

TIP

That additional software is the almost-magical *Virtual PC* from Microsoft (www.microsoft.com). This program emulates a Pentium-based PC on your Mac so you can run genuine Microsoft Windows operating systems (Windows XP Professional or XP Home, Windows 2000, Windows Me, and Windows 98) on your Mac.

So, with a copy of Virtual PC (around $200), your Mac *can* run those .exe files (and most Windows programs as well). Unfortunately, because emulating a Pentium processor and PC video card demands a lot from your Mac, the performance you get is slower than even a cheap PC. So although it's a useful program for running most Windows applications (including Web browsers, which run remarkably well under Virtual PC), fast-moving games (such as Doom, Quake, or Unreal Tournament) are mostly unplayable. Bummer. The Windows bundled Solitaire game, on the other hand, works pretty well under Virtual PC.

Burning CDs and DVDs

Apple, or at least Steve Jobs, refers to the Macintosh as "your digital hub" and has been doing so since January 2001 at Macworld Expo (before Intel started touting the Pentium 4 as the "center of your digital world"). With Mac OS X (10.1 or later), this means you can play, create, and publish audio and video. If your Mac is equipped with a CD-RW or SuperDrive, just insert a blank CD-R, CD-RW, DVD-R, or DVD-RW disc and you'll see the alert (as shown in Figure 7-1) that asks you what you want to do with the disk.

Figure 7-1:
Insert a
blank CD in
your CD-RW
drive and
get ready to
feel the
burn.

Choose what you want to do from the Action pop-up menu. The default choice is Open Finder, unless you've changed that default in the CDs & DVDs System Preference pane.

TIP

The other choices are Open iTunes and Open Other Application. If you choose the first, iTunes automatically opens when you insert a blank CD; if you choose the second, you are first presented with an Open File sheet where you can select the application you want to open; then you select the application and it opens. If you want to make this action the default so it occurs the next time you insert a blank disk (and every time thereafter), click the Make This Action the Default check box.

Let's go with Open Finder for now, though: Click the OK button, and your blank CD mounts (appears as an icon) on the Desktop — just like any other removable disk — but its distinctive icon tells you that it's a recordable CD (or DVD), as shown in Figure 7-2. From that point on, just copy files onto it until you have it the way you want it. When you're ready to create your CD, start to drag the icon, and the Trash will turn into a Burn button (looks like the warning for radioactivity to me), as shown in Figure 7-3.

Figure 7-2:
Recordable
optical
disks get a
distinctive,
labeled
icon.

Figure 7-3:
Just drag
the disk icon
to the Burn
Disc (with
a *c*) button
on the
Dock when
you're ready
to burn
your CD.

Alternatively, you could Control+click the disk's icon and choose Burn Disc (yes, Apple spells it with a *c*) from the contextual menu or select the icon and choose Burn Disc from the File menu (see Figure 7-4). If you choose Eject, either from the contextual menu or from the File menu, you'll be asked whether you want to burn the disk first.

Figure 7-4:
Two more
ways to
burn a disk.

TIP

MP3 players play files in the order that they're written, which will be alphabetically. So, if you want them to play in a particular order, be sure to name them with sequential numbers at the beginning. Fortunately, iTunes makes that easy with the Create File Names with Track Number option in your Importing preferences.

After you've chosen to burn a disk, you see the dialog shown in Figure 7-5. Choose a speed from the Burn Speed pop-up menu; then click the Burn button, and you're done.

Figure 7-5:
The last
step before
the burning
begins.

TIP

I usually use a slower (2x), more reliable burn speed unless I'm in a huge hurry. I have had many discs fail at the higher speeds (we call those discs "drink coasters"). So I avoid them unless I need to burn a disc really quickly.

Click the Save Burn Folder To check box if you think you might want to burn another copy of this disc someday.

Speaking of the Burn Folder, it's a new Tiger feature and a slick one at that. Burn Folders are designed to let you burn their contents on a CD or DVD quickly and easily. There are three ways to create one:

- ✔ Choose File➪New Burn Folder.

- ✔ Choose New Burn Folder from the Action menu in the toolbar of any window in the Finder.

- ✔ Ctl+click and choose New Burn Folder from the contextual menu.

When you drag a file or folder onto a Burn Folder, Mac OS X sneakily creates an alias of that file or folder and sticks that in the Burn Folder instead of the original file. This has two benefits: First, you don't have to have two copies of the file on your hard disk — one to burn and the other stashed wherever it should be stashed. But the second benefit is even more significant: If you've made changes to files in the Burn Folder, when you burn a CD or DVD in the future, it will be burned with the latest versions of the files and folders it contains.

You can use Burn Folders to jury-rig a backup system that's better than nothing. I show you how in Chapter 8.

Getting Disks Out of Your Mac

You now know almost everything there is to know about disks except one important thing: how to eject a disk. Piece of cake, actually. Here are several ways, all simple to remember:

- ✔ Click the disk's icon to select it, and then choose File➪Eject (or use the keyboard shortcut ⌘+E).

- ✔ Drag the disk's icon to the Trash. You'll notice that when you drag a disk's icon, the Trash icon in the Dock changes into an Eject icon, like that shown in the left margin here.

    The preceding method of ejecting a disk is something that used to drive me (and many others) crazy before Mac OS X. In the olden days, the Trash icon didn't change into an Eject icon. And this confused many new users, who then asked me the same question (over and over and over): "But doesn't dragging something to the Trash erase it from your disk?"

- ✔ Click the disk icon while holding down the Control key and then choose Eject from the contextual menu.

There's one more way if you like little menus on the right side of your menu bar, as shown in Figure 7-6.

Figure 7-6:
The last step of all — ejecting the disk.

To install your own Eject menu, navigate to System/Library/CoreServices/ MenuExtras and then open (double-click) the Eject.menu icon. Your Eject menu will appear on the right side of your menu bar.

TIP

There are 23 other handy menus in the MenuExtras folder and they're all installed the same way — just double-click 'em. You can see a few of mine in Figure 7-6; from left to right are my AirPort, Sound, Input (the flag), Battery, and Clock menus.

To move a menu extra after it's installed on your menu bar, hold down ⌘, click the menu, and then drag left or right.

To remove a menu extra, hold down ⌘ and drag the menu off the menu bar and onto the Desktop, as shown on the left in Figure 7-7. It disappears with a little poof as shown on the right in Figure 7-7.

Figure 7-7:
⌘+click and drag, and poof — the Eject menu is gone for good.

Chapter 8

Back Up Now or Regret It Later

Although Macs are generally reliable beasts (especially Macs running OS X), someday your hard drive will die. I promise. They *all* do. And if you don't back up your hard drive (or at least back up any files that you can't afford to lose) before that day comes, chances are good that you'll never see your files again. And if you do see them again, it will only be after paying someone like Scott Gaidano of DriveSavers Data Recovery Service a king's ransom, with no guarantee of success.

DriveSavers is the premier recoverer of lost data on hard drives. They understand Mac hard disks quite well, do excellent work, and can often recover stuff that nobody else could. (Ask the producers of *The Simpsons* about the almost-lost episodes.) Understandably, DriveSavers charges accordingly. Here's the phone number for DriveSavers: 415-883-4232. Now pray that you never need it — and if you back up often, you won't. But if, somehow, none of this sinks in, tell Scott that I said, "Hi."

In other words, you absolutely, positively, without question *must back up* your files if you don't want to risk losing them. Just as you adopt the Shut Down command and make it a habit before turning off your machine, you must remember to back up important files on your hard drive to another disk or device, and back them up often.

How often is often? That depends on you. How much work can you afford to lose? If your answer is that losing everything you did yesterday would put you out of business, you need to back up daily or possibly twice a day. If you would only lose a few unimportant letters, you can back up less frequently.

Backing Up Is (Not) Hard to Do

You can back up your hard drive in basically two ways — the brute force method, or the easy way. Read on to discover both. . . .

Backing up by using the manual, brute-force method

The most rudimentary way to back up your files is to do it manually. Accomplish this by dragging your files a few at a time to another volume — another hard disk or CD-R, CD-RW, DVD-R, or DVD-RW. (Don't forget to actually *burn the disc* if you use any of those three- or four-letter acronyms; a drag is not enough.) By doing so, you're making a copy of each file that you want to protect. (See Chapter 7 for more info on removable storage.)

Yuck! If doing a manual backup sounds pretty awful, trust me — it is. This method takes forever; you can't really tell whether you copy every file; and you can't copy only the files that have been modified since your last backup. Almost nobody sticks with this method for long.

Of course, if you're careful to only save files in your Documents folder, as I suggest several times in this book, you can probably get away with backing up only that. Or, if you save files in other folders within your Home folder, or have any files in your Movies, Music, Pictures, or Sites folders (which often contain files you didn't specifically save in those folders like your iPhoto photos and iTunes songs), you should probably consider backing up your entire Home folder. As you'll read in a moment, it's even easier with backup software.

Backing up by using the manual, brute-force method with Burn Folders

Adding Burn Folders to the mix makes it slightly easier to burn backups of important files and folders using the brute force method. If you're not going to use real backup software (covered in the following section) to protect your valuable files, the brute-force with Burn Folder technique will at least protect your most important files and folders.

As long as you remember to burn discs regularly, of course.

In fact, even though I use Retrospect daily to back up almost everything on my hard disk, I also used a Burn Folder with the Mac OS X 10.4 Tiger For Dummies folder in it as a backup of my backups.

It's easy to do. I just created a new Burn Folder and then dragged the Tiger For Dummies folder onto it. Every day or two I click the Burn button, as shown in Figure 8-1. An alert asks me to insert a blank disc (unless I already put one in the drive), and reminds me that I need a disc capable of holding at least 264.8MB, the size of the Tiger For Dummies folder today.

Figure 8-1: Burning the contents of my Tiger FD Burn Folder.

Another alert asks if I'm sure I want to burn the disc (which, by the way, will be usable on any Mac or Windows computer), and also offers me the opportunity to rename the disc before it's burned and choose a burn speed. I click the Burn button and without any further ado, my backup disc is burned for me.

It's like déjà vu all over again. I just clicked a Burn button (the one in the Burn Folder window shown in Figure 8-1) two seconds ago. I understand the need for consistency, but it seems weird to have to click Burn two or three times before any actual burning occurs. For what it's worth, iTunes does the same thing and worse: If you ignore its flashing Burn icon for long enough, the burn is aborted and you have to start all over again (and click Burn two or three more times, I might add).

Backing up by using commercial backup software

If you ask me, a good backup program is the best investment you can make. Frankly, I like the security of knowing that every document I modify today is being backed up automatically. And that's what backup software is all about.

Backup software automates the task of backing up, remembering what is on each backup disk (if your backup uses more than one disk) and backing up only those files that have been modified since the last backup.

Furthermore, you can instruct your backup software to only back up a certain folder (Home or Documents) and to ignore the hundreds of megabytes of stuff that make up OS X, all of which can be easily reinstalled from the Mac OS X CD-ROM.

Your first backup with commercial software should take anywhere from a few minutes to many hours and use one or more pieces of optical media — CD-R, CD-RW, DVD-R, DVD-RW, magneto-optical disks — or non-optical media such as another hard drive or any kind of tape backup. Subsequent backups, called *incremental backups* in backup-software parlance, should take only a few minutes.

If you do incremental backups, be sure to label all the disks you use during that operation — if you use multiple disks, number them. Your backup software may prompt you with a message such as Please insert backup disk 7. If you haven't labeled your media clearly, you could have a problem figuring out which disk *is* disk 7.

For some unfathomable reason, Apple has almost never seen fit to provide backup software with new Macs or include it with Mac OS. I know that some early-'90s Macintosh Performas had a crummy backup program, and if you pay the 99 bucks for .Mac, you get Apple's decent Backup program. But other than those two attempts, Apple has left millions of Mac owners clueless, for years, giving them nothing more than a brief passage regarding backing up in the Macintosh *User's Guide*.

Information on backing up should be in big red letters, in the first chapter of the guide, and include a warning from the Surgeon General or something. And it wouldn't kill Apple to provide a backup utility with OS X, either. Sheesh, even Windows has a backup command, albeit a lousy one. C'mon, Apple, give Mac owners a fair shake — include Backup with those $129 OS X upgrades.

Fortunately, plenty of very good backup programs are available for well under $150, including the excellent Retrospect family of backup solutions from Dantz Development (www.dantz.com).

Retrospect Desktop protects up to three networked desktops and notebooks for $129; Retrospect Workgroup protects a single server and up to 20 networked desktops and notebooks for $499; Retrospect Server protects up to 100 networked clients, including Windows and Macintosh desktops and notebooks, as well as Mac OS X servers for $799.

Here's a nice touch: The included network client (all three versions of Retrospect use it) runs on Windows XP, Windows 2000 Professional, Windows NT 4.0 Workstation, Windows 95/98/Me, Red Hat Linux (versions 6.2, 7.1, 7.2, 7.3, and 8), and, of course, Mac OS 9 or X. So if you've got any non-Mac computers, chances are Retrospect can back them up over your local-area network at no additional expense.

Other backup offerings include TriBackup 3 (around $50) from Tri-Edre (www.tri-edre.com); and more modest synchronizer programs such as ChronoSync ($20) from Econ Technologies (www.econtechnologies.com), or You Synchronize ($50) from You Software (www.yousoftware.com).

Virus trivia

A computer *virus,* in case you missed it in *Time* or *Newsweek,* is a nasty little piece of computer code that replicates and spreads from disk to disk. Most viruses cause your Mac to misbehave; some viruses can destroy files or erase disks with no warning.

The good news is that most virus scares that you hear and read about won't affect you (O, lucky Mac user!) because they are specific to users of Windows systems. Most viruses are specific to an operating system — Mac viruses won't affect Windows users, Windows viruses won't affect Mac users, and so forth. The one real exception here is a "gift" from the wonderful world of Microsoft Office (Word, Excel, for example) users: the dreaded *macro viruses* that are spread with Word and Excel documents containing macros written in Microsoft's VBA (Visual BASIC for Applications) language. But you're even safe from those if you practice safe computing as I describe.

As it happens, so far almost all the viral activity affecting OS X involved various Windows macro virii. In fact, at the time of this writing, I know of no OS X-specific viruses nor of any that attack Mac OS X exclusively — and (at least so far) none that cause damage. Still, the advice in this chapter is sound — one never knows when the little boys out there will decide to attack the Mac. OS X viruses aren't impossible or nonexistent; they just don't exist in known examples at this moment in time. But they could someday; better safe than sorry.

If you use disks that have been inserted in other computers, you need some form of virus-detection software. If you download and use files from Web and File Transfer Protocol (FTP) sites on the Internet, you need some form of virus detection as well.

You don't have too much to worry about if

- ✔ You download files only from commercial online services, such as America Online, which is very conscientious about viral infections.

- ✔ You use only commercial software and don't download files from Web sites with strange names.

You should definitely worry about virus infection if

- ✔ An unsavory friend told you about a Web site called `Dan'sDenOfPirated IllegalStolenBootlegSoftware. com` — and you actually visited it.

- ✔ You swap disks with friends regularly.

- ✔ You shuttle disks back and forth to other Macs.

- ✔ You use your disks at service bureaus or copy shops.

- ✔ You download files from various and sundry places on the Internet, even ones that don't *sound* as slimy as `Dan'sDen OfPiratedIllegalStolenBootleg Software.com`.

- ✔ You receive e-mail with attachments (and open them).

If you're at risk, do yourself a favor and buy a commercial antivirus program. Although you can choose from many shareware and freeware antivirus solutions, none that I know of are as trustworthy as Virex or Norton. The big advantage of buying a commercial antivirus program is that the publisher contacts you each time a virus is discovered — and provides you with a software update to protect you against the new strain. (Or, for a fee, the publisher can

(continued)

(continued)

send you a new version of the software every time a new virus is found. But that can get expensive; new viruses appear every day.)

On the commercial front, two leading virus-detection utilities are Virex and Norton AntiVirus (NAV; formerly Symantec Anti-Virus). Each has its advocates. I've used NAV for years and I have never been infected with a virus. My editor uses Virex and has also been virus-free. You'll find more info about Virex at: `www.networkassociates.com/us/products/mcafee/antivirus/desktop/virex.htm`, and more info on Norton AntiVirus at `www.symantec.com/nav/nav_mac/index.html`.

If you want the most flexible, top-of-the-line backup software, spend a little more and pop for Retrospect. It can do everything the others can do — and more. It's the only backup software you'll ever need.

One of the best things about good backup software is that you can set it up to automate your backups and perform them even if you forget. I use FireWire hard drives as my backup media of choice, and Retrospect backs up all the important stuff on my main hard disk four times each day, each time to a different backup set and disk. At night my entire boot drive is duplicated to another hard disk, giving me a bootable backup I can use in emergencies. (Where my data is concerned, I sleep pretty well, thanks.)

Why You Need Two Sets of Backups

You're a good soldier. You back up regularly. You think you're immune to file loss or damage.

Now picture yourself in the following scenario:

1. One day you take a DVD disc, or your portable FireWire hard disk to QuicKopyLazerPrintz to print your résumé on the high-resolution laser printer there. You make a few changes while at QuicKopyLazerPrintz and then take the disk home and stick it into your Mac (or connect it if it's a FireWire drive). Unbeknownst to you, the disk or document became infected with a computer virus at QuicKopyLazerPrintz. (I discuss viruses in the sidebar "Virus trivia," elsewhere in this chapter.)

2. When you insert or connect the disk, the infection spreads to your boot drive like wildfire.

3. Then you do a backup. Your backup software, believing that all the infected files have been recently modified (well, they *have* been — they were infected with a virus!), proceeds to back them up. You notice that

the backup takes a little longer than usual, but otherwise things seem to be okay.

4. A few days later, your Mac starts acting strangely. You borrow a copy of an excellent virus-detection software, such as Virex or Norton AntiVirus (formerly Symantec Anti-Virus), and discover that your hard drive is infected. "A-ha!" you exclaim. "I've been a good little Mac user, backing up regularly. I'll just restore everything from my backup disks."

Not so fast, bucko. The files on your backup disks are also infected!

This scenario demonstrates why you need multiple backups. If you have several sets of backup disks, chances are pretty good that one of the sets is clean.

I always keep at least three current sets of backup disks going at any one time. I use one set on even-numbered days, one on odd-numbered days, and update the third set once a week and store it somewhere other than my office (such as a neighbor's house or a safe deposit box). This scheme ensures that no matter what happens — even if my office burns, is flooded, is destroyed by a tornado or a hurricane, or is robbed — I won't lose more than a few days' worth of work. I can live with that.

Part III
Doing Stuff with Your Mac

The 5th Wave   By Rich Tennant

INTERNET ACCESS
.50¢ - Min.

In this part . . .

Moving right along, Part III comprises how to do stuff with your Mac. In this section, it's off to the Internet first — how to get it working and what to do with it after you do. Next, I help you decipher the myriad Print options to help you become a modern-day Gutenberg. You also find out about the applications that come with OS X, the Classic Environment, and how to make your OS X look and feel the way you want it (even if that's retro — ahem — Classic). Finally, I take you on a tour of the System Preferences application, and show you how it lets you customize your Mac so it's just the way you like it. (Tailfins and white sidewalls optional.)

This is an excellent section if I do say so myself . . . and one you definitely don't want to miss.

Chapter 9

Internet-Working

· ·

· ·

*T*hese days, networking online is easier than finding a log to fall off of: You simply use the Internet to connect your Mac to a wealth of information residing on computers around the world. Luckily for you, Mac OS X has the best and most comprehensive Internet tools ever shipped with a Mac operating system. In this chapter, I cover the top two: the *World Wide Web* (that's the *www* you see so often in Internet addresses) and *e-mail* (which stands for *electronic mail*). Okay, with Apple's release of iChat AV, I'm adding a third one: *live chatting.*

A Brief Internet Overview

The *Internet,* which is a giant conglomeration of connected computers, offers innumerable types of services. Sometimes referred to as the *Information Superhighway,* the Internet is a giant worldwide network of computers. With an Internet connection, you can view text and graphics on your computer, even if the text and graphics are sitting on a computer in Tokyo. Via the Internet, you can send and retrieve messages and computer files to and from almost anywhere in the world — in milliseconds.

Other Internet services include bulletin board discussions called *newsgroups,* File Transfer Protocol (FTP), and videoconferencing. After you have your connection set up (I discuss this process in the "Setting Up for Surfing" section later in this chapter), I urge you to check out these nifty features.

Unfortunately, although these other features are pretty cool, going into much detail about them is also beyond the purview of this book.

The most interesting part of the Internet, at least in my humble opinion, is the Web. This is the part of the Internet in which you traverse (that is, surf) to Web sites and view them on your computer with software called a *Web browser*.

Mac OS X offers built-in Internet connectivity right out of the box. For example, your machine comes with

- ✔ Its own built-in **Point-to-Point Protocol** (PPP) client for making modem connections to the Internet.

  If you don't even know what a modem is, don't worry. Skip ahead to the upcoming section "Setting Up for Surfing," and all will become clear.

- ✔ Apple's **Safari** Web browser with which you to navigate the Web, download remote files via FTP, and more.

- ✔ The **Mail** application (for e-mail).

- ✔ **iChat AV** is Apple's live online chatting client that works with other iChat users, people using AOL Instant Messaging [AIM] clients, people using Jabber (an open-source chatting protocol), and Bonjour.

Because most Mac users like things to be easy, Mac OS X includes a cool feature in its Setup Assistant to help you find and configure an account with an Internet Service Provider (ISP). After your Internet connection is up and running, you can use Safari to cruise the Internet (or acquire and use one of the many other free and commercial Web browsers for OS X, such as Firefox or OmniWeb).

But before I can talk about browsers, e-mail software, and chatting, I first have to help you configure your Internet connection. When you're finished, you can play with your browsers, mail, and chat applications to your heart's content.

Setting Up for Surfing

Before you can surf the Internet, you need to get a few small tasks out of the way first. In this section, I walk you through them all.

If you're a typical home user, you need three things to surf the Internet:

✔ A modem or other connection to the Internet, such as Digital Subscriber Line (DSL), cable modem, Integrated Services Digital Network (ISDN), or satellite Internet service.

If you use technology other than a regular (analog) modem, DSL, or cable modem to connect your computer to the Internet, your network administrator (the person who you run to at work when something goes wrong with your computer) or ISP will have to help you set up your Mac because setting up those other configurations is beyond the scope of this book.

✔ An account with an ISP (an Internet Service Provider such as EarthLink or RoadRunner) or America Online (AOL).

✔ Mac OS X Tiger default installation.

It starts with the modem

A *modem* is a small, inexpensive device that turns data (that is, computer files) into sounds and then squirts those sounds across phone lines. At the other end, another modem receives these sounds and turns them back into data (that is, your files). All current Macs include an internal 56 Kbps modem.

Now plug a phone line into the modem. On Macs with internal modems, that simply means plugging one end of the phone cable into the phone plug-shaped port on the side or back of your Mac and the other end into a live phone outlet (or the phone jack on a surge suppressor that has a phone line running to your phone outlet). If you have an external modem, plug the phone cable into the modem and plug the modem cable into a USB port. Finally, plug the modem into an AC power source if it requires AC power (some don't because they obtain power from your Mac's USB port).

The modem port on Macs with internal modems looks a lot like the Ethernet port, but it's smaller. You could plug a phone cable into the Ethernet port, but it wouldn't fit right and it wouldn't get you connected to the Internet. The modem port is the smaller of the two — look for the phone icon next to it. Conversely, the Ethernet port is the larger of the two. Look for an icon that looks something like this: <•••>. Check out the differences: Both ports and their icons appear in the margin (the Ethernet port is on the left).

Just in case you visit a store populated by computer geeks, a phone connector is called an RJ-11, and an Ethernet connector is called an RJ-45.

High-speed connections

If you have a cable modem, digital subscriber line (DSL), or other high-speed Internet connection — or are thinking about getting any of these — you can use them with your Mac. In most cases, you merely connect your Mac to the Internet via a cable plugged into the Ethernet port of your Mac and into an external box, which is either connected to a cable or phone outlet, depending on what kind of access you have to the Internet. Your cable or DSL installer-person should set everything up for you. If they don't, you'll have to call that service provider for help — troubleshooting a high-speed connection is pretty abstruse (which puts it "beyond the purview of this book").

Your Internet service provider and you

After you make sure that you have a working modem, you have to select a company to provide you with access to the Internet. These companies are called *Internet service providers* (ISPs). Just like when choosing a long-distance company for your phone, the prices and services that ISPs offer vary, often from minute to minute. After you make your choice, you can launch and use Internet Explorer, Mail, iChat AV, or any other Internet application. Keep the following in mind when choosing an ISP:

 ✔ If you're using a cable modem, your ISP is your cable company. In most cases, the same applies to DSL — except that your provider is either your local phone company or an ISP that you've chosen to get your service connected. In that case, your ISP usually contacts the phone company and arranges for installation and setup for you.

 ✔ If you subscribe to AOL, AOL is your ISP. You don't need to do anything more than install the AOL software and log on to AOL. You can ignore the rest of this chapter except for the parts about surfing the Web, iChat AV, and Apple's .Mac (dot-Mac) offerings, and preferences.

 You don't need Mail (the e-mail program included with OS X) if you get your mail exclusively through AOL, but if you've opted for a .Mac account, you will want to use the Apple Mail application to access it.

In addition to AOL, check out dedicated Internet service companies such as EarthLink and AT&T. Also investigate what your local cable or phone company offers. In other words, it pays to shop around for the deal that works best for you.

The going rate for unlimited access to the Internet, using a modem, is $10–$25 per month. If your service provider asks for considerably more than that, find out why. (***Note:*** If you have a cable modem, DSL, or other high-speed connection, you'll probably pay at least twice that much.)

For those who don't care for Safari

You can use any Internet browser you choose — such as Netscape, Firefox, OmniWeb, iCab, Opera, or Chimera — but these browsers are not installed automatically with OS X (as Safari is); instead, you have to download and install them first. You'll find the latest version of each by visiting `www.versiontracker.com/macosx` and searching for *browser*.

If you don't like Safari, I recommend taking a look at either OmniWeb or Firefox, which are both filled with features you won't find in Safari.

OmniWeb was the first usable third-party browser for Mac OS X and it's gotten better and

better over the years; Firefox is a cross-platform, open source browser from the Mozilla project and has quickly become the hottest new browser on the OS X scene.

Frankly, all the browsers are pretty darned good, and there's no penalty for installing a second, third, or fourth one on your hard disk. So if you're not totally satisfied with the included browser, try some of the others to decide which you like best.

When you installed OS X (assuming you did, and that it didn't come pre-installed on your Mac), the Installer program asked you a bunch of questions about your Internet connection and then set everything up for you. This process is detailed at the end of the book in the Appendix. If you didn't have an Internet connection (an ISP) at that time, you'll need to configure the Network System Preferences pane yourself. Although I cover the Network System Preferences pane in depth in Chapter 13, how to configure it so that your Mac works with your ISP is something you'll have to work out with that ISP. If you have questions or problems not answered by this book, your ISP should be able to assist you.

And if your ISP can't help, it's probably time to try a different ISP.

Browsing the Web with Safari

In this chapter, I concentrate on Safari because it's the Web browser installed with OS X Tiger. (For the first time in years, Microsoft Internet Explorer is not included, which isn't surprising since Microsoft announced they were discontinuing the Mac version of IE.)

Getting up and running with Safari

Before you can browse the Web, the first step is to open your Web browser. No problem. As usual, there's more than one way. You can launch Safari by

✔ Clicking the Safari icon on the Dock (look for the big blue stopwatch)

✔ Double-clicking the Safari icon in your Applications folder

✔ Single-clicking a URL link in an e-mail or other document

✔ Double-clicking a URL link document in the Finder

When you first launch Safari, it automatically connects you to the Internet and displays the default Apple home page (see Figure 9-1).

Figure 9-1:
The Apple
home page.

If a dialog pops up asking whether you'd like to set Safari as your default browser, click Yes. If you later change your mind and would prefer a different browser to be your default, you can change it in the Internet System Preference pane (covered extensively in Chapter 13).

I don't have room in this book to describe everything about Safari, but I hit the highlights from the top of the Safari screen.

"What's this button do?"

The buttons along the top of the window from left to right — Back/Forward, Reload/Stop, and Add Bookmark — do pretty much what their names imply. Play with them a bit, and you'll see what I mean.

Other available buttons include Home, AutoFill, Text Size, Print, and Bug (report a bug to Apple); you add or delete them using Customize Address Bar in Safari's View menu.

Below the Address field are some "bookmark" buttons that take you directly to pages that may interest you, such as the Apple Web site, the Apple .Mac Web site, Amazon.com, eBay, Yahoo, and others.

The News item in this row of buttons is a pop-up (actually a pop-down) menu, as shown in Figure 9-2. Clicking any of these buttons or choosing one of the items in the News (or a different) menu transports you to that page.

Figure 9-2:
The News button is actually a menu.

"Address me as Sir, rodent!"

To the right of the top row of buttons is the Address field. This is where you type Web addresses, or *URLs* (Uniform Resource Locators), that you want to visit. Just type one in and press Return to surf to that site.

Web addresses almost always begin with `http://www`. But Safari has a cool trick: If you just type a name, you usually get to the appropriate Web site that way — without typing `http`, `//`, or `www`. For example, if you type **apple** in the Address field and then press Return, you go to `http://www.apple.com`. Or if you type **doctormacdirect**, you're taken to `www.doctormacdirect.com`. Try it — it's pretty slick.

Bookmarks

Choosing Bookmarks➪Show All Bookmarks, typing the keyboard shortcut
⌘+Option+B, or clicking the Show All Bookmarks button (shown in margin)
brings up the Bookmarks window, as shown in Figure 9-3.

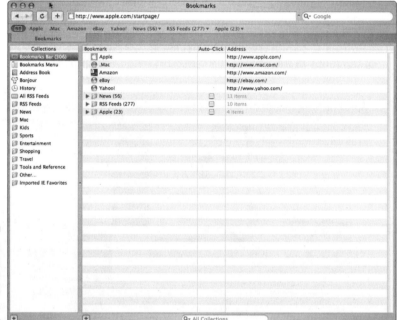

Figure 9-3:
The
Bookmarks
window in
all its glory.

You can view the contents of any Collection (that is, a folder full of bookmarks)
by clicking its name in the Collections pane. (Figure 9-3 shows, in particular,
the contents of the Bookmarks Bar folder.) Here are the basics of navigating
bookmarks:

✔ Open bookmarked pages by double-clicking them.

✔ Use the Bookmarks menu to add bookmarks or folders.

✔ Move bookmarks by dragging them. You can place bookmarks and folders of bookmarks on the Safari Bookmarks Bar or Menu by dragging
them to the appropriate folder. If you drag a folder of bookmarks to the
Bookmarks Bar folder (or directly onto the Bookmarks Bar itself), the
result is a drop-down menu, as shown in Figure 9-2.

✔ To delete a bookmark, select it and then press Delete or Backspace.

Bookmarks are favorites, and favorites are bookmarks. Both words describe the same exact thing — shortcuts to Web sites. In this chapter, I use Bookmark because that's what Safari calls them. Some other browsers call them Favorites.

Your copy of Safari comes pre-loaded with bookmarks that take you to other nifty Mac sites to check out. You'll find links to Apple sites, hardware and software vendors, Mac publications, and more. Take a look at the list of great Web pages that your pals at Apple have put together. Be sure to explore all the included bookmarks when you have some time; most, if not all, are worth knowing more about.

One of the biggest buzzes in Web browsing these days (other than *blogs*, a form of Web-published personal journal) is *RSS*, which stands for Really Simple Syndication (according to most people who know about it). You see synopses of what's available at the site providing the *RSS feed* — which gives you an adjustable-length overview with a link to the full story. When a Web page has an *RSS feed* (that's what the special RSS links are called) associated, you'll see a little RSS icon at the right end of the address bar, just like the one in Figure 9-1. Click it and you'll see all the RSS synopses for the site.

If you like this RSS thing (and why wouldn't you?), Safari includes plenty of interesting feeds to choose from. Click the little book icon (below the Back arrow near the top of the window), and then click All RSS Feeds collection on the left. The list of available RSS feeds will appear on the right; double-click one or more items in the Bookmark list to see its feed.

Searching with Sherlock

Looking for something on the Internet? Check out Sherlock, an application included with Mac OS X that can help you hunt down just about anything on the Internet. You can scour general-purpose Internet search engines with the options under the Internet button or get more specific with one of the nine other Internet buttons.

In this section, you discover how to find Sherlock, how to use it to search the Internet, and how to get help with it when all else fails.

Double-click the Sherlock icon in your Applications folder and the Sherlock window appears, as shown in Figure 9-4.

Figure 9-4:
It's
Sherlock's
Channels
screen.

A quick look at Sherlock's features

Before you use Sherlock, I'd like to point out a few of its more important features.

The top of the Sherlock window sports a series of buttons. From left to right they are Channels, Internet, Pictures, Stocks, Movies, Phone Book, eBay, Flights, Dictionary, Translation, and AppleCare. You click the button that best represents what you're searching for. If you're looking for a Web site, click Internet. If you want to find where and when a movie is playing near you, click Movies. If you want to look up a word's meaning, click Dictionary. And so on.

Although you certainly can use Sherlock's Dictionary (and it is very good), you will probably find Dashboard's Dictionary widget a little more convenient. Check out the Dashboard discussion in Chapter 11. The bottom part of the Sherlock window is *context-sensitive;* it changes in response to the particular button you've clicked in the button bar (before a search). Then it displays the results of your search (after you search, of course).

Searching with Sherlock

You use Sherlock to find things on the Internet. In this section, I first show you how to search with Sherlock.

Although I use an Internet search in the steps, you can follow the same steps to search in any of the other channels. After you know how to search the Internet with Sherlock, you know how to search any Internet channel with Sherlock. To use Sherlock, follow these steps:

1. **Start Sherlock by double-clicking the Sherlock icon in your Applications folder.**

2. **Click one of the 10 Internet buttons to choose a channel.**

   Figure 9-5 shows the Internet channel.

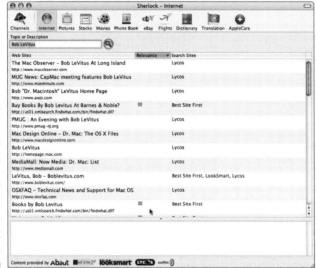

Figure 9-5:
Searching
for myself
by using
Sherlock's
Internet
search.

Yes, I know there are actually 9 icons, but the leftmost icon just describes what the 10 real search icons do, as you can see in Figure 9-4. Those appear to the right of the little dividing line, and are actual buttons that you click to initiate Internet searches.

3. **In the text entry field beneath the Sherlock search buttons (labeled Topic or Description), type a word or a phrase that you want to search for.**

4. **To begin your search, press Return or click the magnifying-glass button to the right of the text-entry field.**

   Sherlock passes your request along to the Web search engines and then displays a list of search results, similar to Figure 9-5.

5. **Click any search site listed along the bottom of Sherlock's window (About, Ask Jeeves, Best Site 1st, and so on) to launch your Web browser and access the search engine directly.**

To start a new search, repeat Steps 2 through 5.

Some channels are slightly different in the way they look and work — for example, the Movies channel (shown in Figure 9-6) doesn't let you search for movies by name. Instead, it asks for your city and state or ZIP code and then displays the movies in a three-column browser. By default, it bases the search on the address you put in your "this is me" card in Address Book, but you can specify a different person or address.

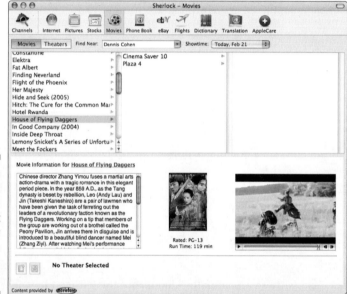

Figure 9-6:
The Movies channel works a bit differently than some of the others.

The Movies channel offers some nifty extras not found in other channels, including the movie poster and a QuickTime preview (lower-right pane of Figure 9-6), plus Add to the Address Book and Map to This Theater buttons (lower-left in the bottom pane of Figure 9-6). If you click the Map to This Theater button, you get not only a map, but also driving directions from the address you gave Movies in the beginning. Slick!

If you like using Sherlock, its Dock icon offers direct access to all of its channels, as shown in Figure 9-7.

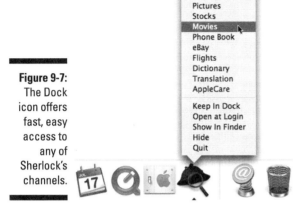

Figure 9-7:
The Dock
icon offers
fast, easy
access to
any of
Sherlock's
channels.

Checking out Help Center

I need to use another weasel-out here. I could write an entire chapter about
using Sherlock, but one of the rules we *For Dummies* authors must follow is
that our books can't run 1,000 pages long. So I'm going to give you the next
best thing: Open the Help Center (by choosing Help⇨Sherlock Help from the
Sherlock menu bar). A special Sherlock Help window appears; you can search
for any topic here.

Getting Your E-Mail with Mail

Mail is a program that comes with Mac OS X that you use to send, receive,
and organize your e-mail. You can also use Mail to access an address book
that includes the addresses of your friends and family.

You can use other applications to read Internet mail. Mozilla (Thunderbird)
and AOL, for example, have their own mail readers, as does Microsoft Office
(Entourage). And lots of power users like the BBEdit-like editing features in
MailSmith (BareBones Software). But for Macs, the easiest and best mail reader
around (meaning, the best one on your hard drive by default) is probably
Mail. And you can't beat the price — it's free!

 Mail is fast and easy to use, too. Click the Mail icon on the Dock or double-
click the Mail icon in the Applications folder to launch Mail. The Mail icon
looks like a cancelled postage stamp, as shown in the margin.

If this is your first time launching Mail, you'll see a Welcome message asking if you'd like to see what's new. If you click Yes, Help Viewer launches and shows you the What's New in Mail page.

Mail's main window looks like Figure 9-8.

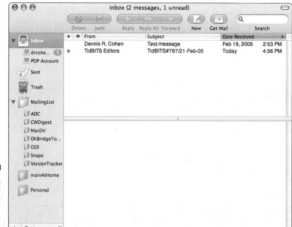

Figure 9-8: Mail's main window.

Composing a new message

Here's how to create a new e-mail message:

1. **Choose File⇨New Message or press ⌘+N.**

   A new window appears; this is where you compose your e-mail message, as shown in Figure 9-9.

2. **Place your cursor in the To field and type someone's e-mail address.**

   Use my address (boblevitus@boblevitus.com) if you don't know anyone else to send mail to.

   After you finish addressing a mail message, you can add the recipient to your address book. After you add an address to your address book, all you have to do is type the first few letters of the recipient's name, and Mail fills in the entire address for you. Neat, huh? (Choose Help⇨Mail Help to find out more about this feature.) You can even have Mail add the names and addresses of people who sent you mail by choosing Message⇨Add Sender to Address Book (press ⌘+Y) when you're reading the mail from them.

3. **Press the Tab key twice to move your cursor to the Subject text field and then type a subject for this message.**

Figure 9-9:
Composing
an e-mail
message.

4. **Click in the main message portion of the window (refer to Figure 9-8) and type your message there.**

5. **When you're finished writing your message, click the Send button to send the e-mail immediately or choose File⇨Save As Draft to save it in the Drafts folder so you can work on it later.**

If you do save your message to the Drafts folder (so you can write more later, perhaps), you can send it when you're ready by opening the Drafts folder, double-clicking the message, and then clicking the Send button.

Checking your mail

How do you check and open your mail? Easy. Just click the Get Mail button at the top of the main Mail window (refer to Figure 9-8).

You can configure Mail to send and receive your mail every x minutes by choosing Mail⇨Preferences and then clicking the General icon at the top of the window. Pull down the Check for New Mail pop-up menu and make a selection — every 1, 5, 15, 30, or 60 minutes — or choose Manually if you don't want Mail to check for mail automatically at all. (The default setting is to check for mail every five minutes.)

Dealing with spam

E-mail is a wonderful thing, but some people out there try to spoil it. If you think you get a lot of junk mail in your regular mailbox, just wait until some purveyor of electronic junk mail gets hold of your e-mail address. These lowlifes share their lists — and before you know it, your e-mail box is flooded with get-rich-quick schemes, advertisements for pornographic Web sites and chat rooms, and all the more traditional buy-me junk mail.

Mail comes with a Junk Mail filter that analyzes incoming message subjects, senders, and contents to determine which ones are likely to contain bulk or junk mail. When you open Mail for the first time, it's running in its training mode, which is how Mail learns to differentiate between what it considers junk mail and what you consider junk mail; all it needs is your input. Mail will identify messages it thinks are junk; click the Not Junk button in the brown bar for any message that *isn't* junk mail. Conversely, if a piece of junk mail slips past Mail's filters and ends up in the Inbox, select the message and then click the Junk button in the Mail window's toolbar.

After a few days (or weeks, depending upon your mail volume), Mail should be getting it right almost all the time. When you reach that point, choose Automatic mode in the Junk Mail tab of Mail's Preference pane and Mail will start moving junk mail automatically out of your Inbox and into a Junk folder, where you can scan the items quickly and trash them when you're ready.

If (for some reason that escapes me) you prefer to receive and manually process your junk mail, you can turn off Junk Mail processing by disabling it in the Junk Mail tab of Mail's Preference pane.

Changing your preferences

Actually, Mail's Preferences are more than you may expect from the name. This is the control center for Mail — where you

- ✔ Create and delete e-mail accounts
- ✔ Determine which fonts and colors are used for your messages
- ✔ Decide whether to download and save attachments (such as pictures)
- ✔ Decide whether you send formatted mail or plain text
- ✔ Decide whether to turn on the spell checker
- ✔ Decide whether to have an automatic signature appended to your messages
- ✔ Establish rules to process mail that you receive

If you really want to tap the power of Mail, learn to set *Rules.* With some cool rules, you can automatically tag messages with a color, file them in a specific mailbox, reply to/forward/redirect the messages automatically (handy when you're going to be away for a while), automatically reply to messages, or *kill-file* them (just delete them without even bothering to look at them — what better fate for mail from people you hate?).

But wait — there's more!

As I've said before, I can offer you some starting points here, but space limitations put a bunch of these features beyond the scope of this book. Even so, you should find everything perfectly straightforward, possibly with the assistance of Help⇨Mail Help.

I recommend you read the What's New in Mail entries to learn more about cool new Tiger features like Smart Mailboxes, Photo Slideshows, improved searching options, Parental Controls, .Mac synchronization, a connection doctor, account-specific signatures, and more.

And don't forget Address Book

Another freebie from Apple is Address Book, which Mail and many other applications use as a repository for names, addresses, phone numbers, e-mail addresses, and other information about people. Address Book is where you should store information about your contacts — relatives, friends, or the odd enemy that you keep in touch with for self-punishment purposes.

So while it's not technically part of Mail and isn't essential to using the Internet, it is an essential companion to Mail, so I'll pause here for a quick look at the multi-talented Address Book.

Follow these steps to create a new entry in the Address Book:

1. **Launch the Address Book application by double-clicking its icon in the Applications folder or clicking its Dock icon.**

   The Address Book appears. The first time that you open Address Book, you see two cards: Apple Computer and the one with the personal identification information you supplied when you created your account.

2. **To create a new entry, click the Plus button at the bottom of the Address Book's Name column.**

   An untitled address card appears. The First name text field is initially selected. (You can tell by the border it now has, as shown in Figure 9-10.)

3. **Type the person's first name in the First text field.**

   Here I type **Doctor**.

4. **Press Tab.**

   Your cursor should now be in the Last text field.

   You can always move from one field to the next by pressing Tab — in fact, this shortcut works in almost all Mac programs that have fields like these. (You can move to the previous field by pressing Shift+Tab.)

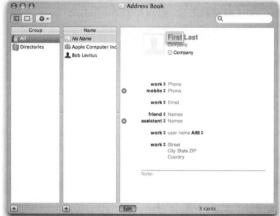

Figure 9-10:
A new
address
card in
Address
Book.

5. **Type the last name for the person you're adding to your Address Book.**

   Here I type **Mac**. Continue this process, filling in the rest of the fields
   shown in Figure 9-11.

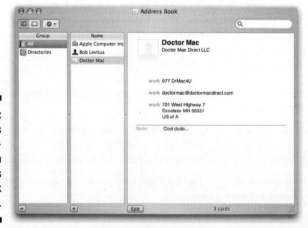

Figure 9-11:
The address
card dis-
played in
the Address
Book
window.

6. **When you're done entering information, click the Edit button to exit
   the editing mode.**

   The contact I created with this step appears in Figure 9-11.

   The little contact card is called a *vCard* (virtual business card).

   To add more info about any Address Book entry, select the name in the
   Name column (<No Name> in Figure 9-10; you can tell when a name is
   selected because it has a gray field behind it), click the Edit button at
   the bottom of the Address Book window, and then make your changes.

You can do scads of pretty neat stuff with Address Book that (you can all say it along with me this time) I just don't have room to cover in this book. Just for starters, you can organize your contacts into groups so you can e-mail everyone in a group (that you define) with one click. And you can create a blank e-mail message to a contact by clicking and holding the label next to the e-mail address and choosing Send Email from the pop-up menu that appears, as shown in Figure 9-12.

Last but not least, when someone sends you an e-mail message, you can add that person's address to your Address Book by choosing Message⇨Add Sender to Address Book (shortcut: ⌘+Y).

Figure 9-12:
Sending
e-mail to
someone
in your
Address
Book is as
easy as
clicking
here.

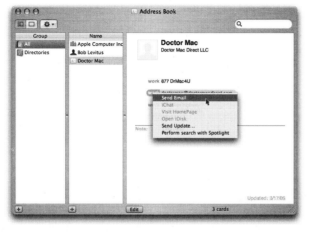

Adding a sender to your Address Book has an additional benefit — it guards messages from that person against being mistaken for junk mail. In other words, your Address Book is a *White List* for the spam filter; if specific senders appear in your Address Book, their messages will never be mistakenly marked as junk mail.

A Quick Overview of .Mac

.Mac (pronounced *dot-Mac*) is a set of optional, Internet-based services that integrate nicely with Mac OS X and cost around $100 a year. Although .Mac isn't specifically a Mac OS X feature, it is an Internet-based service that I happen to think is worth paying for (and I do pay for it). So I'd be remiss if I didn't at least tell you a little bit about it.

At the time of this writing, .Mac offers seven services:

- **Mac.com and Webmail:** An e-mail service that lets you have an e-mail address in the form of `yourname@mac.com`. For OS X users, Apple has added IMAP support and an SMTP server (is that enough geek-speak for you?). In plain English, that means you can now maintain your messages on the Apple mail servers. You can also access your Mac.com e-mail from any computer with an Internet connection and a Web browser (that's the *Webmail* part.)

- **iDisk:** Your own personal 250MB Internet-based virtual disk. You can divide your 250MB proportionally between your e-mail and virtual-disk file storage; initially, each gets a 125MB allocation.

- **HomePage:** The easiest way I know of to build your own home page. You can also use iPhoto to build really nice photo gallery pages with thumbnail images and everything if you're a .Mac subscriber.

- **Backup:** A utility to back up folders on your hard disk to either your iDisk or a CD-R or DVD-R disk.

- **iCards:** Electronic greeting cards that you can e-mail to your friends.

- **Anti-Virus:** A copy of the Virex virus-scanning and protection utility, including regular updates.

- **Support:** A consolidated link to a variety of support services, such as Network Status, online discussion boards concerning Apple hardware and software products, the AppleCare Knowledge Base, and Apple's customer Feedback page.

The first two services — Mac.com and iDisk — are beautifully integrated with OS X. For example, the aforementioned Mail program is set up to work perfectly with a Mac.com e-mail account. All you have to do is supply your username and password. And iDisk is a choice in the Finder's Go menu, although you can't use it until you visit the Apple Web site and create your own Mac.com account ($100/year).

You can even create a local copy of your iDisk on your hard drive and have it automatically synchronize with the remote iDisk via the Internet. (See the .Mac System Preference pane for details.)

Here's another nice touch: Apple provides a folder full of useful freeware, shareware, and demonstration versions of software on every iDisk — and it doesn't count against your 250MB, either. You may download and try out the programs at your leisure at no extra cost.

Finally, as the icing on the goodies already mentioned, you also get discounts and free copies of different programs and games throughout the year. Some deals are better than others; a few have been particularly sweet.

I could go on and on, but I won't. Just surf to `http://www.Mac.com` if you want to know more (or to check on the special deals available today).

Communicating via iChat AV

Instant messaging and chat rooms provide for interactive communication between users all over the world. If you're into instant messaging, iChat AV gives you immediate access to all the other users of AOL Instant Messaging (AIM), Jabber, and .Mac. All you need is their screen name and you're set to go. You can even join any AOL chat room just by choosing Go To Chat from the File menu.

OS X's built-in Bonjour (Apple used to call it Rendezvous) support makes it even better. With Bonjour, which offers configuration-free connections, you don't have to do anything to be part of a Bonjour network because your Mac configures itself and joins up automatically. For example, with Bonjour enabled, I've sent and received messages from/to my AirPort-equipped PowerBook from/to my desktop computer without any network configuration. Just choose Bonjour from the Window menu and select the person with whom you want to chat from the Bonjour window.

Your text chats can be one-to-one or they can be group bull sessions. Each participant's picture (or icon) appears next to anything he says, which is displayed in a cartoon-like thought bubble, as shown in Figure 9-13.

If you've attached a picture to a person in your Address Book, you'll even see that picture when you iChat with that person. Neat! If you find the thought bubbles a little too childish, you can turn them off from the View menu.

Figure 9-13:
A chat with myself. (I have two Macs on the same network.)

iChat AV even lets you transfer files, giving you a very convenient way to share photos or documents without resorting to file sharing or e-mail. Just drag the document's icon to the message box, as demonstrated in Figure 9-14, press Enter or Return, and the file will zip across the ether.

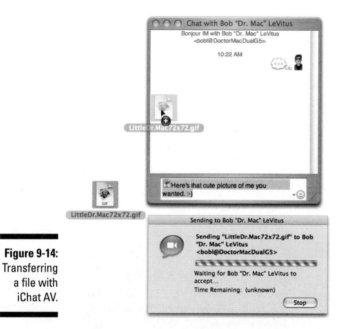

Figure 9-14:
Transferring
a file with
iChat AV.

iChat AV is integrated with the Address Book, so you don't have to enter your Buddies' information twice. It also communicates directly with the Mail application. Just select a Buddy in iChat AV's Buddy List, and then choose Send Email from the Buddies menu (or use the keyboard shortcut ⌘+Option+E), and Mail will launch (if it's not already open), and address a new message to the selected buddy, ready for you to begin typing.

Gimme an A! Gimme a V!

The greatest iChat feature is audio/video chatting, which is what the *AV* in its name stands for. To conduct a video or audio chat, connect a FireWire camera and/or a supported microphone to your Mac. That's it — you're all set to chat using video and/or audio.

And, the latest enhancement to iChat's AV capabilities is that you can now conference a video chat with up to three other people at once and audio chat with up to nine other folks at the same time.

Although many FireWire camcorders work fairly well for video chatting, Apple's $149 iSight camera/microphone combination is designed just for this purpose (and works even better in most cases).

When you've got appropriate hardware connected to your Mac, your buddies' names in the Buddy lists will display little green telephone or camera icons if they've got the right hardware on their end. To start an audio- or video-conference, click the appropriate green icon(s). Your buddies will receive an invitation to begin an audio or video chat. If they accept the invitation, a Video Chat window appears, as shown in Figure 9-15.

Figure 9-15: I'm iChatting with my buddy Dave Hamilton.

iChat's audio and video features are easy to set up and use.

If you've got a FireWire camcorder handy, give it a try. My chat handle is **levi-tus**; feel free to invite me to video chat if you see me online.

Chapter 10

Publish or Perish: The Fail-Safe Guide to Printing

In This Chapter

▶ Connecting a printer

▶ Using Page Setup to prepare your document for printing

▶ Printing to most printers

▶ Mastering the printing process

*P*rinting is the process of getting what's on your screen onto paper. I know you probably know that, but my editor insisted I start this chapter by defining printing. And so I have.

Printing under OS X should be as simple as pressing the keyboard shortcut ⌘+P and then pressing the Return or Enter key. Happily, that's usually just how easy printing something is; when it isn't, printing can turn into a raging nightmare. If you configure your printer and printing software properly, however, printing is as easy as can be. And that's pretty darn simple. In this chapter, I scare away the bogeymen to help you avoid any printing nightmares. I walk you through the entire process as if you just unpacked a new printer and plugged it in.

If you're upgrading from a 9.*x* version of Mac OS, you probably want to work through these steps because things have changed in OS X.

Before Diving In . . .

Before I even start talking about hooking up printers, you should know a few essential things. So here's a little list that tells you just what those things are:

> ✔ **Read the documentation that came with your specific printer.**
> Hundreds of different printer makes and models are available for the Mac, so if I contradict something in your printer manual, follow your manual's instructions first. If that effort doesn't work, try it my way — use the techniques that you'll be reading about in the rest of this chapter.

✔ **The Print and Page Setup sheets differ slightly (or even greatly) from program to program and from printer to printer.** Although the examples I show you in this chapter are representative of what you will probably encounter, you may come across sheets that look a bit different. For example, the Print and Page Setup sheets for Microsoft Word include choices I don't cover in this chapter (such as Even or Odd Pages Only, Print Hidden Text, and Print Selection Only). If you see commands in your Print or Page Setup sheet that I don't explain in this chapter, they're specific to that application; look within its documentation for explanation. Similarly, Adobe Illustrator CS has added numerous gadgets, list boxes, radio buttons, and so forth to the Print dialog to the point where you might not even recognize it as a Print dialog.

✔ **I use Apple's bare-bones word processor, TextEdit, for the examples in this chapter.** If you want to follow along, you'll find TextEdit in your Applications folder.

✔ **Don't forget about Mac OS Help.** Many programs support this excellent Apple technology, which can be the fastest way to figure out a feature that has you stumped. So don't forget to check the Help menu before you panic. (I cover the Help menu way back in Chapter 3.)

So, with those things in mind, get ready, set, print!

Ready: Connecting and Adding Your Printer

Before you can even think about printing something, you have to connect a printer to your Mac and then tell OS X that the printer exists. Here's how.

Connecting your printer

Once again, I must remind you that there are thousands of printer models that you could connect to your Mac. And each one is a little different from the next. In other words, if what you're about to read doesn't track with the printer you're trying to connect, I again implore you to RTFM (that's *Read The Fine Manual*, in case you're wondering). It should tell you how to load your ink or toner cartridges.

Remove all the packing material and little strips of tape, some of which you won't even see if you don't know where to look.

That said, here are some very general steps to connect a printer:

1. **Connect the printer to your Mac with the cable snugly attached at both ends (printer and Mac).**

   For your printer to work, you have to somehow connect it to a data source. (Think of your phone — you can't receive calls without some sort of connector between the caller and the callee.)

2. **Plug the printer's AC power cord into a power outlet (yup, the regular kind in the wall, on a power strip, or best of all, on a UPS [Uninterruptible Power Supply]).**

   Some printers require you to plug one end of the AC power cord into the printer; others have the AC power cord attached permanently. The point is that your printer won't work if it's not connected to a power source.

3. **Turn on your printer (check out your manual if you can't find the switch).**

4. **If your printer came with software, install it on your hard drive, following the instructions that came with the printer.**

5. **(Optional) Restart your Mac.**

   You need to do this only if you had to install software and the Installer told you to restart.

   That's it!

Any port on a Mac

Before you can print, you need to plug the printer cable into the appropriate port on the back of your Mac, or (in the case of USB or networked printers) into a USB or Ethernet hub. Therein lies the rub. Mac technology has changed dramatically since the previous editions of this book, when I used to say, "Begin by connecting the printer to the Printer port on the back of your Mac (with both the Mac and the printer turned off, of course — but you knew that, didn't you?)." Ah, nostalgia. Now I tell you, "You need to plug the printer cable into the appropriate port. . . ." Why am I being so vague? Because I have to be. You see, these days, printers don't always connect to the same port. Some printers connect to the Ethernet port or to an Ethernet hub (which is, in turn, connected to the back of your Mac). Others connect through the Universal Serial Bus (USB) port. I've even seen a few that connect via the FireWire port. So read the instructions that came with your printer — and plug your printer into the appropriate hole (port) for your Mac.

Typically, your printer connects to your machine via a USB, Ethernet, or FireWire cable. Don't confuse this item with your printer's AC power cord (the kind you find on everyday appliances). If your printer didn't come with a cable that fits into one of the ports on your Mac, contact your printer manufacturer and ask for one; it's cheesy not to provide the proper cable with a printer. Unfortunately, some manufacturers make printers with different kinds of connectors on the back (to sell to those poor souls stuck using Windows) and expect you to buy your own cable. Asking one of these manufacturers for a cable will be an exercise in futility.

Checking for AppleTalk if you don't see your printer

If you have an AppleTalk printer but don't see it on the list when you click the AppleTalk option from the pop-up menu (look for the pop-up reading AppleTalk in Figure 10-2), check in System Preferences to see whether AppleTalk is active. I cover System Preferences in more detail in Chapter 13, but here's a quick rundown on how you check this:

1. **Choose System Preferences from the Apple menu or by clicking its icon in the Dock.**

   The System Preferences window opens.

2. **Open the Network Preferences pane by clicking the Network icon in the System Preferences window.**

   The System Preferences window turns into the Network pane.

3. **Select Built-in Ethernet from the Show pop-up menu.**

4. **Click the AppleTalk button of the Network pane and check to see whether the** Make AppleTalk Active check box is selected.

5. **If the AppleTalk Active check box is not marked, check (select) it.**

   You may have to click the padlock icon at the bottom-left of the window and enter an Administrator password to make this selection.

6. **After you make AppleTalk active, quit System Preferences and go back to the Printer Setup Utility application (click its icon on the Dock; or, if you quit or restarted, launch it — it's in the Utilities folder inside your Applications folder) and add your AppleTalk printer.**

   For the full story, see the section "Setting up a printer for the first time," where I detail adding your AppleTalk printer.

7. **When you've added and configured a printer, you can quit Print Center.**

Setting up a printer for the first time

After you connect your computer and printer with a compatible cable, provide a power source for your printer, and install the software for your printer, you're ready . . . to configure your Mac. (No rest for the weary. You have to do that so your Mac and your printer can talk to each other.)

The Printer Setup Utility application (which I am about to discuss) is the tool you use to tell your Mac what printers are available.

Many of the steps involving Printer Setup Utility require that your printer be turned on and warmed up (that is, already run through its diagnostics and startup cycle) beforehand.

Follow these steps to set up a printer for the first time:

1. **Launch Printer Setup Utility.**

   You'll find Printer Setup Utility in the Utilities folder, which is inside your Applications folder. Click the Applications button in the Sidebar of any Finder window to open the Applications folder. Now open the Utilities folder and double-click Printer Setup Utility. (Or, if you're taking my advice about learning keyboard shortcuts, press Shift+⌘+U to go directly to the Utilities folder.)

   Now, Tiger's a pretty smart cat — often it will have already recognized your new printer. If you see your printer listed in the Printer List window (shown in Figure 10-1), you're golden and can skip straight to the material following Step 3.

Figure 10-1: Printers that Printer Setup already knows about show up here.

If you have never set up a printer on this Mac, Step 2 may be superfluous — you'll see an alert that says, *You have no printers available,* and asks, *Would you like to add to your list of printers now?* If you click the Add button at the bottom of this alert, the Printer Browser window and sheet shown in Figure 10-2 appear.

2. **Choose Add Printer from the Printers menu or click the Add button in the Printer List window's toolbar.**

   The Printer Browser window appears. You have two choices:

   • If you see your printer's name and model number in the Printer Browser list, go on to Step 3.

   • If you don't see your printer in the list, first click the Add button (the one with a printer and a little plus sign) and then click the More Printers button: The sheet shown in Figure 10-2 appears.

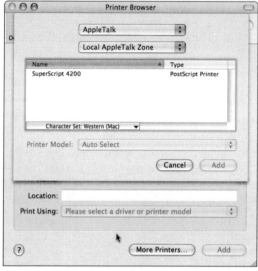

Figure 10-2:
Available
printers,
listed
with their
specified
connection
types,
appear here.

3. **In the sheet that appears in front of the Printer Browser window, click the top pop-up menu to select your printer's connection type.**

   • Most printers connect in one of two ways: directly to your Mac (via a USB port) or over a network, using AppleTalk.

   • Many USB printers (such as most of the compatible printers from Epson, Canon, Lexmark, and Hewlett-Packard) are recognized immediately without your having to perform this step.

   • For my example, I choose AppleTalk because the printer I work with here is an NEC SuperScript 4200N PostScript model, connected to the Mac via an Ethernet network.

If your printer isn't recognized at this point, you may have to install its driver software first, either from the CD that came with the printer or by downloading the latest driver software from your printer manufacturer's Web site.

AppleTalk and USB are by far the most common kinds of printer connections for Macs. Another option available in the Printer Browser window is IP Printing. If your printer is on a Transmission Control Protocol/Internet Protocol (TCP/IP) network, you may need to configure the printer by using its network address. IP printers usually connect via Ethernet and are almost always found on large corporate networks. Fortunately, your network administrator should be able to help you set up an IP printer; administrators almost always troubleshoot and maintain such large networks.

If you encounter trouble setting up a printer for Mac OS X, you may want to contact your printer's manufacturer about getting the latest, greatest driver. Many printer manufacturers are offering new drivers with enhanced functionality. You can usually find new drivers for your printer on the Web or a major Internet service provider, such as America Online. Apple often includes such new drivers in the Software folder on your iDisk. And the Mac OS X 10.4 Installer disk may have additional printer drivers as well. Check with your printer manufacturer for details.

After you choose your printer connection type, you see the names and kinds of available printers in the Printer Browser sheet's list. In Figure 10-2, my PostScript printer's name, SuperScript 4200, appears.

4. **Click the name of the desired printer on the list, and then click the Add button.**

The sheet closes. A new sheet appears in front of the Printer Browser window, telling you that your new printer is being configured. When that sheet closes, close the Printer Browser: The Printer List window reappears, showing the printer that you just added. (If you've added printers before, they appear here, too.)

Now you can print your first document! Before you do, though, make sure you have the document set up to look just the way you want it to print. Read through the appropriate section ("Set: Setting Up Your Document with Page Setup") later in this chapter for more info.

Set: Setting Up Your Document with Page Setup

After you set up your printer, the hard part is over. You should be able to print a document quickly and easily — right? Not so fast, bucko. Read here how the features in the Page Setup sheet can help you to solve most basic printing problems.

Become familiar with Page Setup — you may not need to use it right this second, but it's a good friend to know.

Almost every program that can print a document has a Page Setup command on its File menu. Note that some programs use the name *Page Setup*, and others use *Print Setup*. (Print Setup is the quaint, old-fashioned term, more popular in the System 6 era and in Windows than on today's Macs.) Either way, this is the sheet where you can choose your printer, paper size, page orientation, and scaling percentage (as shown in Figure 10-3).

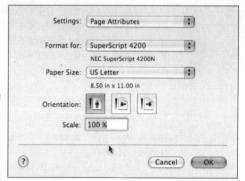

Figure 10-3:
The Page
Setup sheet
in TextEdit.

Users of network printers or PostScript printers may see slightly different versions of the Print and Page Setup sheet. The differences should be minor enough not to matter.

Click the little question mark in the lower-left corner at any time for additional help with the Page Setup sheet. If you do, Page Setup help opens immediately in the Help Viewer. (Okay, maybe not *immediately*, but Help Viewer in Tiger is much faster than previous incarnations. . . .)

The options within the Page Setup sheet are as follows:

✔ **Settings:** When the default Page Attributes show up in this pop-up menu, you see what configuration options are available.

✔ **Save As Default:** When you have everything configured the way you want it to be for most documents, choose this option to save the configuration as your Page Setup defaults.

✔ **Format for:** In this pop-up menu, you find the name of the active printer. If you have several printers configured, you can choose any of them from this list. As you can see in Figure 10-3, the NEC SuperScript 4200 printer that I set up earlier in this chapter (see the "Ready: Connecting and Adding Your Printer" section) is on the menu.

✔ **Paper Size:** Use options in this pop-up menu to choose the type of paper currently in the paper tray of your printer or to choose the size of the paper that you want to feed manually. The dimensions of the paper that you can choose appear below its name.

Page Setup sheet settings (including Paper Size) remain in effect until you change them. For example, when you print an envelope, don't forget to change back to Letter before trying to print on letter-sized paper.

- ✔ **Orientation:** Choose from options here to tell your printer whether the page you want to print should be *portrait-oriented* (like a letter, longer than it is wide) or *landscape-oriented* (sideways, wider than it is long). Click the icons of the little person for the following (from left to right): Portrait, Landscape facing left, and Landscape facing right. You can see them in Figure 10-3 to the right of the Orientation heading.

- ✔ **Scale:** Use the Scale control percentages to enlarge or reduce your image for printing. Just type a new value into the Scale text-entry box, replacing the default number 100 (shown in Figure 10-3).

Some programs also offer additional Page Setup choices. If your program offers them, they usually appear in the Settings pop-up menu in the Page Setup sheet. (Adobe Photoshop and Microsoft Word have them; TextEdit doesn't.)

Go: Printing with the Print Sheet

After you connect and configure your printer and then set up how you want your document to print, you come to the final steps before that joyous moment when your printed page pops out of the printer. Navigating the Print sheet is the last thing standing between you and your output.

Although most Print sheets that you see look like the figures I show in this chapter, others may differ slightly. The features in the Print sheet are strictly a function of the program with which you're printing. Many programs choose to use the standard-issue Apple sheet as shown in this chapter, but not all do. If I don't explain a certain feature in this chapter, chances are good that the feature is specific to the application or printer you're using (in which case, the documentation for that program or printer should offer an explanation).

Printing a document

If everything has gone well so far, the actual act of printing a document is pretty simple. Just follow the steps here and in a few minutes, pages should start popping out of your printer like magic. (In the sections that follow, I talk about some print options that you'll probably need someday.)

1. **Open a document that you want to print.**

2. **Choose File⇨Print (or use the keyboard shortcut ⌘+P).**

   You see the basic Print sheet, as shown in Figure 10-4.

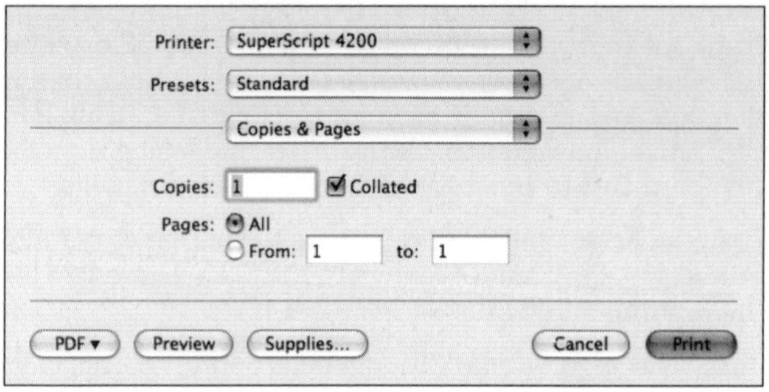

Printer:	SuperScript 4200
Presets:	Standard
	Copies & Pages
Copies:	1 ☑ Collated
Pages:	⦿ All
	○ From: 1 to: 1

(PDF ▾) (Preview) (Supplies...)   (Cancel) (**Print**)

Figure 10-4:
Your basic
Print sheet.

3. **Change any settings that you like in the Print sheet and then click Print.**

Wait a few minutes for the network to tell the printer what to do, and then walk over to your printer to get your document.

RANT & RAVE

Dictating perfection . . . sort of

The Print command appears in the File menu in the vast majority of the Mac programs you'll see and use. Every so often you may come across a program that doesn't follow these conventions, but I would say at least 98+ percent of commercial Mac programs put the Print command in the File menu and use ⌘+P for its keyboard shortcut.

One of the best things about the Mac is that Apple has published a set of guidelines that *all* Mac programs should use. Consistency among programs is one of the Mac's finest features. Notice how 98+ percent of all programs house the Open, Close, Save, Save As, Page Setup, and Print commands in their File menus and the Undo, Cut, Copy, and Paste commands in their Edit menus. That's the kind of convenience and consistency that the Macintosh Human Interface Guidelines recommend.

Macintosh Human Interface Guidelines also recommend that the keyboard shortcut ⌘+P should be reserved for the command "plain text" unless it is used for Print, in which case ⌘+T should be used for Plain Text (which works much like the

keyboard shortcuts ⌘+B and ⌘+I, used to format bold and italic text, respectively). Bottom line: ⌘+P is almost always the shortcut for the Print command in the File menu.

My point: Choosing File➪Print (⌘+P) *won't* work for you if any one of the following is true for the software you're using:

✔ The Print command is on a different menu.

✔ There *is* no Print command. (Hey, it could happen.)

✔ The Print keyboard shortcut is anything but ⌘+P.

If any of the above is true for a program you're using, you just have to wing it. Look in all the menus and check out the product's documentation to try to get a handle on the Print command for that pesky program. You can also write the software company a brief note mentioning that it could make things easier on everyone by putting the Print command in the proper place and using the generally agreed-upon keyboard shortcut.

Choosing from among different printers

Just as you can in the Page Setup sheet, you can choose which printer you want to use from the Printer pop-up menu of the Print sheet.

You can choose only from the printers that you have added via the Printer Setup Utility, as I describe in the section earlier in this chapter (the one I lovingly refer to as "Setting up a printer for the first time").

Choosing custom settings

If you've created a custom group of settings previously, you can choose from them in the Presets pop-up menu of the Print sheet. I touch more on this feature in the "Save Custom Settings" section later in this chapter.

The Print sheet also features another pop-up menu initially displaying Copies & Pages (refer to Figure 10-4) — that offers additional options.

I go through these options and their sub-options, one at a time, in the following sections.

Copies & Pages

When you select Copies & Pages in the pop-up menu, you can choose how many copies to print and the page range that you want to print.

Click in any of the fields in this sheet and then press the Tab key. Your cursor jumps to the next text field in the sheet; likewise, pressing Shift+Tab and the cursor jumps to the previous field. This shortcut works in almost any program, window, dialog, or Web page that has fields for typing information.

- ✓ **Copies:** In this text field, set how many copies you want to print. The Print sheet defaults to one copy (1) in most applications, so you'll probably see the numeral 1 in the Copies field when the Print sheet appears. Assuming that's the case, don't do anything if you want to print only one copy. If you want to print more than one copy of your document, highlight the 1 that appears in the Copies field and replace it by typing in the number of copies you want.

- ✓ **Pages:** Here you find two radio buttons: All or From. If you want to print your entire document, select the All option. If you want to print only a specific page or range of pages, mark the From radio button and then type the desired page numbers in the From and To text-entry boxes.

For example, suppose you print a 10-page document — and then notice a typo on page 2. After you correct your error, you don't have to reprint the whole document — only the page with the correction. Reprint only page 2 by typing a **2** in both the From and To fields. You can type any valid range of pages (um, you can't print out page 20 if your document is only 15 pages long) in the From and To fields.

Layout

Choose Layout from the pop-up menu to set the number of pages per printed sheet, the layout direction, and whether you prefer a border. (See Figure 10-5.)

- ✔ **Pages per Sheet:** Choose from preset numbers here in this pop-up menu to set the number of pages that you want to print on each sheet.

  Pages appear on-screen smaller than full size if you use this option.

- ✔ **Layout Direction:** Choose from one of four buttons that govern the way the small pages are laid out on the printed page.

  Click any of these buttons, and the *proxy* (the rectangle on the left displaying the numbers 1–16 in sequential order in Figure 10-5) also changes to show you the effect of your choice.

- ✔ **Border:** Your choices from this pop-up menu are none, single hairline, single thin line, double hairline, and double thin line.

- ✔ **Two-Sided:** If your printer supports two-sided (known as *duplex*) printing, the three radio buttons will allow you to specify whether you're going to use two-sided printing and, if so, whether you'll be binding (or stapling) along the long or short edge of the paper.

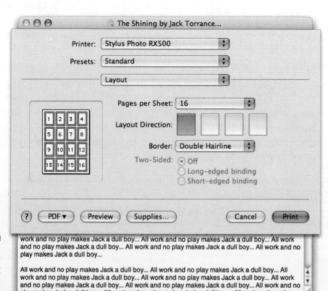

Figure 10-5:
The Layout
sheet.

Scheduler

The Scheduler lets you set a later time for printing (say, while you're asleep, at lunch, or in a meeting). The Scheduler is shown in Figure 10-6.

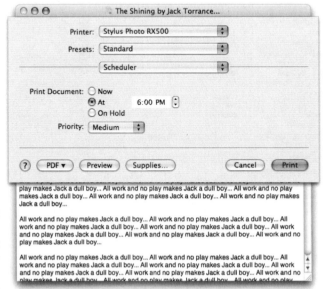

Figure 10-6: The Print Scheduler sheet.

Printer Features

The options on this sheet vary from printer to printer, but typically include such settings as print resolution, media type, and whether you're printing in color, grayscale, or black and white. Some printers may not offer this sheet.

Summary

When you select Summary in the pop-up menu, you can see the printing details for your document, as shown in Figure 10-7. Look here for one final check to verify your print-job settings — how many copies you want, whether you want them collated, the page range of your print job, your layout choice(s), whether to save a file as a PDF, plus any settings specific to your particular printer or the application you're printing from.

Paper Handling

Use this pane to reverse the order your pages print, or, if you want to print only the odd or even numbered pages. You can also specify whether the document's paper size is to be used (in which case you might have lines that break across pages) or whether the output should be scaled to fit the chosen paper size (this last feature — Destination Paper Size — is new in Tiger).

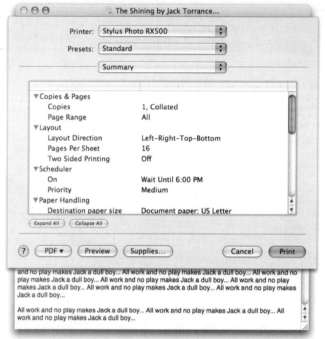

Figure 10-7:
Summary
for the
about-to-
be-printed
document.

ColorSync

Use this pane to choose a color-conversion method and/or to add a Quartz filter. The idea here is to get the printed page to look as much like what's on your screen as possible.

Quartz filters include Black & White, Blue Tone, Gray Tone, Lightness Decrease, Lightness Increase, Reduce File Size, and Sepia Tone. They do pretty much what they say they do when you apply them to a print job.

Print Settings

This pane, if present, offers printer-specific choices such as type of paper, type of ink, and other settings specific to the selected printer.

Save custom settings

After you finalize the printer settings for Copies & Pages, Layout, Output Options, and any other options your printer driver provides, choose Save As from the Presets pop-up menu. Name the settings and from now on, that setting appears as an option in the Presets pop-up menu. Just choose your saved set before you print any document with which you want to use it.

Previewing Your Documents

When you click the Preview button, you see a version of the page or pages that you're about to print, displayed by the Preview application at a size small enough to allow you to see the whole page at once, as shown in Figure 10-8.

Figure 10-8:
A Print Preview of a TextEdit document.

If you have any doubt about the way a document will look when you print it, check out Preview first. When you're happy with the document preview, just click the Print button, choose Print from the File menu, or press ⌘+P.

Print Preview works with the Preview application that Apple includes with Mac OS X. With the Preview feature, you do cool things like these:

- ✔ **See all the pages in your document one by one.**
- ✔ **Zoom in or out to get a different perspective on what you're about to send to the printer (pretty cool!).**
- ✔ **Rotate the picture 90 degrees to the left or right.**
- ✔ **Spot errors before you commit to printing something.** A little up-front inspection can save you a lot of paper, ink (or toner), and frustration.
- ✔ **Add headers and footers.** Many applications include (or allow you to include) header or footer fields to fill in. *Headers* include information or page numbers that run at the top of each page, like the ones this book uses. *Footers* — you guessed it — are the same thing, but they appear at the bottom of a page. They aren't visible while you're working on the text of your document, but they do appear in the printed version (if you set them to). Use Preview to get a look at the header or footer before you print your document. Just zoom in on that area of the page to take a closer look; make any desired changes within the application that created the file.

Check out the Preview program's View menu and its toolbar. Here you can zoom in or out, rotate your document, move forward or backward (through multipage documents), and other stuff. So I urge you to pull down the View menu and check it out. If you have a multipage document (or multiple documents) open, a drawer pops out of the side of the window to let you move through the pages.

To hide and show the drawer, click the Drawer button, choose View➪Drawer, or use the keyboard shortcut Shift+⌘+D.

Just the Fax . . .

OS X includes the capability to fax a document right from the Print sheet. Just choose Fax from the PDF pop-up menu button at the bottom of every Print sheet and the sheet becomes the Fax sheet, as shown in Figure 10-9.

To fax a document, choose Fax from the menu that appears when you press and hold the PDF pop-up menu button on the Print sheet and then type the fax phone number of the recipient in the To field.

If you click the button with the silhouette on the right of the To field, you can select a recipient from the OS X Address Book.

Type a subject name in the Subject field if you so desire, add a dialing prefix if your phone requires one (such as 1, which most U.S. phones require to dial a ten-digit, long-distance phone number). Select your modem from the modem pop-up menu if it's not already selected (as mine is in Figure 10-9).

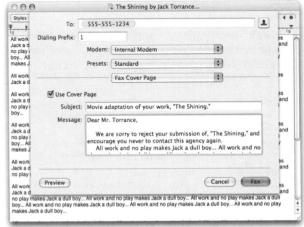

Figure 10-9: In Tiger, faxing is just as easy as printing.

Everything else in the Fax sheet is just the same as in the Print sheet, which you can read all about in the previous sections. Just click the Fax button, and your fax will be sent.

Before you try to fax something out into the world, make sure you have a functioning modem — and that it's configured, set up properly, connected to a phone line, and turned on. If you don't, this whole faxing process will (of course) fail.

Font Mania

Jazz up your documents — or make them a little more serious — with different fonts. To a computer user, *font* means typeface — what the characters look like. Although professional typographers will scream at my generalization, I'll go with that definition for now.

Tens of thousands of different fonts are available for the Macintosh. You don't want to use the same font that you'd use for a garage-sale flyer as you would for a résumé, right? Lucky for you, Mac OS X comes with a bunch of fonts, as shown in Figure 10-10. Some are pretty predictable, such as Times New Roman (it's the font of this paragraph), but OS X gives you some artsy ones, too, such as Brush Script. If you *really* get into fonts, you can buy single fonts and font collections anywhere you can buy software. Plenty of shareware and public-domain fonts are also available from online services and user groups. Some people have *thousands* of fonts. (Maybe they need to get out more.)

The pre-installed fonts live in two different folders, both called Fonts. One is in the Library folder at root level on your hard disk; the other is in the Library subfolder within the System folder. Both are shown in Figure 10-10.

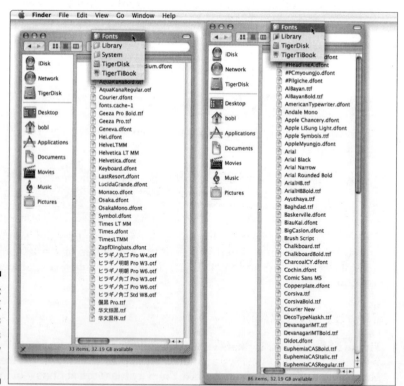

Figure 10-10:
Mac OS X includes these fonts and plenty more.

OS X actually has four different Font folders. A third one, also called Fonts, is in the Library in your home directory. The upcoming section explains the subtle distinctions among those three locations. The fourth one is in the Network/Library folder, and you see it only when you're connected to a network server.

Installing new fonts

To install any new font, drag its icon into one of the two Fonts folders that you have access to, as follows:

✔ **If you want other users to be able to access the new font,** drag the font's icon to the Fonts subfolder inside the Library folder, which is at the root level of your hard drive. This Fonts folder has universal access. (The two Library folders are covered in Chapter 6.)

✔ **If you want to limit access to the new font solely to yourself,** drag the font's icon to the Fonts subfolder (located in the Library folder inside your home folder — just keep digging and you'll get there).

The Fonts folder on the right in Figure 10-10 — the one in the Library inside the System folder — is reserved for OS X and can't easily be modified. If you try to remove a font from it — or add one, for that matter — you'll first have to "authenticate" yourself as an Administrator.

If you've designated a Classic System Folder, OS X will also load any fonts in its Fonts folder, for a total of five different folders named Fonts. (Some applications — in particular, high-end design applications like Adobe Illustrator and Adobe InDesign — add yet *another* Fonts folder to the mix: the Application Support folder within the Library folder at the root level of your hard drive.) You can access any fonts in these out-of the-way-places only when you're running the program that installed them.

Types of fonts

There are many font formats with names like OpenType, Mac TrueType, Windows TrueType, PostScript Type 1, bitmap, and dfont. No problem — Mac OS X supports them all. In fact, the only font format I know of that OS X *doesn't* support is PostScript Type 3.

That said, the three most common formats for Macs are TrueType, PostScript Type 1, and OpenType.

- **TrueType fonts:** These standard-issue Apple fonts come with Mac OS X. They're in common use on Macs as well as on Windows machines. That's partly because these fonts are *scaleable:* They use only a single outline per font, and your Mac can make their characters bigger or smaller when you choose a font size in a program.

- **Type 1 fonts:** These fonts are often referred to as *PostScript Type 1* fonts, and they are the standard for desktop publishing on the Mac (as well as Windows and UNIX). Tens of thousands of Type 1 fonts are available. (Not nearly as many high-quality TrueType fonts exist.)

  Type 1 fonts come in two pieces: a *suitcase* to hold the bitmap that tells the computer how to draw the font on your screen, and a second piece (called a *printer font*) that tells the printer how to print the font on a page. Some Type 1 fonts come with two, three, or four printer fonts, which usually have related names. Just toss all the parts in the appropriate library folder, and you'll have those fonts available in every program you use.

- **OpenType fonts:** OpenType fonts are really TrueType fonts where PostScript information is embedded. This gives you the greater typographic control that high-end typesetters require — while still keeping the one-file convenience of TrueType.

And that's about it for printing and fonts. Onward!

Chapter 11

Application Overload

In This Chapter

▶ Checking out applications included with Mac OS X

▶ Tips for getting the most out of some of them

▶ A folder chock-full of useful utilities

M ac OS X comes with a whole folder full of applications — software you can use to do everything from surfing the Internet to capturing an image of your Mac's screen to playing QuickTime movies to checking the time. In this chapter, I give you a thumbnail view of each application — the ones I don't cover here get their due in other chapters — and tell you a bit about working with applications in Mac OS X.

As is often the case with feature-rich tech, you could write a whole book about many of the applications I'm about to mention. And once again, space considerations forbid me to offer more than a brief description of each.

Technically, most of these applications aren't even part of Mac OS X. Rather, the vast majority of them are what are known as *bundled* apps — programs that come with the operating system but are unrelated to its function. Readers (bless them) tend to complain when I skip over these goodies, so I mention them all — but only provide details on those I consider a vital part of the operating system. Programs that have little or nothing to do with the operating system (such as TextEdit, iCal, and iTunes) are described only briefly; programs I consider joined at the hip to Mac OS X Tiger (such as Automator, AppleScript, Font Book, and many items in the Utilities folder) get the lion's share of the ink.

Many software developers often get ideas for cool shareware and commercial applications from what they find in the Mac OS Applications or Utilities folders. They look at what Apple has provided for free and say, "Hey, I can add some cool features to that!" The next thing you know, you have new and improved versions of Mail, Terminal, Grab, TextEdit, and others. If you use an Apple-supplied application but find it lacking, check your favorite shareware archive (www.versiontracker.com or www.macupdate.com are my two favorites) for a better mousetrap.

Shareware, for those of you who haven't experienced the joy, is freely distributed try-before-you-buy software. There's a lot of it written for Tiger, much of which is as good as (or better than) commercial software.

Folder Full of Apps

The applications that you get with Mac OS X are all stored in (where else?) the Applications folder. Hang with me as I run 'em down!

If you want to see them, though, first you need to open the Applications folder. You can get there in three ways:

- ✔ Click the Applications folder in the Places sidebar in any Finder window
- ✔ Choose Go⇨Applications
- ✔ Use the keyboard shortcut ⌘+Shift+A

Address Book

 Just what you'd expect: The Address Book is the place to store contact information for your family, friends, and anyone else of whom you want to keep track. It works with the Mail application, enabling you to quickly look up e-mail addresses when you're ready to send a message. Use it with iChat, too, to help you quickly chat with your online friends. It can also work with any other application whose programmers choose to make the connection.

 For example, my Sony Ericsson wireless phone can obtain my contact information (wirelessly!) from Address Book (through the magic of Bluetooth). I talk about the Address Book a bit in Chapter 9. For more on Bluetooth, see the sidebar entitled "Whither Bluetooth?" elsewhere in this chapter.

Apple Graphing Calculator

 This venerable piece of visual eye-candy showing off the PowerPCs computational power disappeared when Apple introduced OS X. But, it has now returned, better than ever. A quick, visual math instructor, Apple Graphing Calculator can graph equations in two or three dimensions. You can even plot out and analyze linear and differential equations, compute integrals, and then create and save the result.

AppleScript

AppleScript is "programming for the rest of us." It can record and play back things that you do (if the application was written to allow the recording — Finder, for example, was), such as opening an application or clicking a button. You can use it to record a script for tasks that you often perform and then have your Mac perform those tasks for you later. You can write your own AppleScripts, use those that come with your Mac, or download still others from the Web. The following sections should give you some indication as to how much — or how little — you care about AppleScript.

Discovering whether you give a hoot about AppleScript

Describing AppleScript to a Mac beginner is a bit like three blind men describing an elephant. One man may describe it as the Macintosh's built-in automation tool. Another may describe it as an interesting but often-overlooked piece of enabling technology. The third may liken it to a cassette recorder, recording and playing back your actions at the keyboard. A fourth (if there were a fourth in the story) would assure you that it looked like computer code written in a high-level language.

They would all be correct. *AppleScript,* a built-in Mac automation tool, is a little known (at least until recently) enabling technology that works like a cassette recorder for programs that support AppleScript recording. And scripts do look like computer programs (could that be because they *are* computer programs? Hmm . . .).

If you're the kind of person who likes to automate as many things as possible, you may just love AppleScript because it's a simple programming language that you can use to create programs that give instructions to your Mac and the applications running on your Mac. For example, you can create an AppleScript that launches Mail, checks for new messages, and then quits Mail. The script could even transfer your mail to a folder of your choice. Of course, Tiger also introduces Automator, which includes a whole lot of preprogrammed actions that makes a task like the one just described even easier.

I call AppleScript a time-and-effort enhancer. If you just spend the time and effort it takes to understand it, using AppleScript will save you oodles of time and effort down the road.

Therein lies the rub. This stuff is far from simple — entire books have been written on the subject. So it's far beyond the purview of a 408-page *For Dummies* book. Still, it's worth learning about if you'd like to script repetitive actions for future use.

You can put frequently used AppleScripts on the Dock or on your Desktop for easy access. Apple also provides a script-menu extra that you can install in your menu bar by double-clicking the AppleScript Utility — along with a number of free scripts to automate common tasks, many of which are in the Example Scripts folder. (An alias to that folder is present in the AppleScript folder.) Furthermore, additional scripts can always be downloaded from www.apple.com/applescript. Many AppleScripts are designed for use in the Toolbar of Finder windows, where you can drag and drop items onto them quickly and easily. There are even more available to enhance your use of iTunes, iPhoto, and iDVD.

Checking out AppleScript

The Applications folder contains an AppleScript folder, which in turn contains the Script Editor program (plus an alias that takes you to a folder full of sample AppleScripts).

Script Editor is the application you use to view and edit AppleScripts. Although more information on Script Editor is beyond the scope of this book, it's a lot of fun. And the cool thing is that you can create many AppleScripts without knowing a thing about programming. Just record a series of actions you want to repeat — and use Script Editor to save them as a script. If you save your script as an application (by selecting Application from the Format menu in the Save sheet), you'll be able to run that script by just double-clicking its icon.

If the concept of scripting intrigues you, I suggest that you open the Example Scripts folder and rummage through it to check out the scripts available at www.apple.com/applescript. When you find a script that looks interesting, double-click it to launch the Script Editor program where you can examine it more closely.

Automator

Programming without coding, putting prefabricated activities (known as *actions*) together to automate repetitive or scheduled tasks — how cool is that? Well, if you agree that it's cool, you'll want to know more about Automator.

Automator does just what you'd expect: It enables you to automate many common tasks on your Mac. If it sounds a little like AppleScript to you (which I discuss in the preceding section), you're not mistaken — the two share a common heritage. But this all-new tool (in Tiger) is a lot simpler to use (albeit less flexible) than AppleScript.

For example, in AppleScript you can have *conditionals* (if this is true, do that, otherwise do something else), but Automator is purely *sequential* (take this, do that, then do the next thing, and then . . .).

The big difference is that conditionals allow AppleScripts to do things involving *decision-making* and *iteration* (while this is true, do these things); Automator Workflows can't make decisions or iterate.

The upside to Automator is that you don't have to know anything about programming and you don't have to type any archaic code. Instead, if you understand the process you want to automate, you can just drag and drop Automator's prefab "Actions" into place and build a *Workflow* (Automator's name for a series of Actions).

There is one thing you do need to know about programming (or computers), though: Computers are stupid! You heard me right — even your top-of-the-line dual processor G5 is dumb as a post. Computers only do what you tell them to do, though they can do it faster and more precisely than you can. But all computers run on the G.I.G.O. principle — Garbage In/Garbage Out — so if your instructions are flawed, you're almost certain to get flawed results.

Another similarity between Automator and AppleScript is that it's up to the developers of the applications you want to automate to provide you with the actions or with scripting support. Not all developers do so. For example, in Apple's wonderful iLife '05 suite of multimedia applications, iTunes, iPhoto, and iDVD are all AppleScriptable — and they've supplied actions for Automator users. Neither iMovie nor GarageBand, however, support AppleScript or Automator at this time.

When you launch the Automator application, you see the window in Figure 11-1. The Library list on the left contains all the applications Automator knows about which have actions defined for them. It also contains some example Workflows and any Workflows you've created. Select an application or Workflow on the left and its related actions appear in the Action list. When you select an action the pane at the bottom of the window (Ask for Confirmation in Figure 11-1) explains what that action does, what input it expects, and what result it produces. Just drag actions from the Action list into the pane on the right to build your workflow.

The Workflow shown in Figure 11-1 is one I created and tested in less than 10 minutes, and it works! Plus, it's a useful shortcut I use a lot and one I suspect you may like and use, too. I call it *Scale & Mail* because that's what it does — it takes a selected image file, shrinks it to 25 percent of its original size, opens the Mail application, creates a new message, and inserts the shrunken image as an enclosure/attachment. And it all happens automatically, with no human intervention.

To create this Workflow, I dragged the seven items you see in Figure 11-1 from the Actions list on the left to the Workflow pane on the right. I clicked the Run button to test it and it worked. I wanted to make using it easy, so I chose File⇨Save As and saved the Workflow as an Application (by choosing *Application* instead of *Workflow* in the Save As dialog's File Format menu).

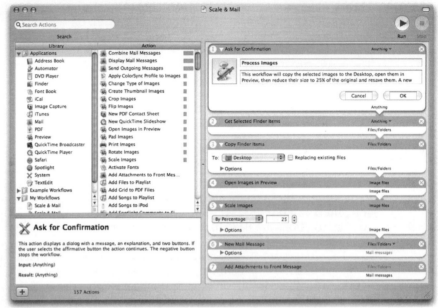

Figure 11-1:
An
Automator
workflow
I built in
10 minutes.

I saved the application to a convenient location (my desktop) and gave it a try by dragging and dropping a picture onto it (as shown in Figure 11-2): I dragged and dropped Picture 9 onto the Scale & Mail Workflow application icon (top left); the Ask for Confirmation dialog appeared and I clicked OK (top right); the picture was then reduced in size and enclosed in a new Mail message (bottom center).

Now, any time I have a big digital picture on my hard disk and want to send it someone via e-mail, I just drag it onto my handy little Scale & Mail icon and it's shrunken and attached in the blink of an eye.

If you like this automation thing, I encourage you to spend some quality time messing around with the Example Workflows included in your Automator Library. They show you a lot about the cool things you can do with your Automator Workflows.

If you use a Workflow often, you might want to add it to your Dock for even easier access. (I discuss the Dock in Chapter 2.)

Automator is a very useful addition to Mac OS X; it's deep, powerful, and expandable, yet relatively easy to use and master. Do yourself a favor and spend some time experimenting with ways Automator can save you time and keystrokes. You won't regret it.

Figure 11-2:
Testing
my new
application.

Calculator

Need to do some quick math? The *Calculator* application gives you a simple calculator, with all the basic number-crunching functions that your pocket calculator has. To use it, you can either click the keys with the mouse or you can use your numeric keypad (on your keyboard) to type numbers and operators (math symbols such as +, –, and =). Check out the Calculator in Figure 11-3.

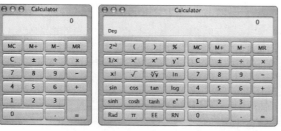

Figure 11-3:
The
Calculator,
Basic (left),
Scientific
(middle), and
Programmer
(right).

Calculator now has three modes, Basic, Scientific, and Programmer. Pressing ⌘+2 (View⇨Scientific) turns the formerly anemic calculator into a powerful scientific calculator, and View⇨Programmer (⌘+3) turns it into the programmer's friend, letting you display your data in binary, octal, hexadecimal, ASCII, and Unicode as well as performing programming operations like rotate, shifts, and byte-swaps (the programmers among you know what all that means, and it really won't matter to the rest of you). Calculator also offers a paper tape (View➪Show Paper Tape) to track your computations and if you want, provide a printed record. It can even speak numbers aloud (Speech➪ Speak Button Pressed and Speech➪Speak).

I find it interesting that until the advent of Mac OS X version 10.2 Jaguar, the only thing that had changed about the Calculator since the Mac was invented was the interface. Then, in Panther, Apple added the paper-tape-and-scientific mode (called Advanced at the time); now, in Tiger, it's called the Programmer mode. No functionality had been added or removed in almost 20 years — how many computer programs can say that? (For the curious: Calculator was a Desk Accessory in early versions of the Mac OS and an Apple Menu Item in versions 8 and 9.)

Chess

This is a visual implementation of the GNU (stands for Gnu's Not UNIX, but don't ask me why) chess-playing game. You can play against the computer at a variety of settings. Chess is a fairly strong player and should provide a good contest for any chess player who has less than a master ranking. You can see what it looks like in Figure 11-4.

Figure 11-4:
The super-snazzy
Mac OS X
3-D Chess
game.

Notice that in the figure, the Dock is hovering over the window. Don't forget that you can auto-hide the Dock by choosing ⌘⇨Dock⇨Turn Hiding On/Off (or by pressing ⌘+Option+D).

To play a game, launch Chess and then choose Game⇨New. If you're playing against the computer, you play as white — click a white piece and move it. The computer responds by moving a black piece, making it your turn again. Because this is *Mac OS X Tiger For Dummies* rather than *Chess For Dummies*, I won't even attempt to tell you how to improve your chess game here.

You can tinker with a couple of preferences in the Chess program. To make the computer a more formidable opponent, choose Chess⇨Preferences and drag the Level slider toward the word *Hard*. You can also choose to play human-versus-human or change the name that the computer uses from the rather unimaginative *Computer* to something more evocative (maybe *Kasparov*). The last option in the Preferences dialog lets you turn Voice Recognition on or off. (The default is On, which is why you see the circular Speech Recognition window on the right in Figure 11-4.) If you choose to use it, you press the Esc key, and then speak your moves ("Knight G1 to F3," and so on). It works pretty well but, of course, requires that you have an appropriate microphone connected to your Mac.

If you need a hint (as I often do) to make a good next move, choose Move⇨Hint or press ⌘+Shift+H. The program shows you the move that it calculates to be your best choice, blinking both the piece it thinks you should move *and* the square to which you should move it. You don't have to take the program's suggestion — just make a different move if you decide to decline the suggestion.

Dashboard

This is the application icon for Dashboard. You could double-click it to get immediate access to Dashboard. You probably won't use it much — clicking its Dock icon or pressing its keyboard shortcut, F12 by default, are easier ways to invoke Dashboard.

Dashboard is a way-cool set of *widgets*, which is what Apple calls mini-applications that live inside the Dashboard layer. Dashboard takes over your screen when invoked through any of the three possible ways (as shown in Figure 11-5).

Widgets function much like desk accessories or Sherlock channels in earlier versions of Mac OS. Some widgets talk to applications on your hard disk, such as Address Book, iTunes, or iCal. Others, including Flight Tracker, Stocks, and Weather, gather information for you via the Internet.

When you activate Dashboard, your Widgets are displayed in a gray overlay floating above the Finder and any open applications (iCal in Figure 11-5).

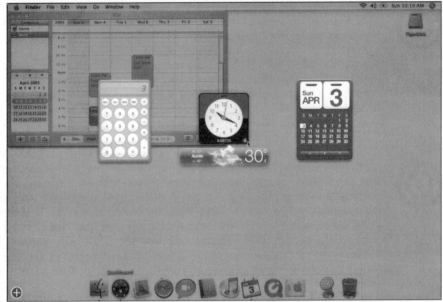

Figure 11-5:
Dashboard,
with the
Default
Widgets:
Calculator,
Clock,
Calendar,
and
Weather.

Each time you invoke Dashboard, widgets that were open last time you used it will be on your screen. To use other widgets other than the four on your screen by default, click the Open button (shown in the lower-left corner of Figure 11-5) to open the Widget Bar, which is shown in Figure 11-6.

Figure 11-6:
Click a
widget
(Translation
here) and it
appears
mid-screen.

Widget Bar sounds like a trendy watering hole downtown, but I assure you that's the official, Apple-sanctioned name. Really.

By the way, you can't remove widgets from the Widget Bar, nor can you change their order, so don't bother trying.

To place a widget on-screen, click its icon and it appears in the middle of your screen, all set to do your bidding, as shown in Figure 11-6. Or, you can click and drag a widget anywhere on your screen if you prefer.

Click almost anywhere on a widget to move it around on your screen. To put a widget away, click its Close button — the large X at the upper-left corner of the widgets in Figure 11-6. If you don't see an X, press the Option key and move the pointer over the widget and you will. Also, a close button appears automatically on all widgets when the Widget Bar is open.

Note that the Dashboard Dock icon is slightly different from other Dock icon menus. In addition to the familiar Remove from Dock item, you also find More Widgets, Dashboard Preferences, and Show Dashboard:

- **More Widgets** launches your Web browser and shows you additional widgets that you can download and use. (The More Widgets button in Figure 11-6 does the same.)
- **Dashboard Preferences** opens the Dashboard System Preference pane (which I cover in Chapter 13) immediately.
- **Show Dashboard** is the same as clicking the Dock icon. Dashboard and all your widgets appear on-screen.

Think of your Dashboard widgets as handy yet potent mini-programs available at any time with a keystroke or click. Widgets are just so danged cool, I want to give a quick look at a couple I consider particularly useful before moving along.

Translation

The Translation widget could be a lifesaver. You've been able to do this trick on the Web for a while, but now you can do it right on your desktop. This widget translates words from one language to another. It offers more than a dozen language choices including French, German, Spanish, Russian, Dutch, Chinese (shown in Figure 11-7), and more, and can translate in either direction.

I love the Translation widget so much sometimes, it hurts.

It's fun at parties, too. Try this: Type a paragraph or two of your purplest prose into Translation. Now translate back and forth to any language a few times. Howl when prose written as, "It was a dark and stormy night when our heroine met her untimely demise," turns into something like, "It was one night dark and stormy where our heroin met an ugly transfer." It doesn't get much better than this, folks.

I used to leave my PowerBook at home if I wasn't going to absolutely need it. But the Translation widget is so wicked-cool and useful, lately I've been taking my PowerBook almost everywhere I go.

Flight Tracker

Flight Tracker, shown in Figure 11-8, can find flights on most airlines and report the flight's status in real time — a terrific timesaver when you've got to meet a flight.

Figure 11-8:
The Flight
Tracker
widget does
what its
name
implies — it
tracks a
flight or
flights for
you in real
time.

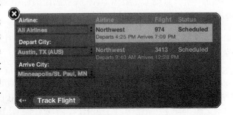

This is a good one; you can open more than one instance of a widget. So if you're trying to track two flights, or want to know the weather in more than one city, just click the appropriate widget in the Widget Bar and another instance of it appears.

Phone Book

Phone Book (shown in Figure 11-9) is like a yellow page directory. It can quickly find local (or not local) phone numbers.

Some widgets have More Info buttons, usually in the lower-right corner. Click it and the widget appears to flip around, exposing its backside and additional options (see Figure 11-9).

Figure 11-9:
Click the
little "i"
button (left)
to expose
Phone
Book's
options
(right).

I expect to see lots of Dashboard widgets appear in fairly short order. They can easily be written in JavaScript, making their development readily accessible to any competent Web developer. Meanwhile, Figure 11-10 shows you all the included Widgets at once. Enjoy!

Figure 11-10:
Dashboard
and the
complete
widget
collection.

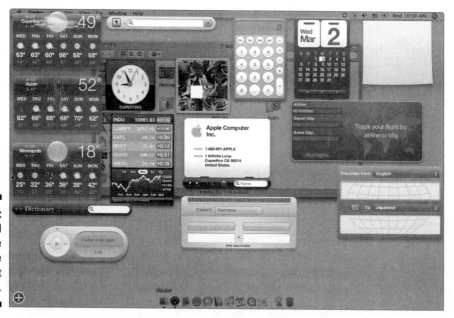

Dictionary

 An application version of the dictionary and thesaurus found in Dashboard, Dictionary provides phonetic listings, definitions, and etymologies for the words you type into the search box — as well as providing a set of synonyms and, often, antonyms. The supplied reference works are *The New Oxford American Dictionary* and *The Oxford American Writer's Thesaurus*.

DVD Player

 This application is present only on Macs that have an Apple-recognized DVD player or SuperDrive DVD burner installed. Inserting a DVD into such a Mac automatically starts the DVD Player. You can then watch the movie on your Mac, unless you've changed the default in the CDs & DVDs System Preferences (which is to Open DVD Player when you insert a video DVD).

Many external DVD players aren't recognized and you'll need to use the software that came with it or a tool like *vlc* (VideoLAN Client) to watch DVDs inserted into those players.

The System Profiler application (in the Utilities folder) can tell you whether you've got a DVD drive in your Mac. Just launch it and then click the IDE (ATA) item in the contents column on the left; the details appear on the right.

 If you choose ⌘⇨About this Mac in the Finder, there's a More Info button. Click it and System Profiler opens.

The DVD Player comes with a snazzy little on-screen remote control, as shown in Figure 11-11.

To choose between the vertical (the two on top in Figure 11-11) and the horizontal (bottom two) controllers, choose Controls⇨Use Vertical/Horizontal Controller or use the keyboard shortcut ⌘+Option+C.

To open or close the little Controller drawer (as shown top right and bottom in Figure 11-11), choose Controls⇨Open/Close Control Drawer, use the keyboard shortcut ⌘+], or click the little pull tab (where you see the arrow cursor in Figure 11-11) and drag.

The controls themselves should be self-explanatory to anyone who has ever used a set-top DVD player. If they're not familiar to you, hover the cursor over any control and a tool tip will pop up, as shown in Figure 11-12.

Figure 11-11:
DVD Player's
on-screen
remote-
control
gadget.

Figure 11-12:
Hover your
cursor to see
a tool tip.

Font Book

 Font Book lets you view your installed fonts, install new fonts, group your fonts into collections, and enable and disable installed fonts. If you ever used the commercial program Extensis Suitcase, Font Book does much the same job.

To install a new font, choose File➪Add Fonts or use the shortcut ⌘+O. A standard Open dialog allows you to select a font or fonts to be installed. Previously (that is, in Panther), you chose whether the font was to be installed for all users, just you, or into the Classic environment's Fonts folder in this Open dialog. In Tiger, you install new fonts into your Home folder's Library➪Fonts folder. You can change the default installation location in the Font Book Preferences dialog. As shown in Figure 11-13, you can select multiple fonts in the Open dialog and install them all at once.

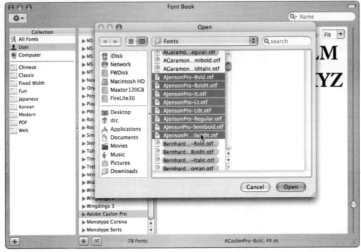

Figure 11-13:
Font Book's
Open dialog
lets you
install new
fonts — one
or many.

To view a font, click its name in the Font list. To change the size of the viewed font, choose a new size from the drop-down menu in the upper-right corner (it says "Fit" in Figure 11-14) or move the blue slider on the right side of the window up or down.

To disable a font so it no longer appears in applications' Font menus, choose Edit⇨Disable or click the Disable button (the check mark in a square button) at the bottom of the window.

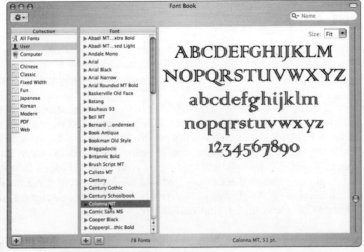

Figure 11-14:
Click a font
in the Font
list on
the left to
display it in
the pane on
the right.

To enable a previously disabled font, choose Edit⇨Enable or click the Enable button (same as the Disable button) at the bottom of the window.

To create a new font collection, click the + button at the bottom of the Collection pane, choose File⇨New Collection, or use the keyboard shortcut ⌘+N. To add a font to a collection, first choose the All Fonts collection and then drag the font from the Font list onto the collection in which you want it placed. To remove a font from a collection, select the Collection, select the font in the Font list, and choose File⇨Remove Font.

If you remove a font from the All Fonts collection, it disappears permanently. This action cannot be undone, so be careful when you remove fonts.

iCal

iCal is a wonderful utility that's a daily/weekly/monthly pocket and desktop calendar equivalent. You can publish your calendar(s) to a .Mac account or other compatible (WebDav) server as well as subscribe to calendars that others publish. Integrated with the Address Book, you can select people who you want to invite to a scheduled event. Figure 11-15 shows me inviting some friends to a small shindig.

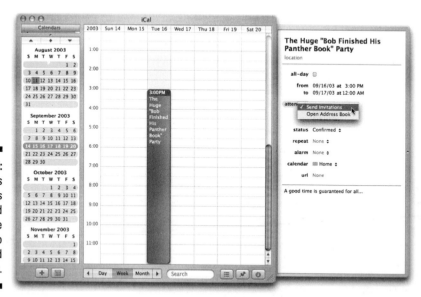

Figure 11-15:
iCal uses Address Book and Mail to invite people to scheduled events.

iChat

 Text-based chatting on the Internet is an old and popular pastime. Numerous protocols abound with names such as IRC (Internet Relay Chat), ICQ (a mnemonic play on *I Seek You*), AIM (AOL Instant Messenger), and many others. *iChat* supports AIM and lets you communicate with other Mac.com members, Jabber chat users, and users on your local network via Bonjour. You can even hook up online with anyone connected to AOL's massive AIM network, including joining AOL chat rooms, even if you aren't an AOL subscriber. (*Note:* You do have to know the chat room's name.) Figure 11-16 shows me having a brief conversation with someone we both know and love.

Figure 11-16: I'm not schizo-phrenic, and neither is the other Bob "Dr. Mac" LeVitus.

You can even drag and drop files (such as photos from iPhoto) onto the message area when you're chatting with someone, and the file will be sent right to his or her iChat window! This is way easier than creating an e-mail to send the file while you're chatting.

Furthermore, if you have a FireWire DV camcorder or Apple's iSight camera connected, you can conduct video chats with iChat, and see and hear the person on the other end.

 Apple has really extended iChat's AV features by adding conference-call support to audio and video chats. You can now video-chat with up to three other users (as shown in Figure 11-17) and audio-chat with up to ten users at once.

Online meetings: Blessing or curse?

That's a serious, four-way video conference with me (bottom center, small), and (top — left to right) Bare Bones Software's Rich Siegel, Macworld's Jason Snell, and John Popper, Blues Traveler's vocalist and harp player.

 Just kidding. That's actually noted author, opinion writer, humorist, Chicago Sun Times columnist, and fellow Wiley book author Andy Ihnatko on the right in Figure 11-17. But I had you going there for a second, didn't I?

Figure 11-17:
A serious
four-way
video
conference.

Image Capture

Use this program to transfer images from your Universal Serial Bus (USB) digital camera, various SmartMedia readers, or from many supported scanners. If you don't have such a device, don't worry about it. If you do have one — and the software that came with it doesn't work with OS X (or even if it does) — try Image Capture.

I discuss Image Capture in a bit more detail in Chapter 19.

Internet Connect

This program replaces the old Point-to-Point Protocol (PPP) application in earlier versions of Mac OS. It is used to configure dial-up telephone modem connections.

iSync

iSync is Apple's hot synchronizing software that lets you synchronize your Address Book entries and iCal calendars with over 20 cell phone models, your iPod, and/or your PDA (such as Palm, Visor, and others). It also lets you synchronize your Address Book entries, iCal calendars, and Safari Bookmarks between multiple Macs in different locations via a .Mac account.

iTunes

 iTunes is a great piece of multimedia software from Apple. It lets you play CDs, create your own audio or MP3 CDs (assuming that you have a CD burner), play MP3, AIFF, AAC, WAV, and Audible.com files, integrate with your iPod or other MP3 player, listen to Internet radio stations, and view some rather pretty visual displays. It is also your interface to the iTunes Music Store, the world's leading (legitimate) source of downloadable music. (Whew!)

Mail

 Mail is the free e-mail program that comes with OS X. I cover Mail in Chapter 9.

Preview

 You use Preview to open, view, and print PDFs as well as most graphics files (TIFF, JPEG, PICT, and so on). *PDF files* are formatted documents that include text and images. User manuals, books, and the like are often distributed as PDF files. You can't edit a PDF file with Preview, but you can leaf through its pages or print it and you can select text and graphics from it, copy them to the Clipboard, and paste them into documents in other applications. It's also the application that pops open when you click the Preview button in the Print dialog, as described in Chapter 10.

 Any OS X program that offers PDF as a file format is one you can print your own documents from. You do so via the Output Settings pop-up menu choice, or by using the Save As PDF button found in all OS X 10.2 (and later) Print dialogs.

QuickTime Player

 Use the QuickTime Player to view QuickTime movies or streaming audio and video. The quickest way to launch it is by clicking its icon on the Dock. It also opens automatically when you open any QuickTime movie document file.

Safari

 Safari is Apple's Web browser, discussed in some detail in Chapter 9.

Sherlock

I mention Sherlock — the cool search tool you can use to find Web sites, people, software, stuff to buy, and lots more — in several chapters of this book. (I will not say "Elementary." Real Sherlock Holmes fans know he didn't either.)

Stickies

Stickies are electronic Post-it™ Notes for your Mac. They're a convenient place to jot notes or phone numbers. Some Stickies are shown in Figure 11-18.

Stickies are supremely flexible. Move them around on-screen (just drag 'em by their title bars) and change their text to any font and color you desire by using the Note menu. Make your Stickies any color you like by using the Color menu. You can collapse a Stickie by double-clicking its title bar, or print it and import or export text files from the Stickies application.

If you hover the cursor over a Stickie note (but don't click), the creation and modification dates and times pop up in a little tool-tip-style window.

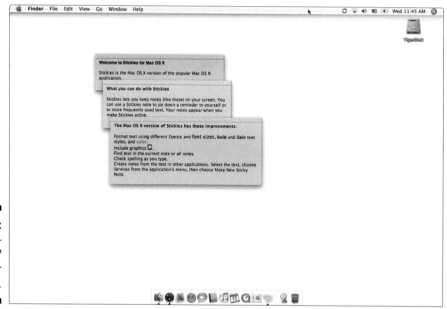

Figure 11-18:
Stickies —
Post-it™
Notes for
your Mac.

Anything that you type on a Stickie is automatically saved as long as you keep that note open. But when you close a note (by clicking its close box, choosing File➪Close, or using the keyboard shortcut ⌘+W), you lose its contents forever. Fortunately, Stickies give you a warning and a second chance to save the note in a separate file on your hard drive. You can also export Stickies (choose File➪Export Text) and save Stickies as plain text, rich-text format (RTF) files, or as rich-text format with attachments (RTFD) files. The last two formats support fonts and other formatting that plain-text format does not.

Stickies have grown up in Mac OS X. They work pretty much as they always have, but now you have more options available, such as a spell checker. You can also import pre-Mac OS X Stickies and plain-text files. The old Stickies application supported colors, but not fonts (as Mac OS X Stickies do).

System Preferences

 I mention System Preferences throughout this book. For complete details on setting them, though, check out Chapter 13.

You can open the System Preferences application in any of these three ways:

- ✔ Double-click its icon in the Applications folder.
- ✔ Click its icon on the Dock.
- ✔ Choose System Preferences from the menu.

TextEdit

 TextEdit is a word processor/text editor that you can use to write letters, scribble notes, or open Read Me files. Although it's not as sophisticated as Apple-Works, Pages, or Microsoft Word, you can use it for some text formatting and to check your spelling. TextEdit supports images, too. (Just copy an image in another program and paste it into a TextEdit document. Or you can use drag-and-drop to drop an image into a TextEdit document from many applications.)

TextEdit can open Microsoft Word documents. This is fabulous if you don't happen to have a copy of Microsoft Word on your hard drive. Neat!

Utilities

 Here's another folder full of stuff. Most of the items in the Utilities folder work with other applications to do some useful thing. You may never even open a lot of these applications. The Utilities folder appears in Figure 11-19; stick with me for a brief tour of each application you find there.

Figure 11-19:
The Utilities
folder.

Activity Monitor

In *UNIX* (the operating system behind Mac OS X), applications and other things going on behind the scenes are called *processes*. Each application (and the operating system itself) can run a number of processes at once.

Activity Monitor was introduced in Panther, but its capabilities will be familiar to users of previous versions of OS X — it combined the functions of Process Viewer and CPU Monitor (both discontinued in Panther) and a little bit more, all in one convenient, easy-to-decipher application.

In Figure 11-20, you see 45 processes running. Interestingly, only four applications are open (the Finder, Snapz Pro X, Dashboard, and Activity Monitor itself).

To display the three CPU monitor windows on the right of the Activity Monitor window in Figure 11-20, choose Monitor⇨ Show CPU Usage (keyboard shortcut ⌘+2), Floating CPU Window (no keyboard shortcut), and/or Show CPU History (keyboard shortcut ⌘+3).

You also select what appears in the Activity Monitor's Dock icon — CPU Usage, CPU History, Network Usage, Disk Activity, Memory Usage, or the Activity Monitor icon — from the Dock Icon submenu in the Monitors menu. All but the Activity Monitor icon appear "live," meaning they update every few seconds to reflect the current state of affairs.

To choose how often these updates occur, use the Monitor⇨Update Frequency submenu.

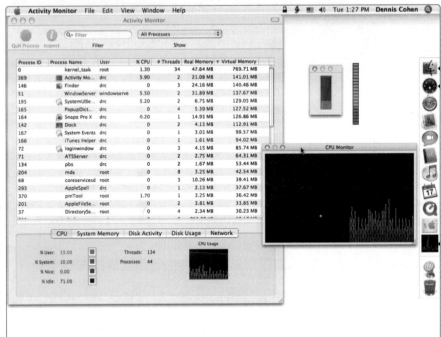

Figure 11-20:
The Activity
Monitor
(left) and its
three little
CPU Monitor
windows
(right).

But be careful — shorter durations cause Activity Monitor to use more CPU cycles, which can decrease overall performance.

Finally, the bottom portion of the Activity Monitor window can display one of five different monitors. Just click the appropriate tab — CPU, System Memory, Disk Activity, Disk Usage, or Network — to see that particular monitor.

Geeks and troubleshooters can use Activity Monitor to identify what processes are running, which user owns the process, and how much CPU capacity and memory the process is using. You can even stop a process that you think may be causing problems for you.

Messing around in Activity Monitor is not a good idea for most users. If you're having problems with an application or with Mac OS X, try quitting open applications, force-quitting applications (press ⌘+Option+Esc — the Mac "three-finger salute"), or logging out and then logging back in again before you start mucking around with processes.

AirPort Admin Utility

You use *AirPort Admin Utility* to change individual Internet settings of an AirPort Base Station, such as the phone number of your Internet service provider (ISP).

Whither Bluetooth?

Bluetooth is an upcoming standard for wireless communication between intelligent devices over short distances. At least that's my definition. One of the first devices that came on the market is the Sony Ericsson T68i wireless phone I've been using.

Bluetooth is a smart protocol. When two Bluetooth devices have been prepared (actually, paired), they recognize each other when they're within range — 20–30 feet — and then they automatically perform whatever task they were instructed to perform when they were paired.

My phone can receive calendar items, contacts, and little pictures from my Mac. And I can back up the phone's memory to my Mac's hard disk as well. If I attach the Bluetooth adapter to my PowerBook, I can use the phone as a wireless modem and surf the Internet or check my e-mail from the beach if I want to, just like on TV. (Now, where's that cold beer?)

What AirPort is to wireless networking, Bluetooth is to intelligent wireless peripheral connections.

Bluetooth isn't very fast and has a limited range (around 20–30 feet from your Mac). But it's swell for sending small amounts of data back and forth between devices. Watch for devices that you currently use via USB (digital cameras, printers, and such) to offer Bluetooth connectivity soon.

Warning: If your Mac doesn't have Bluetooth built-in (or a Bluetooth adapter connected to it) and you try to launch any of the three Bluetooth utilities, they alert you that your Mac doesn't have the proper Bluetooth hardware connected to it — and they refuse to launch.

AirPort Setup Assistant

The name is pretty self-explanatory. You run this program to configure your AirPort card for wireless networking.

Audio MIDI Setup

This program is the control center for any MIDI devices built into or connected to your Mac.

Bluetooth File Exchange

If you have a Bluetooth device and your Mac has a Bluetooth adapter connected to a USB port (or has Bluetooth built in, although no Mac has it at the time of this writing), you can drag icons for Address Book items (vCard files), iCal items (vCal files), and pictures (.gif files) onto the Bluetooth File Exchange icon to copy the file from your Mac to the Bluetooth device — wirelessly — via Bluetooth.

ColorSync Utility

This single-purpose program verifies the contents of the color-matching profiles installed on your Mac. If you don't use ColorSync (Apple's color-matching technology to ensure what you see on-screen is the same as what you print on any device), don't worry about it.

Console

Mac OS X is based on an operating system called *UNIX,* a powerful operating system with lots of incredibly geeky features and capabilities that most Mac users don't really want to know about (and that Apple hides from you unless you want to work with them). But for those who want to find out what's going on under the hood of Mac OS X (or even to tinker around with the engine), the Console application provides a window into the deep, dark world of UNIX. Console displays system messages that can help you troubleshoot problems with Mac OS X — provided you know how to interpret them. If you've never learned conversational UNIX, don't let it scare you — most folks never need Console.

DigitalColor Meter

This is a little program that displays what's on your screen as numerical color values, according to two different systems: RGB (red-green-blue) or CIE (the abbreviation for a chromaticity coordinate system developed by the Commission Internationale de l'Eclairage, the international commission on illumination). If you're not a graphic artist or otherwise involved in the production of high-end color documents, you'll almost certainly never need it.

Directory Access

This little program is meant for system administrators on large networks. If your computer is connected to a campus or corporate network, talk to your network administrator about these settings.

If you're a home user with no vast cube farm to manage, just ignore this program.

Disk Utility

If you're having problems with your hard drive or need to make changes to it, Disk Utility is a good place to start. This application has five active components: First Aid, Erase, Partition, RAID, and Restore.

First Aid

If you suspect something's not quite right with your Mac, the First Aid portion of Disk Utility should be among your first stops. Use First Aid to verify and (if necessary) repair an ailing drive. To use it, click the First Aid button on the left side of the Disk Utility window. Click a volume's icon and then click Verify. You get information about any problems that the software finds. If First Aid doesn't find any problems, you can go on your merry way, secure in the knowledge that your Mac is A-OK. If verification turns up trouble, click Repair to have the problem fixed. You can also use First Aid to fix disk permission problems.

You won't be able to use the copy of Disk Utility in your Applications/Utilities folder to repair your OS X boot disk. To do that, you must reboot from the Mac OS X CD and run the copy of Disk Utility found on that CD-ROM.

You can't use Disk Utility First Aid to fix a CD-ROM or DVD-ROM disk, nor can it fix most disk image files. These disks are read-only and can't be altered. You *can* fix Zip disks, SuperDisks, DVD-RAM discs, or any other writeable media that can be mounted by your Mac.

Erase

Use Erase to format (completely erase) a disk. You can't do this to the startup disk — the one with *Mac OS X* on it.

When you format a disk, you erase all information on it, permanently. Formatting can't be undone — unless you are absolutely sure this is what you want to do, don't do it. Unless you have no use for whatever's currently on the disk, make a complete backup of the disk before you format it. If the data is critical, you should have at least two (or even three) known-to-be-valid backup copies of that disk before you reformat.

Partition

Use this tab to create disk partitions (multiple volumes on a single disk), each of which is treated as a separate disk by OS X.

RAID

By using Redundant Array of Individual Disks (RAID), you can treat multiple disks as a single volume, which is sort of the opposite of partitioning.

Of partitions and volumes

Partitioning a drive lets you create multiple volumes. A *volume* is a storage space that (from the Mac's point of view) looks and acts just like a hard drive; a *partition* is simply a designated volume on a drive, completely separate from all other partitions (volumes). You can create any number of partitions, but it's a good idea to limit yourself to no more than a small handful. Lots of people, including me, use one partition for Mac OS X and another for Mac OS 9.

You can only create drive partitions on a newly formatted drive. So to partition a drive, first format it in Drive Setup and then create partitions. Before you do that, give some thought to how large a partition you want to create. You won't be able to change your mind about it later.

I think that partitions should be no smaller than 2GB. You can get away with 1GB if you have a 6GB or smaller drive, but you don't need to create a lot of little partitions just to store your stuff. Instead, use folders: They work just great for organizing things the way you like. The one exception to this rule is if you burn a lot of CDs with your CD-RW drive. In that case, a 650MB or 700MB (if you use that size CD) partition lets you *prototype* your CDs before you burn them — set up the content and check to see just how much stuff *will* fit on a single 650MB or 700MB disk. Of course, creating disk-image files of those sizes would leave the space free for other uses when you aren't prototyping.

By the same token, you should limit the number of partitions you create. A PowerMac G4 with a 20GB drive does just fine with two (or maybe three) partitions.

Restore

Use the Restore tab to restore your Mac to factory-fresh condition from a CD-ROM or disk-image file.

Speaking of disk images (and I will be in a minute), Disk Utility contains the functionality formerly found in the now-discontinued Disk Copy program.

In most cases, you install new software on your Mac from a CD-ROM, DVD-ROM, or by downloading it from the Internet. Software vendors typically use an installer program that decompresses and copies files to their proper places on your hard drive. After you've installed the software, you're back in business.

Apple's variation on this theme is a humongous file called the *disk image* — everything you'd normally find on a disk, without the disk. These days more developers are adopting the disk-image format for their downloadable installers and updaters. When mounted on your Desktop (more on what *mounting* means in a minute), a disk image looks and acts just like a real disk. You can open it and see its contents in a Finder window, copy files from its window to another disk, drag it to the Eject button to remove it from your Desktop — go wild. To make a disk image appear on your Desktop, you double-click the image file. At that point, the Disk Utility application takes over and puts an icon (which for all intents and purposes looks like a disk) on your Desktop.

Disk Utility not only mounts images when you double-click them, it can also be used to create your own disk-image files and burn them onto CD-ROMs and DVD-ROMs.

 Because disk images can be transferred via the Internet — and because they act just like disks — they're a great substitute for a CD-ROM or other disk-based software installer. A software maker can create both a CD version of an installer and a disk image that can be downloaded.

Grab

 Want to take a picture of your screen? I used to do this a lot so that I could bring you the screen shots (what you see in the figures) in this book. You can use Grab to take a picture of all or part of the screen, and then save that file for printing or sending around (say, to all your screaming fans who want to see your Desktop pattern or how you've organized your windows). The first edition of this book used Grab, but I used the superb Snapz Pro X utility (Ambrosia Software; www.ambrosiasw.com) for the figures in subsequent editions. It's definitely worth the shareware fee.

 Grab's best feature is its capability to do a timed screen capture. Like those cameras that let you start the timer and then run to get into the shot, Grab gives you ten seconds to bring the window you want to the front, pull down a menu, get the cursor out of the way, or whatever you need to do to get the screen just right.

Grab's default behavior is to display no cursor. If you want to show a cursor in your screen shots, choose Grab⇨Preferences and then select a pointer (from the ten choices in the Preference dialog) by clicking it. To have no cursor, click the topmost, leftmost item, which is an empty box (that indicates *no cursor*).

Installer

Here's an application that you'll never need to open yourself. But don't get rid of it — software developers, including Apple, write installer scripts that automate the process of putting software on your Mac (that's what all those .pkg and .mpkg file extensions are about). These scripts know where everything should go and in what order — and in order to run, those installer scripts need to find this little program. If you simply leave this critter alone to snooze in peace, everything will be hunky-dory.

Java

This folder contains three tools for using the versatile and powerful Java language with your Mac:

- ✓ **Input Method Hot Key:** This is what you use to designate a hot key that allows you to select from multiple input methods in a pop-up menu.

  The hot key is available only while a Java application is the active application.

- ✓ **Java Plugin Settings (one for version 1.3.1; another for version 1.4.2):** This is a control panel for Java and plug-ins that you may run in your Web browser.

- ✓ **Java Web Start:** This nifty little tool lets you launch full-featured applications written in the Java language with a single click from within your Web browser. One big advantage of an application written in Java is that you don't have to wait for the publisher to create a Mac OS X version. The same Java code that runs on Windows or Linux or Solaris (Sun's version of UNIX) will run on Mac OS X and inherit the Mac OS X interface.

Keychain Access

A *keychain* is a way to consolidate all your passwords — the one you use to log into your Mac, your e-mail password, and passwords required by any Web sites. Here's how it works: You use a single password to unlock your keychain (which holds your various passwords) and then you don't have to remember all your other passwords. Rest assured that your passwords are secure because only a user who has your keychain password can reach the other password-protected applications.

To create a new keychain, choose File⇨New Keychain.

To add passwords to the keychain, you must first create a keychain and a password for it. Then you can add passwords to the chain.

After you set up a keychain, you can just open Mail or another application that supports the keychain. When the program asks for your password, supply it and choose Yes to add the password to the keychain.

How do you know which programs support the Keychain utility? You don't until you're prompted to save your password in a keychain in that Open dialog, connect window, or so forth. If a program supports Keychain, it offers a check box for it in the user ID/password dialog or window.

The Keychain utility is particularly cool if you have multiple e-mail accounts and each one has a different password. Just add them all to your keychain, and you can get all your mail at once with one password.

To add a Web site password to a keychain, open the Keychain Access application and click the Password button. In the New Password Item window that opens, type the URL of the site in the Keychain Item Name text field, type your username in the Account Name field, and then type your password in the Password text field, as shown in Figure 11-21.

Keychain Item Name:

https://www.banking.wellsfargo.com

Enter a name for this keychain item. If you are adding an Internet password item, enter its URL (for example: http://www.apple.com)

Account Name:

71077345

Enter the account name associated with this keychain item.

Password:

dotodotododt

Enter the password to be stored in the keychain.

☑ Show Typing

Cancel   Add

Figure 11-21: Add a URL to the keychain in Keychain Access.

To use the new URL password, double-click the URL in the Keychain Access window. A small Get Info window will pop up. Click the Go There button to launch your browser (if it isn't already running) — you're whisked away and logged in to the Web site you choose.

Migration Assistant

This is pretty much a one-trick pony, but that pony is a prizewinner. You use the Migration Assistant to transfer your account and other user information from another Mac or another volume on the current Mac to this one. You need to authenticate as an Administrator to use it, but it's a pretty handy way to transfer an account without having to recreate all the preferences and other settings. When you first installed Tiger (or when you booted your nice new Tiger-based Mac for the first time), the setup utility asked you whether you wanted to transfer your information from another Mac — if you answered in the affirmative, it ran the Migration Assistant.

NetInfo Manager

 Here's another little program for system administrators on large networks or power-user administrators of shared Macs. If you're a home user who hasn't set up an empire yet, just ignore it.

Network Utility

 And here is yet another little program for system administrators on large networks. But unlike the others (the ones I've told you to ignore if you're a home user), this one can come in handy if you're a veteran Internet user. It offers common Internet utility functions such as ping, traceroute, whois, finger, and such. If those terms look like gibberish, you can ignore this program and you'll still be fine.

ODBC Administrator

 If you have to access corporate databases using Open Database Connectivity (ODBC), your database administrator will give you the settings that you need to plug into this tool. If you're not going to be doing that, skip this tool.

Printer Setup Utility

 Printer Setup Utility is the program that you use to configure your Mac to use printers and to manage print jobs. I discuss Print Center in Chapter 10.

System Profiler

 System Profiler is a little program that gives you information about your Mac. (What a concept!) If you're curious about arcane questions such as what processor your Mac has or what devices are currently connected to it, give the Profiler a try. Poke around the Commands menu and check it out; this little puppy is benign and won't hurt anything.

 If you ever have occasion to call for technical support for your Mac, software, or peripherals, you're probably going to be asked to provide information from System Profiler. So don't get rid of it just because you don't care about this kind of stuff.

Terminal

 Mac OS X is based on UNIX. If you need proof — or if you actually want to operate your Mac as the UNIX machine that it is — Terminal is the place to start.

Because UNIX is a command-line-based operating system, you use Terminal to type in your commands. You can issue commands that show a directory listing, copy and move files, search for filenames or contents, or establish or change passwords. In short, if you know what you're doing, you can do everything on the command line that you can do in Mac OS X. For most folks, that's not a desirable alternative to the windows-and-icons of the Finder window. But take my word for it; true geeks who are also Mac lovers get all misty-eyed about the combination of a command line *and* a graphical user interface.

If you do decide to tinker with Terminal and the UNIX-y innards of Mac OS X, please take some time to bone up on UNIX itself. Everything you learn about UNIX will work on your Mac OS X. A good book on the subject is *Learning the UNIX Operating System (Nutshell Handbook)* by Jerry Peek, Grace Todino, and John Strang. Or try *UNIX Visual QuickStart Guide* by Deborah S. Ray and Eric J. Ray — the UNIX book I keep on my own desk, just in case.

VoiceOver Utility

The Mac, from its very introduction in 1984, has been vocal. Concurrent with the Quadra line, Apple introduced text-to-speech capability — and Casper, its voice-recognition software — back in 1991.

VoiceOver is the next evolutionary step for text-to-speech. In addition to reading what's on the screen to you, VoiceOver integrates with your keyboard so you can navigate around the screen until you *hear* the item you're looking for. Once you're there, you can use Keyboard Access to select list items, click check boxes and radio buttons, move scrollbars and sliders, resize windows, and so on — with a simple keypress or two. (I discuss this in Chapter 13 on System Preferences.)

Apple considers the VoiceOver Utility so important that it received one of the pre-canned keyboard shortcuts: Ctrl+Option+F8.

Rather than waste a bunch of words on a feature designed for those with impaired vision, let me show you all the options in one picture, Figure 11-22. It ought to be worth at least a thousand words.

I can only give you a hint of how cool this is; you can't hear what's happening from reading this book. VoiceOver Utility Help is extensive, clear, and really shows off the power-and-cool factor. Of course, you might get the machines-are-taking-over willies when your Mac starts to talk to you or make sounds — but if you give it a try, it could change your mind.

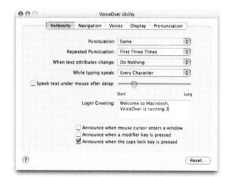
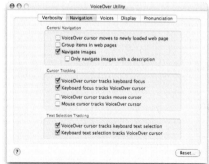
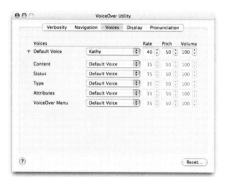

Figure 11-22:
Use these five tabs to set up your Mac to talk to you just the way you like.

Chapter 12

The Classic Environment: Like Mac OS 9, Only Better

Mac OS X is capable of running two different operating systems. Mac OS X, of course, runs your machine, but Mac OS 9.2.2 — the Mac OS version that was in use just before Mac OS X — is available too, if you need it.

Why would Apple give you two operating systems, and what in the world do you do with more than one? I explain this in the following section, and later I explain how two operating systems on one computer work together, how you can use them, and why you would want to.

Mac OS X version 10.4 Tiger requires version 9.2.2 of Mac OS to provide the Classic environment. But most (if not all) programs don't distinguish between Mac OS 9, 9.0.1, 9.0.2, 9.0.3, 9.0.4, 9.1, 9.2, 9.2.1, and 9.2.2. So when I call a program a *Mac OS 9 program,* what I mean is that it's not an OS X program and that it will (usually) run under any version of Mac OS 9.

In essence, when I talk about stuff that works with (or appears in) all versions of Mac OS 9, I say *Mac OS 9* or *Mac OS 9.x.* When I'm talking about Classic — or another feature or program that requires OS 9 version 9.2.2 — I say *Mac OS 9.2.2.*

If you're not sure whether to — or how to — install Classic on your system, see the Appendix of this book, where I discuss the different ways to install Classic.

You Can Call It Classic

Mac OS X is the software that controls your Mac (as I describe in Chapter 1) — it's the magic that starts your computer, displays the Desktop, and gives you access to all the tools you use every day to work with your files and applications.

Mac OS 9.2.2, called *Classic* when running under Mac OS X, actually runs inside an operating system (OS) *emulator* — software that does most, but not all, of what an operating system does by pretending to be one. When you launch an older application, it's as if you've booted a computer within your computer; that is, Classic first emulates the OS 9 startup process, loading all the extensions and control panels that it needs to mimic Mac OS 9.2.2 and run the application.

Retail boxed copies of Mac OS X version 10.4 Tiger don't include a Mac OS 9 installation CD. Classic is supported fully, but you have to come up with your own Mac OS 9 installation CD (or a copy of your Mac OS 9 System Folder) to use Classic. Also, Macs sold after January 1, 2003 won't be able to boot into Mac OS 9, although they will still be able to run Mac OS 9 programs in Classic.

If your current hard disk has an OS 9 System Folder on it already, you're golden. If not, and you have access to a Mac with a Mac OS 9 System Folder on it, you can copy that System Folder to a CD or DVD, and then copy it onto your startup disk.

If you have an older Mac OS 9 installation CD (Version 9.0.x or 9.1.x) lying around, you should be able to install that version and then use the OS 9 Software Update control panel to update it to 9.2.2. It's worth trying if you don't have another way of getting an OS 9 System Folder on your Mac. And, of course, you must have an OS 9 (9.2.2) System Folder on an attached hard disk to use Classic.

Running under Mac OS X, Classic behaves like any other application, just like AppleWorks, Internet Explorer, or TextEdit. With Classic running, you can use Mac OS 9.2.2's Apple menu (as long as at least one Classic program is running) and you can run Mac OS 9 applications.

You also have access (by switching to any OS X window) to your Mac OS X Home, Desktop, and applications. Finally, you can switch to another program (when a Classic program is active) by choosing it from the Application menu at the far right of the Mac OS 9.2.2 (Classic) menu bar.

Most Macs sold after January 1, 2003 can't start up in Mac OS 9. Which means the *only* way to run older software on newer Macs is via Classic.

All currently open applications — including any Classic apps — appear in your Dock for easy access.

What's so great about Classic?

If you're a Mac newbie or don't have applications or other tools that work with Mac OS 9, you may wonder why Apple would go to the trouble of including Classic in Mac OS X and why you'd want to use it. Well, I think Classic makes OS X a lot better by making available a panoply of older programs that would otherwise be relegated to the slag heap. And long-time Mac users love Classic because it provides access to programs that haven't been updated for Mac OS X. (The following section discusses this in much greater detail.)

Doin' the Classic dance

If you're a former Mac OS 9 user, you probably have lots of applications and documents that ran under Mac OS 9. For example, suppose that you have Adobe's Photoshop 6.5. You don't have the Mac OS X-native version of Photoshop (version 7, Photoshop CS, or Photoshop CS2) yet, but you do have your copy of Photoshop 6.5, which worked perfectly with Mac OS 9. Classic lets you use version 6.5 until you decide to upgrade to the OS X version of Photoshop. Are you with me? Old software, old files, new operating system.

Although you certainly will want programs written for OS X (often called *OS X-native* applications) rather than programs that run as Classic applications, sometimes you have no choice: The program you want isn't available as a native OS X app — it either runs in Classic or not at all.

When emulation *isn't* the sincerest form of flattery

Sometimes it's the only way to go — and emulators aren't just for Mac OS 9/Classic. Some, like Classic, do everything that an operating system does except boot up the computer. Some bridge the PC/Mac gap: With Pentium emulators (such as Virtual PC) for Mac OS, for example, you run Windows software on your Mac in a window that looks like, well, Windows. Other kinds of emulators — such as those used in companies in which a Mac or PC needs to connect to a mainframe or other big computer — run the mainframe's software in a window on your desktop computer. Most emulators, including Classic, enable you to use the keyboard shortcuts and commands that the emulated system (Mac OS 9, in the case of Classic) uses.

To make software work with Mac OS X, the folks who write it *(developers)* have to rewrite *(port)* OS 9 programs for Mac OS X. Or they have to create them from scratch by using special programming tools designed to create *native* Mac OS X applications. Not all developers have done this yet — partly because lots of people still use older Macs with older versions of Mac OS, and because rewriting programs costs money and takes time.

But Apple has encouraged them, and they have responded. These days, there are no new OS 9 (Classic) apps being released; 99.9 percent of software for the Mac today is OS X-native.

Working with Classic

Frankly, there's not much to working with Classic. If you launch an old program, Classic launches itself and everything just works. But, in the inimitable *For Dummies* tradition, I'm going to tell you all about it anyway. First I talk about launching Classic, then I talk about opening Classic applications, then I take a coffee break (kidding). Last but not least, I show you how to boot up with OS 9.2.2 for those occasions where Classic just won't do the job.

Launching Classic (or letting it launch itself)

You don't really have to launch Classic, per se. It launches itself whenever you open any Mac OS 9 application (or a document that belongs to that application). When you do, your Mac figures out that the program or document is a *classic,* and the Classic environment launches automatically.

That's not exactly true. Although you can't launch it in the traditional sense (by opening its icon), you can make it launch from the Classic System Preferences pane. In the upcoming "Setting Classic Preferences" section, I show you how.

The first time that you launch Classic, a dialog appears, asking you to allow Mac OS X to install some files in the Mac OS 9.2.2 System Folder (that's the folder that runs the Mac OS 9.2.2 environment). These files are needed to bridge the gap between Mac OS X and Mac OS 9.2.2, so click OK when you see the dialog.

After you launch Classic, you first see a small status window (shown in Figure 12-1) with a progress bar and a Stop button . . . just in case you change your mind and don't want Classic to launch.

Figure 12-1:
Opening
Classic
launches the
Mac OS 9.2
emulator.

After you start Classic, you can watch the emulator load by clicking the right-pointing triangle below the progress bar (under the arrow cursor in Figure 12-1). Clicking this triangle expands the window to show you the progress of the startup process (as shown in Figure 12-2). If you're a Mac OS 9 user, you'll recognize the welcome screen.

Figure 12-2:
Expand the
window and
view the
familiar OS 9
welcome
screen.

If you don't choose to view the startup process by expanding the Classic window, just wait a bit and watch the progress bar inch its way along until Mac OS 9.2.2 launches and is ready to use. At that point, the Classic window disappears, your Classic application becomes active, and you see the Mac OS 9.2.2 menu bar. You can see it all in Figure 12-3; note the way the menu bar changes to the old 9.2-style when Classic is active.

Figure 12-3:
The Classic
program,
iCalc, is
active;
the OS X
Desktop
and Finder
window (my
Home) are
inactive but
can still be
seen in the
background.

Opening a Classic app

With Classic, you can launch any pre-Mac OS X application by double-clicking its icon. If Classic isn't already running, double-clicking a Classic application automatically launches both Classic and the application. When you double-click a MacWrite (or other document) file associated with a Classic app, for example, the Classic application launches — and so does MacWrite (or whatever Classic application created the file).

You can tell when you're using a Classic program because when it's active (front-most on your screen), you see the old OS 9-style menu bar, complete with a multi-colored Apple menu in the upper-left corner of your screen. Figure 12-4 shows the old striped Apple menu and its blue OS X counterpart.

If you select the Graphite Appearance in the General System Preferences pane, the OS X Apple icon will be gray instead of the default blue. In any event, it's always a solid color in the OS X menu bar — and always rainbow-colored in the Classic menu bar.

Figure 12-4:
The Classic
Apple menu
(right) and
the OS X
Apple
menu (left).

Getting oriented ("Toto, we're not in OS X, anymore . . .")

Classic is a strange bird, combining things that are familiar from each of the two operating systems on your Mac. In the following sections, I walk you through what to expect when Classic is active.

Menu bar

The menu bar that you see when working in a Classic application is the Mac OS 9.2.2 version. You'll know it by the multi-hued Apple logo in the top-left corner. Compare that with the Mac OS X Apple, which is a solid color (either blue or gray, depending on your choice in the General System Preference Pane).

The Mac OS 9.2.2 menu bar appears when you have a Mac OS 9 application open and active. If Classic has been launched but no Classic application is running, you'll see the Mac OS X menu bar.

Okay, space is limited here (and I can't find my giant shoehorn), so instead of going over all the features you can access from the Classic menu bar, I point out just a few — and encourage you to explore them on your own. Although most of the menus on the menu bar belong to the Classic application that's open (iCalc in Figure 12-3), a couple — sometimes more — are part of Mac OS 9.2.2.

The first feature of the Mac OS 9.2.2 menu bar is the Apple menu (topped by that rainbow Apple logo, as shown in Figure 12-4). The old customizable Apple menu is among the coolest of all Mac OS 9 features — and one that lots of Mac OS X users miss. This menu contains all sorts of goodies — such as tools for working with parts of Mac OS 9 (control panels, the calculator, and so forth), as well as aliases to folders (or files, if you've put them there). The beauty of the Apple menu is that it's available in all Classic Mac applications.

Another menu I want to tell you about is the Application menu, located at the top far-right corner of the OS 9.2.2 menu bar. You'll know it by the application's name and icon — iCalc in Figure 12-5. The Application menu displays a listing of all applications that are currently running, including both Classic and Mac OS X applications.

Figure 12-5:
You can use
the OS 9
Application
menu to
switch
between
programs
when the
Classic
menu bar
is active.

Dock and icons

As in Mac OS X, the Finder's Desktop and windows are visible when you're working in the Classic environment — that includes the Dock and any icons you have on the Desktop. The Dock is pretty smart about Classic: When you open a Classic application, the application's icon appears on the Dock; the icon disappears when you quit the application. In Figure 12-6, you can see the Dock with one Classic application icon in the middle of some Mac OS X application icons. Telling them apart is tricky — the Classic application icons are, well, sometimes a little *uglier* than the Mac OS X ones. Where OS X icons have clean lines, OS 9 icons can look jaggy and . . . well . . . ugly. (That's because they're old, lower-resolution icons.) Check out Figure 12-6 to see for yourself.

Finder windows

Whether a Classic application or the Mac OS X Finder is active, you might see Mac OS X Finder windows (assuming that any are open and that your Classic application isn't blocking your view of them). You can use them to open or move files as you normally would with Mac OS X alone. If you double-click a file that belongs to a Mac OS 9 application, that program opens when you launch the Classic application.

Figure 12-6:
ResEdit's
jack-in-the-
box icon
doesn't look
so good
when it's
surrounded
by beautiful
photo-
realistic
OS X icons
on the Dock.

Getting back to OS X

To get out of Classic and back to OS X, just click the Desktop, any OS X icon in the Dock, any OS X application in the Application menu, or any Finder window, and you're back to good ol' Mac OS X as quick as a bunny.

To quit the Classic application, you'll need to use the Classic System Preference Pane as described in the next section.

Setting Classic preferences

In Chapter 13, I talk about System Preferences panes, but because the preferences for Classic are important to this discussion, I cover them here and now.

If you have multiple hard drives or partitions with Mac OS 9.2.2 installed on them, you can choose which one to use as the operating system for the Classic environment. You make that choice in the Classic pane of System Preferences. (See Chapter 13 for more on System Preferences.) Just select the drive or partition (mine is TigerDisk in Figure 12-7), and the next time that you launch Classic, it uses that volume's copy of Mac OS 9.2.2. Volumes that don't include Mac OS 9.2.2 appear dimmed in the Preferences window.

By selecting the Start Classic When You Log In check box, you tell Mac OS X to do just that. The advantage is that you won't have to wait a minute or two for Classic to launch the first time you launch a Classic application. The disadvantage here is that Classic uses a hefty amount of RAM and other system resources.

Figure 12-7:
Classic
System
Preferences.

If you select the Warn Before Starting Classic check box, when you open a Classic application or a document owned by a Classic application, OS X will present a dialog warning you that Classic is about to start up and offers the choice of starting or not starting it, as shown in Figure 12-8.

Figure 12-8:
OS X tells
you that
Classic is
starting and
asks what
you'd like
to do.

The third check box — Show Classic Status in Menu Bar — adds a useful Classic status indicator and menu to the right side of your menu bar, as shown in Figure 12-9.

Running Classic when you don't need it can slow OS X's performance, so I prefer to keep Start Classic When You Log In disabled — and Warn Before Starting Classic enabled. Classic then only runs when I'm sure I want and need it — and never when I don't.

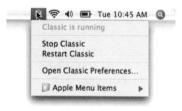

Figure 12-9:
The Classic status menu adds a useful shortcut to your OS 9 Apple Menu Items.

Note the three buttons at the bottom of the System Preferences Classic pane's Start/Stop tab. (The last two are used mostly when the Classic environment crashes, freezes, or otherwise acts improperly.)

- ✔ **Stop/Start:** Launches Classic without first launching a Classic program. (If Classic is not running, this button toggles to Start.)

In the earlier section "Launching Classic (or letting it launch itself)," I offer this tip: *Although you can't launch it (Classic) in the traditional sense (by opening its icon), you can make it launch by using the Classic System Preferences pane.* The Start/Stop button is what I was talking about.

- ✔ **Restart:** Restarts Classic (big surprise), which is like rebooting OS 9.2.2 without having to reboot OS X.

You can continue to work in OS X — listen to iTunes, edit movies in iMovie, surf the Web, get your mail, and so on — while Classic starts or restarts. Which is just another reason OS X is better.

- ✔ **Force Quit:** Forces the Classic environment to quit, even if it's crashed or frozen.

Getting more info on Classic

To get the most from Classic, take a look at the version of this book that was written especially for Mac OS 9: *Mac OS 9 For Dummies* (well, duh!). I'm very proud of it. Read the chapters on the Apple menu and those that cover the contents of the System Folder. You'll discover a lot more about the wonders available to you in the Classic environment.

Booting from Mac OS 9.2.2

Before I finish with Classic, here's one more thing you may want to know — how to boot your Mac so it runs OS 9.2.2 instead of OS X.

As I mention earlier in the chapter, if you bought a Mac after January 1, 2003, it may not be capable of booting OS 9 at all. If that's the case, Classic is the only way you can run OS 9 software.

And as I mention earlier in the chapter, some programs — mostly games — just won't work when you try to run them in the Classic environment under OS X. When that happens, you'll have to start up your Mac with OS 9.2.2 if you want to use that program.

No problem; it's a snap. Here's how:

1. **Open System Preferences by clicking its icon in the Dock or choosing System Preferences from the menu.**

2. **Click the Startup Disk icon to open the Startup Disk pane.**

3. **Click a Mac OS 9.2.2 icon to select it, as shown in Figure 12-10.**

   If you've installed OS 9.2.2 on two or more volumes, you'll see two or more OS 9 System Folders; select the one you want to boot from.

Figure 12-10: Choose Mac OS 9.2.2 to start up your Mac (while running Mac OS X).

You can restart most Macs in *Target Disk mode* by holding down the T key during startup. When your Mac is in Target Disk mode, it acts like a FireWire hard drive — and can be connected to another computer via a FireWire cable for fast file transfers. What's new is that Mac OS X 10.4 has a button in the Startup Disk Preference pane that lets you restart in Target Disk mode. I guess it's there in case you forget the keyboard shortcut (holding down the T key during startup).

4. **Restart your Mac by choosing Restart from the menu or by clicking the Restart button.**

   That's all there is to it. When your Mac comes back to life, you'll be running Mac OS 9.2.2.

If you have both OS 9.2.2 and OS X on the same volume or disk, be careful *not* to rename any of OS X's folders or throw any of OS X's folders in the Trash while you're running OS 9.2.2. The results could be catastrophic — you could easily render OS X inoperable.

When your Mac runs OS 9.2.2 and you want to run OS X again, you can't open the Startup Disk System Preferences pane because it's part of Mac OS X and it isn't available while running OS 9.2.2. Now what? Again, no problem. You do it the old-fashioned way — by using the Startup Disk control panel; just follow these steps:

1. **Open the Startup Disk control panel by choosing Control Panels⇨Startup Disk from the menu.**

2. **Click the folder representing Mac OS X, as shown in Figure 12-11.**

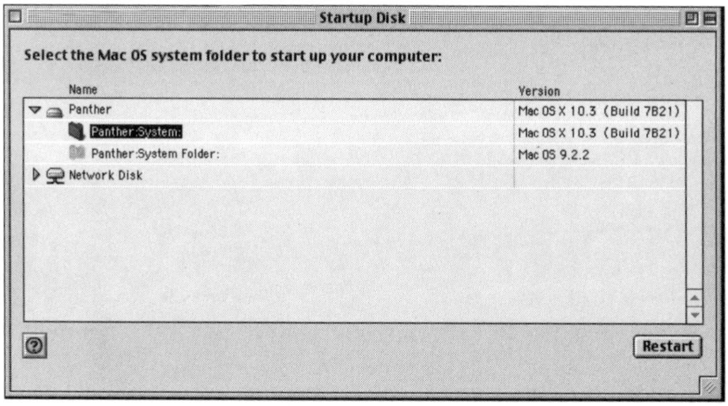

Figure 12-11:
Choose
Mac OS X to
start up your
Mac (while
running
Mac OS
9.2.2).

Startup Disk	
Select the Mac OS system folder to start up your computer:	
Name	**Version**
▽ 🗀 Panther	Mac OS X 10.3 (Build 7B21)
📄 Panther:System:	Mac OS X 10.3 (Build 7B21)
📁 Panther:System Folder:	Mac OS 9.2.2
▷ 🖥 Network Disk	
⑦	**Restart**

3. **Click the Restart button in the Startup Disk window.**

   That's it. In a few moments, you'll be up and running in Mac OS X.

Chapter 13

What Your Mac Prefers

*E*veryone works a bit differently, and we all like to use our Macs in a certain way. System Preferences is the place in Mac OS X where you can set options that are just right for you. You can set everything from the appearance of your screen to the kind of network or Internet connection that you have — and a whole lot more. In this chapter, I take you on a tour of all the Mac OS X System Preferences panes. Hang on; it's gonna be a long, but informative, ride — and you'll end up with a Mac that works the way you want it to.

Introducing System Preferences

You find System Preferences on the Apple (⌘) menu and in the Dock. Choose System Preferences from the ⌘ menu or click it in the Dock to get a look at all the options that I discuss in this chapter. Check out all the features you can change from the System Preferences window, as shown in Figure 13-1.

What you see in Figure 13-1 is the System Preferences window. But when you click any of the icons here, the bottom part of the window changes to reflect the options for the icon that you click. When this happens, I call the bottom part of the window a *pane.* So, for example, when you click the Date & Time icon in the System Preferences window, the bottom part of the window becomes the Date & Time System Preference pane.

Figure 13-1:
The System
Preferences
window:
Change
your world.

System Preferences are similar to those of the OS 9 (or — gasp — Windows) Control Panels, but OS 9 Control Panels (for the most part) load at start up, displaying an icon on the screen when they loaded. System Preference panes don't load at startup; they're just there.

Just where? The actual files for Preference Panes are stored in the Preference Panes folder, in the Library folder in the System folder. (*Note:* This is the OS X System folder, small *f*, not the OS 9 System Folder-with-a-capital-F.) If you choose to install third-party preference panes, they can go either in the Preference Panes folder in the Library folder at the top level of your startup disk (if you want them to be available to all users) or in the Preference Panes folder in the Library in your Home folder (if you want to keep them to yourself).

Some System Preferences relate to topics I cover in other chapters. I'll let you know any time I skip a preference that you can read about in another chapter.

In all previous versions of OS X, the System Preferences window had a customizable toolbar, and I ranted about Apple's choices in the default population of said toolbar. Maybe they got tired of that rant, because they totally eliminated the System Preferences toolbar in Tiger. Cool beans.

Using System Preferences

Before I examine the items in the System Preferences window, I need to explain a couple of things about using them. This info applies to all System Preferences, so listen up.

To use a System Preference, just click it once to open its pane. You can double-click if that habit is ingrained in your mouse finger, but there's no need.

Okay, so you've finished working with a System Preferences pane, but you want to open another one. You could simply close the one that you've been working on, or you could cut to the chase by clicking the Show All button, located at the far left of the top row of icons on the System Preferences window (as shown in Figure 13-1). Clicking the Show All button returns the icons for all available System Preferences to view on the screen. You can also press ⌘+L as a Show All Preferences keyboard shortcut.

Here's an even more convenient way: Choose the System Preferences that you want from the View menu. All the icons that you see in Figure 13-1 also have an entry on this menu; choose one, and its System Preference pane appears immediately.

Here's another nifty tip: You can get rid of the categories altogether and display the icons in alphabetical order. As a bonus, it makes the System Preferences window roughly 25 percent smaller on-screen.

When you choose View⇨Organize Alphabetically, the categories disappear, the window shrinks, and the icons are alphabetized, as shown in Figure 13-2.

Figure 13-2:
Alphabetical
or cat-
egorical —
how do you
prefer
your Pre-
ferences?

To switch from alphabetical view back to category view, choose View⇨Organize by Categories.

Unlocking a preference

Many System Preferences have to be unlocked before you can use them. That's because some of these settings are applicable for *all* users — so they require an Administrator password. After all, you can't have just any user of your Mac change the Network configuration and break it for everyone. See Figure 13-3 to see what a locked preference looks like. Notice the locked lock icon in the lower-left corner and that everything is grayed out and unavailable. Now compare that with Figure 13-4, where the lock has been unlocked (by supplying an administrator user name and password) and all items are enabled.

You don't have to unlock all System Preferences to change them, just some of them. When I come to a System Preference that must be unlocked before you can use it, I'll let you know up front. Deal? Good.

Figure 13-3:
A locked
System
Preferences
pane.

Only users with Administrator privileges can unlock some System Preferences. (See Chapter 14 for more info on administrators and permissions.)

To unlock a preference, do the following:

1. **Click the lock icon in the lower-left corner of the System Preferences pane (also shown in the margin).**

   Mac OS X responds with an Authenticate dialog in which you enter your user name and password.

   The user name and password that you use here must be a user with administrator privileges on this Mac. If your user account isn't set up with administrator privileges, you can't unlock locked panes or change them. You'll need to supply an administrator's user name and password — or learn to live with it the way it is.

   The first user that you create with OS X (when you first install it) is always an administrator.

2. **Enter this user information and then click OK.**

   Mac OS X unlocks the System Preference that you're working with.

In Figure 13-4, you see the Sharing System Preferences pane after being unlocked. Notice that you can now make changes to it; before it was unlocked, all its options were grayed out and impossible to change.

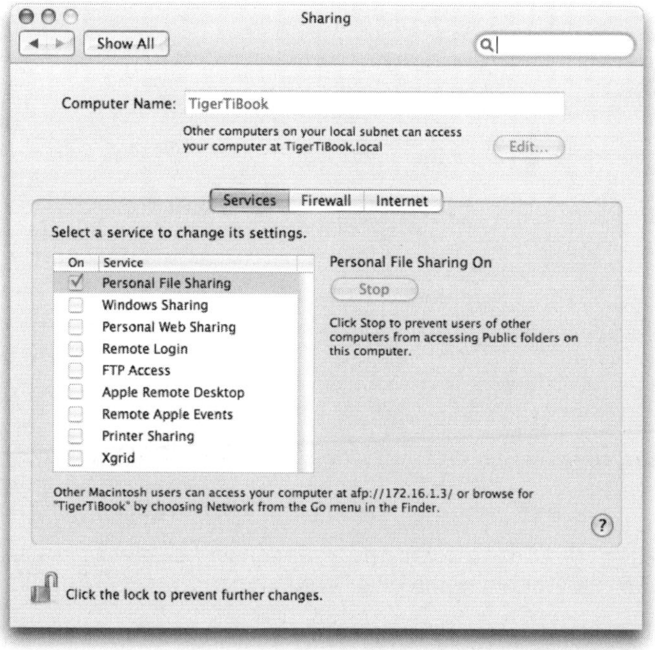

Figure 13-4:
An unlocked System Preference pane displays its options.

(Screenshot of the Sharing System Preferences pane)

Sharing

Computer Name: TigerTiBook

Other computers on your local subnet can access your computer at TigerTiBook.local   Edit...

Services | Firewall | Internet

Select a service to change its settings.

On	Service
✓	Personal File Sharing
	Windows Sharing
	Personal Web Sharing
	Remote Login
	FTP Access
	Apple Remote Desktop
	Remote Apple Events
	Printer Sharing
	Xgrid

Personal File Sharing On

Stop

Click Stop to prevent users of other computers from accessing Public folders on this computer.

Other Macintosh users can access your computer at afp://172.16.1.3/ or browse for "TigerTiBook" by choosing Network from the Go menu in the Finder.

Click the lock to prevent further changes.

Locking a preference

To relock a System Preferences pane (after you unlock it), simply click the lock icon again. The pane locks itself instantly.

Setting Preferences

Ready to dig into each of the System Preferences? Great. I start with the first category (Personal, as shown in Figure 13-1) and work from left to right across the screen.

Personal preferences

The following preference panes are displayed in the Personal category.

Appearance

In the Appearance pane, you can choose specific aspects of how your Mac looks and feels (see Figure 13-5).

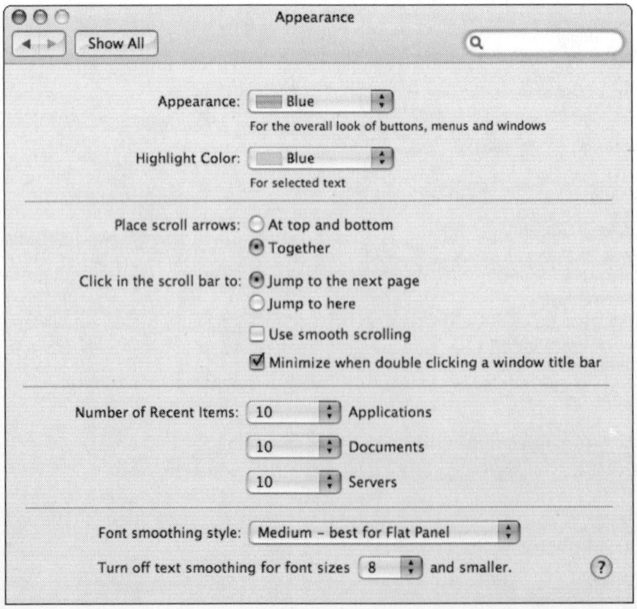

Figure 13-5:
The Appearance System Preferences pane.

Appearance

Show All

Appearance: Blue
For the overall look of buttons, menus and windows

Highlight Color: Blue
For selected text

Place scroll arrows: ○ At top and bottom
● Together

Click in the scroll bar to: ● Jump to the next page
○ Jump to here

☐ Use smooth scrolling

☑ Minimize when double clicking a window title bar

Number of Recent Items: 10 Applications

10 Documents

10 Servers

Font smoothing style: Medium – best for Flat Panel

Turn off text smoothing for font sizes 8 and smaller.

Appearance options

Computers don't care about appearances, but if you want your Mac to look a bit more festive (or, for that matter, businesslike), you can use these menus:

- ✔ **Appearance pop-up menu:** Use choices from this menu to choose from different appearances, changing the overall look of buttons and window controls (the jellybeans in the scroll bars).

  Apple, however, in its infinite wisdom, provides only two choices — Blue and Graphite.

- ✔ **Highlight Color pop-up menu:** From here, you can choose the color that text becomes surrounded by when you select it in a document or in an icon's name in a Finder window. This time Apple isn't so restrictive. You have seven highlight colors to choose from, plus Other, which brings up a color picker from which you can choose almost any color.

Scroll bar behavior

The Place Scroll Arrows radio buttons let you choose whether you have the traditional single arrow at either end or the default (introduced in OS 8) of both arrows together at the bottom or to the right of the scroll bars.

Select from two radio buttons next to the Click in the Scroll Bar To heading to move your view of a window either up or down by a page (the default behavior for OS 9) or to the position in the document roughly proportionate to where you clicked in the scroll bar.

Select the Jump to Here radio button if you often work with long (multi-page) documents. You'll find it quite handy for navigating long documents. And don't forget — the Page Down key on your keyboard does the same thing as selecting the Jump to the Next Page choice, so you'll lose nothing by selecting Jump to Here.

Using smooth scrolling makes documents more legible while you scroll. Give it a try; if you think it's making things feel sluggish, turn it off.

Minimize When Double-Clicking a Window Title Bar does just what it says — it shrinks a window to the Dock when you double-click its title bar. And yes, the yellow gumdrop button does the exact same thing.

The Number of Recent Items pop-up menus control how many applications, documents, and servers are remembered in your ⌘⇨Recent Items submenu.

The Font Smoothing Style pop-up menu offers four settings for anti-aliasing (smoothing) fonts on screen. The categories are

- ✔ **Standard – Best for CRT:** You know, your standard, clunky tube-type monitor. If your monitor isn't a flat-panel LCD, this is probably your best bet.

- ✔ **Light:** Just a hint of the essence of smoothing for your text.

- ✔ **Medium – Best for Flat-Panel:** For those sleek, flat-panel monitors and notebooks, too.

- ✔ **Strong:** Mondo-smoothing. I happen to like it on my flat-panel display, but you might not.

Ignore Apple's editorial comments and try all four. Then choose the one that looks best to your eyes.

The Turn off Text Smoothing for Font Sizes *x* and Smaller pop-up menu (where *x* is the pop-up menu setting) does just what it says. Fonts that size and smaller are no longer *anti-aliased* (smoothed) when displayed.

Dashboard & Exposé

Exposé is a cool feature, introduced with Panther (OS X 10.3). Dashboard is Tiger's glitzy interface to the widgets I mention in Chapter 11 when discussing the Applications folder.

Exposé shows you all open windows (or all the windows open in the application you're currently using) by rearranging the windows on-screen and "graying out" everything else. It can also hide all windows so you can see your desktop (what a concept). Both features can be controlled via keyboard or mouse, and this preference pane (Figure 13-6) is where you tell Tiger how you want to access Dashboard and Exposé.

Figure 13-6:
The Dashboard & Exposé preference pane.

By default, you use the function keys to choose the way Exposé displays your windows:

- ✔ To see all open windows, press F9.
- ✔ To see all open windows belonging to the current application, press F10.
- ✔ To hide all open windows and display the desktop, press F11.
- ✔ To summon forth the Dashboard, press F12.

A picture is worth a thousand words, so take a gander at Figure 13-7, where I've got several applications running with multiple windows open in each of them.

While using Exposé, if you point to a window but don't click, the window's title appears. If you click any window — even one that's grayed out — at any time, Exposé deactivates and that window becomes active.

The four Active Screen Corners pop-up menus allow you to configure the corners of your screen to activate and deactivate Exposé and Dashboard features.

The four Keyboard pop-up menus let you change the keys Exposé and Dashboard use from F9, 10, 11, and 12, or disable the keyboard commands completely (by choosing the dash in any of the pop-up menus).

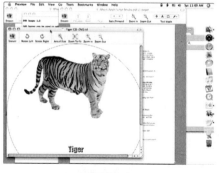

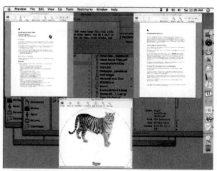
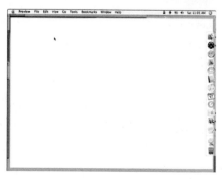

Figure 13-7: Clockwise from top left: Exposé off; F9 — All open windows; F11 — Desktop only; F10 — All applications windows (Preview here).

The four Mouse pop-up menus let you assign alternate mouse buttons to activate or deactivate Exposé and Dashboard features, for those of us who use multibutton mice.

Desktop & Screen Saver

 The Desktop & Screen Saver pane lets you set your Desktop color or picture, as well as choose a screen saver for your Mac.

Desktop

Click the Desktop tab to specify a desktop picture or pattern. Apple provides a number of collections; you choose one via the Collection pop-up menu, or you can choose a different folder of images if you want. You can also drag an image file into the *well* (that indented box in the upper-left corner of the pane).

When you choose a picture, from your Pictures folder or elsewhere, a pop-up menu appears to the right of the well, allowing you to specify how you want the picture displayed. You can

- ✔ **Tile** multiple copies of the image to fill the screen.

- ✔ **Fill Screen** enlarges the image, if necessary, until it fills the screen (this might result in some clipping if the image and your screen don't have the same proportions).

- ✔ **Stretch to fill screen** keeps everything in view, but will distort the image if the image and screen don't have the same proportions.

- ✔ **Center** just places the image in the center of the screen and, if it is smaller than the screen, provides it with a surrounding color that you specify from the Color Picker.

When you select a folder of images, you can tell Tiger to change the desktop picture at predefined intervals (Change Picture Every *xx* check box and pop-up menu). You can even click the Random order check box so you won't always get the pictures in the same order.

Screen Saver

Click the Screen Saver tab to choose a screen-saver module.

Mac OS X comes with several screen-saver modules. To see what the selected module looks like in action, click the Test button. Press any key to end the test.

To set up the screen saver, first choose a screen saver from the list on the left side of the pane. Next, drag the Start Screen Saver slider to the number of minutes you want the Mac to wait before activating the screen saver.

Click the Use Random Screen Saver check box to have your Mac choose a new screen saver at random each time the screen saver kicks in.

You can require a password to wake your Mac from sleep or a screen saver. This option appears in the Security System Preference pane as a check box: Require a Password to Wake This Computer from Sleep or Screen Saver.

Finally, click the Hot Corners button to choose which corner(s) of your screen activates the screen saver and which deactivates it. Now when you move your mouse to a selected corner, you activate or deactivate the screen saver.

That's it. You're done!

If you like Screen Savers/Effects, find plenty more available at your favorite downloadable software repository (mine's `www.versiontracker.com`). Many are free, and some cost a few bucks. Some of those, like Marine Aquarium in Figure 13-8 (from `www.order-n-dev.com`), are even worth paying for.

Figure 13-8:
Search the
Web for
other cool
screen
savers.

I paid my $21.95, and it was worth every penny. It's so lifelike, I sometimes believe those are real fish in my monitor. Plus, unlike other fish I've owned, these never float belly-up (or explode from overeeding). I love this saver/effect; it's the only one I use anymore.

Dock

 I cover the Dock and its preferences in great detail in Chapter 2. Rather than waste any more trees, I'll just move along to . . . .

International

 If you're in the U.S., you might assume that you don't need to set anything in the International System Preferences pane. After all, you chose to see your Mac's menus and commands in U.S. English when you first installed Mac OS X, right? But wait — the International System Preferences pane has more in it than just a choice of language. Here's where you can set date and time formats — probably the most useful feature for U.S. folks — and yes, you can choose a new language here, too.

The International System Preferences pane has three tabs: Language, Formats, and Input Menu. I describe each in the following sections.

Language

This is where you set your Mac's order of preference for languages used in applications. Choose the languages you want your Mac to use by clicking the Edit button and checking or unchecking check boxes; to organize your choices, drag an entry up or down in the list on the left. If an application uses the first language you indicate in this list, you see the application's commands and menus in that chosen language. If your first language choice isn't available, the next option is used, and so on.

The Order of Sorted Lists pop-up menu lets you select a language whose sorting order will be used for lists.

The Word Break pop-up menu is where you specify the language whose rules determine where words begin and end so your software knows (for example) where to wrap a line of text.

Formats

First choose your present location from the Region pop-up menu. Then you select a format for the way dates, times, and numbers are displayed by clicking appropriate Customize button. A sheet appears, showing all the options available. Make your choices and click OK.

When specifying a date format, you can also choose which calendar system to employ. Some of the supplied calendars include Gregorian (the one we think of as standard in the U.S.), Hebrew, Japanese, and Islamic.

Note that when you change an option in any of these sheets, the way it will look if you click OK appears in a gray rectangle near the bottom of the sheet.

In the Numbers section, you'll also see a drop-down list for specifying the currency units you wish to employ by default, and it is quite a list. You can easily find some crossword puzzle answers in this collection. Additionally, there is a pop-up menu where you specify your preferred units of measurement: U.S. and Metric are the choices. (What's called U.S. used to be called "English," but the U.S. is the last holdout from the worldwide conversion to the metric system.)

Input Menu

Use the Input Menu tab to select keyboard layouts, input methods, and palettes that appear in the input menu, which you can display in the menu bar by clicking the Show Input Menu in Menu Bar check box, as shown in Figure 13-9.

While many users will never need an alternative keyboard layout, two of the palettes — the Character and Keyboard Viewer — can be quite handy, as shown in Figure 13-10.

Figure 13-9: The Input Menu tab in the International pane (left) and the Input Menu menu (right).

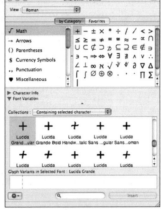
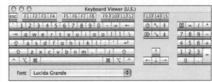

Figure 13-10:
The
Character
Palette
(left) and
Keyboard
Viewer
palette
(right).

Do not under any circumstances click the Options button on the Input Menu tab unless you have good reason to use foreign keyboard layouts on occasion. The ⌘+Option+spacebar keyboard shortcut, when turned on, can cause unpredictable behavior if (later on) you forget that you turned it on. Use this thingy with caution — especially if you use Photoshop (which uses ⌘+Option+ spacebar as the shortcut for Zoom Out).

Security

At the top of the pane, you see the FileVault section. I really can't explain what FileVault does any more clearly than the expository text. If Apple explained all their features as well as they do FileVault, I'd probably have to look for other work — but they don't (as can be seen even in the bottom half of this pane).

In addition to FileVault, this pane offers five check box items that deal with your Mac's security:

✔ **Require Password to Wake This Computer from Sleep or Screen Saver:**
This item causes your Mac to require a password to wake it from sleep or to dismiss the screen saver.

Turning this preference on won't prevent another user from turning off the computer, restarting it, and then logging into their account. If you think this sort of thing could happen, be sure to save your work before you leave your computer.

✔ **Disable Automatic Login:** This item causes your Mac to require every user to provide a user name and password each time the Mac is started up or restarted.

If you want your Mac to start up to the Finder without first asking for a user name or password, select the Automatically Log In option in the Accounts preference pane — and (of course) keep this item unchecked.

✔ **Require Password to Unlock Each Secure System Preference:** This item locks all the System Preference panes that affect all users so they cannot be changed without an administrator name and password.

✔ **Log Out After __ Minutes of Inactivity:** This item causes your Mac to log out automatically after a set number of minutes pass without any keyboard or mouse activity.

✔ **Use Secure Virtual Memory:** This item encrypts your virtual-memory storage and decrypts the data when it's paged back into RAM.

Spotlight

This preference pane is your control center for the incredibly slick (and fast) searching technology that Apple has given the name Spotlight. Using Spotlight, you can find anything on your Mac virtually instantaneously.

Yep, this is a new feature. Because Apple has provided hooks to Spotlight, applications also have access to the fast searching, as Apple shows off in the Tiger versions of Mail, Address, iCal, and other applications. You can even use Spotlight searches in Open dialogs and Save sheets.

The Spotlight pane's two tabs (Figure 13-11) let you control which categories are displayed and in what order (Search Results) and locations that aren't to be searched (Privacy).

Figure 13-11:
Search Results lets you specify which results get shown in what order and Privacy lets you specify which locations not to search.

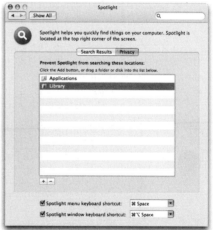

Hardware preferences

Here's where you teach your Mac to play nice with all the gadgets connected to it. The following preference panes are displayed in the Hardware category.

CDs & DVDs

 Introduced with Mac OS X version 10.2 Jaguar, this preference pane lets you decide what your Mac should do when you insert a blank or pre-recorded CD or DVD. Choose here from five pop-up menus; you can also set your Mac to launch certain applications, run AppleScripts, or nothing at all.

Displays

 This pane has two tabs — Display and Color — to set various options for your monitor.

Display

The Colors pop-up menu lets you choose the number of colors your monitor displays.

The list of resolutions governs how much stuff you see on your monitor. The smaller the numbers, the less you'll see and the bigger you'll see it. Bigger numbers mean you see more, but it's smaller. Got it? Most monitors and video cards support multiple resolutions, and some also allow you to choose from multiple refresh rates.

Many monitors offer settings to adjust their brightness; some also enable you to adjust their gamma settings in this tab. If your monitor supports these features, you will see Brightness and/or Gamma Control slide bars in this tab. If you have these features, adjust them the way that looks best to your eyes.

The Show Displays in Menu Bar check box gives you the little menu that you see at the upper-right of most of the figures in this book, so you can change the resolution and color depth without opening the System Preferences application.

If you have a laptop, you see a Detect Displays button; if you have a desktop Mac, you won't have that button. It does just what its name implies: When you connect an external display to your laptop Mac, if that display isn't recognized automatically (which it usually is), you can click this button (or choose Detect Displays from the Displays menu), and the monitor will be instantly recognized without restarting!

 This OS X-only detail is good to remember if you use several different external displays or projection systems in different locations. It saves you from shutting down/restarting and makes the whole process a little sweeter. Just click and you're done.

Color

Choose a pre-configured profile for your monitor (for Apple-brand monitors) and calibrate your display (any brand, including Apple). To calibrate, click the Calibrate button; an assistant will walk you through the process.

Arrange

Finally, if you have two video cards or are using a PowerBook and external monitor together, you'll see a third tab called Arrange. Drag the little pictures that represent your monitors to arrange your screens. Make the on-screen arrangement match the physical set up of your monitors as closely as possible. If you want to place the menu bar on the other screen, drag the little picture of the menu bar from one little screen to the other.

The Arrange tab appears only on PowerBooks with an external display connected to them, and on desktop Macs with either more than one graphics card installed or more than one monitor connected to a graphics card (lots of G4 and G5 desktop Macs contain video cards that can support two monitors simultaneously).

Energy Saver

All Macs are Energy Star-compliant (and have been for years), allowing you to preset your machine to turn itself off at a specific time or after a specified idle period. It offers three tabs: Sleep, Schedule, and Options.

If you have a battery-powered Mac, you'll also have a check box to enable or disable the battery-status indicator in the menu bar.

Sleep

To enable Sleep mode, move the slider to the desired amount of time. You can choose any number between 1 minute and 3 hours, or turn Sleep off entirely by moving the slider all the way to the right to Never.

You can also set separate sleep times for your Mac's display and choose whether to let your hard disk go to sleep if it supports sleep mode. Setting the display to sleep might come in handy if you want your Mac to keep doing what it's doing and you don't need to use the monitor. The hard drive's sleep option is less useful unless you've got a PowerBook or an iBook. Checking this option forces your hard drive to sleep after a few minutes of inactivity, which saves you some battery power.

To activate display sleep, select the Put the Display to Sleep when Computer is Inactive for check box and then drag the slider to the idle-time interval you want.

To wake up your Mac from its sleep, merely move your mouse or press any key on the keyboard.

Drag the slider to 30 or 45 minutes for sleep; remember to turn off your Mac manually when you're not going to need it for a day or more.

Schedule

To start up, shut down, or put your Mac to sleep at a predetermined time, check the appropriate check box and choose the appropriate choices from the Schedule tab's pop-up menus.

Options

The Options tab is home to a small collection of useful settings. On this tab, you'll find check boxes telling the Mac to wake up automatically when the modem detects an incoming call (useful for fax software), to automatically wake for Ethernet network administrative access (handy in a corporate setting where an IT person maintains system configurations), and to restart automatically after a power failure.

PowerBook and iBook users get additional Energy Saver options — including whether to display a battery-status indicator in the menu bar near the clock, as well as a pop-up menu called Processor Performance that offers two options: Highest and Reduced.

Choose Highest when AC power is connected and Reduced when you need to conserve battery power.

Keyboard & Mouse

This pane lets you modify how your keyboard and mouse respond. It offers three tabs (plus a fourth tab — Trackpad — for iBooks and PowerBooks):

Keyboard

Drag the Key Repeat Rate slider to set how fast a key repeats when you hold it down. This feature comes into play when (for example) you hold down the dash (-) key to make a line or the asterisk (*) key to make a divider.

Drag the Delay Until Repeat slider to set how long you have to hold down a key before it starts repeating.

You can type in the box at the bottom of the window to test your settings before exiting this tab.

The Show Eject in Menu Bar check box lets you add an Eject menu to your menu bar, which can come in handy when you've got a recalcitrant disk that doesn't want to come out of your CD or DVD drive.

Mouse

The Mouse tab is where you set your mouse speed and double-click delays. Move the Tracking Speed slider to change the relationship between hand movement of the mouse and cursor movement on the screen. A faster tracking speed setting (moving the slider to the right) sends your cursor squirting across the screen with a mere flick of the wrist; slower mouse speed settings (moving the slider to the left) make the cursor crawl across in seemingly slow motion, even when your hand is flying. Set this setting as fast as you can stand it — I like the fastest speed. Try it: You might like it.

The Double-Click Speed setting determines how close together two clicks must be for the Mac to interpret them as a double-click and not as two separate clicks. Move the slider arrow to the leftmost setting (Very Slow) for the slowest. With this setting, you can double-click at an almost leisurely pace. The rightmost position (Fast) is the fastest setting, which I prefer. The middle area of the slider represents a double-click speed somewhere in the middle.

Changes in the Mouse System Preferences pane take place immediately, so you should definitely play around a little and see what settings feel best for you. You can test the effect of your changes to the Double-Click Speed setting in the Double-Click Here to Test text box at the bottom of the window before you close this preference pane.

Trackpad

If you have a portable Mac with a trackpad (the mouse that is not a mouse) — such as a PowerBook or iBook — you'll see an additional tab — Trackpad — where you can set the tracking speed and double-clicking behavior of your trackpad.

Note: If you have a PowerBook or iBook, there will also be a tab for trackpad settings with the same two settings and options to specify just what tasks the trackpad can be used for, such as tapping it rather than pressing the button when you want to click something. You can even tell OS X to ignore the trackpad while you're typing. But all these goodies are only for notebook Macs — the only kind that include trackpads.

Keyboard Shortcuts

The Keyboard Shortcuts tab was a new feature in Panther and a welcome one at that. Tiger evolves Keyboard Shortcuts to something even better and brighter. It lets you add, delete, or change keyboard shortcuts for many operating system functions such as taking a picture of the screen and using the keyboard to choose menu and dock items. It also allows you to add, delete, or change keyboard shortcuts for your applications.

To change a shortcut, double-click it and then hold down the new shortcut keys. To add a new shortcut, click the + button; to delete a shortcut, click the – button.

The Turn on Full Keyboard Access check box lets you use the keyboard to access all the controls in a window or dialog, which lets you use the Tab key to select buttons and check boxes, allowing you to avoid using the mouse for the most part, if that's your preference.

When Full Keyboard Access is enabled, you press the key combination specified to use the Tab and arrow keys to move among items in the menu bar, Dock, any window's toolbar, or most palettes (floating windows). If you really hate to use your mouse or if your mouse is broken, these keyboard shortcuts can come in really handy. I tend to use them more on my PowerBook when I'm traveling and don't have room to hook up a mouse because I really don't like using the built-in mouse-thing (technically called a *trackpad*).

Print & Fax

This pane lets you configure printers and the built-in Fax capability. It offers three tabs: Printing, Faxing, and Sharing. Also see Chapter 10, which is all about printing.

Printing

Click the Printer Setup button to launch the Printer Setup Utility and configure a new printer.

The Selected Printer in Print Dialog pop-up menu lets you choose which printer is selected by default in Print dialogs and sheets.

The Default Paper Size in Page Setup pop-up menu lets you choose the default paper size your Mac will use in Page Setup dialogs and sheets.

Faxing

Click the Receive Faxes on This Computer check box to enable faxing. Type your fax line's phone number into the My Fax Number field. Set the number of rings you want the software to wait before answering a fax call in the Answer after __ Rings field. Click the Save To check box to enable a pop-up menu that lets you select which folder incoming faxes will be saved to. Click the Email To check box to send an email to yourself (or anyone) when a fax arrives. Click the Print on Printer check box to print incoming faxes automatically (which you choose from the pop-up menu next to the check box).

Sharing

The Share These Printers with Other Computers check box allows printers connected to this Mac to be made available to other Macs on the local-area network. When you activate this check box, the printers directly connected to this Mac are listed in the list box — and you can select other check boxes for the ones you want to share.

Finally, the Let Others Send Faxes through This Computer check box allows other Macs on the local-area network to send faxes through this Mac.

Sound

This pane controls the way your Mac plays and records sound — and offers three tabs: Sound Effects, Output, and Input.

To make your Mac's volume louder or softer, use the Output Volume slider at the bottom of the window. Select the Mute check box to turn off all sound. Click the Show Volume in Menu Bar check box to add a volume control menu to your menu bar.

These three items appear at the bottom of the Sound pane no matter which of the three tabs is active.

Sound Effects

Choose an alert (beep) sound by clicking its name; set its volume using the Alert Volume slider control.

You can also specify the output device through which they play (if you have more than one) by selecting from the Play Alerts and Sound Effects Through pop-up menu.

The Play User Interface Sound Effects check box turns on sound effects for actions such as dragging a file to the Trash.

The Play Feedback When Volume Keys Are Pressed check box tells your Mac to beep once for each press of the increase or decrease volume keys (usually the volume keys on a standard Apple extended keyboard, but the F4 and F5 keys on laptops and other keyboards).

A shortcut to the Sound System Preference pane is to press Option while pressing any of the volume keys.

You can find new sounds on the Internet at your favorite shareware archive (www.versiontracker.com and www.macupdate.com are the two that I like best).

To install new sounds, move them into the Sounds folder inside the Library folder at root level on your hard drive if you want them to be available to all users of this Mac. Or put them in the Sounds folder inside the Library folder in your home folder if you want to be the only one that can use them. (See Chapter 6 for more info on these two Library folders.)

Output

Use the Balance slider in the Output tab to make either stereo speaker louder than the other.

Two that won't show (unless . . .)

Two more preference panes might appear in the Hardware section, but only if your Mac has the appropriate hardware connected to it.

Bluetooth

Bluetooth is wireless networking for low-bandwidth peripherals introduced in Mac OS X version 10.2 Jaguar. If your Mac is equipped with a Bluetooth adapter, you can synchronize wirelessly with phones and Palm devices, print wirelessly to Bluetooth printers, and who knows what else (it's very new technology).

Bluetooth is designed to work with iSync — Apple's synchronization technology — to let you synchronize your address book, calendar, and bookmarks wirelessly with Bluetooth phones such as the Sony Ericsson T68i.

Ink

Ink is Mac OS X's built-in handwriting recognition engine, also introduced in Version 10.2 Jaguar. If you have a stylus and tablet connected to your Mac, just turn it on in this pane and you can write anywhere you can type with the keyboard.

The Ink pane is another one you'll only see if you have one of the handful of tablets that Ink supports connected to your Mac.

All currently supported tablets come from Wacom (`www.wacom.com`) with prices starting under $100 for a small wireless stylus and tablet.

Internet & Network preferences

The following preference panes are displayed in the Internet & Network category. Also see Chapter 9, which covers networking and the Internet.

.Mac

The .Mac pane lets you configure your .Mac subscription and iDisk (if you have them). It offers four tabs:

✔ **Account:** If you have a .Mac account, you can type your name and password here so that you don't have to type them every time that you use your iDisk or Mail. (See Chapter 9's section on .Mac if you want to know what that's all about.)

Click the Sign Up button, and your Web browser will open and take you to the Apple .Mac Sign Up page.

✔ **Sync:** The Sync tab is where you can specify which synchronization services you wish to employ. You can use iSync to manage Safari bookmarks, iCal calendars, Address Book information, keychains, mail accounts, and Mail rules, signatures, and smart mailboxes.

✔ **iDisk:** This tab shows how much of your iDisk (your remote disk maintained on Apple's servers for .Mac members) is used, how much is available, and how you have allocated space between disk storage and mail storage. It also allows you to keep a local copy of your iDisk on your hard disk and synchronize it automatically or manually, and make your Public Folder Read/Write or Read-Only with or without a password.

✔ **Advanced:** Use this pane to register several Macs for synchronization through your .Mac account.

Network

This pane offers options for connecting your Mac to the Internet or to a network. Although I talk a little about this pane in Chapter 9, here's some fast-and-dirty detail to give you the gist.

If you're part of a large office network, check with your System Administrator before you change anything in this pane. If you ignore this advice, you run the risk of losing your network connection completely.

At the top of this pane is the Location pop-up menu. If you use your Mac in more than one place, you can set up a separate configuration for each location and then choose it from this menu. A *location,* in this context, consists of all settings in all tabs in the Network System Preferences pane. After you have this entire pane configured the way that you like, pull down this menu and choose New Location. Type in a name for the new location and then click OK. Then you can change all the settings in this pane at once by choosing that location from the pop-up menu.

If your Mac has a single network or Internet connection (as most home users have), just choose Automatic from the Location menu and be done with it.

Below the Location menu is the Show pop-up menu. Here you choose your network status, Internet connectivity method, and port configuration. If you use a modem to connect to the Internet, choose Internal Modem. If you have another type of Internet access, such as ISDN, cable modem, or Digital Subscriber Line (DSL), choose either Ethernet or Built-in Ethernet.

Depending on which type of connection you choose in the Show menu, you'll see four or five tabs. You'll need to talk to your ISP or network administrator to find out how to configure them; I can't tell you how in this book (there are just too many configurations that depend on your particular ISP and service). But here's a brief rundown on the most important ones:

- ✔ **TCP/IP:** *TCP/IP* is the language of the Internet. On this tab, you specify things such as your IP Address, Domain Name Servers, and Search Domains.

- ✔ **PPP or PPPoE:** These acronyms stand for Point-To-Point Protocol and Point-To-Point Protocol over Ethernet. Which one you see depends on what you've selected from the Show menu. All modems use PPP; some cable and DSL modems use PPPoE. Your ISP will tell you whether you need to do anything with this tab.

- ✔ **AppleTalk:** *AppleTalk* is a homegrown network protocol invented by Apple. Some (but not all) networked printers require it to be turned on for them to function. For more information about AppleTalk in general, this tab in particular, and printers, see Chapter 10.

- ✔ **Proxies:** If you're on a large network or your Mac is behind a firewall, you might need to specify one or more proxy servers. If so, your network administrator can help you with this tab's settings. If you're a home user, you'll probably never need to touch this tab. Finally, some ISPs require you to specify proxy servers; if you need to do this, ask your ISP what to do.

QuickTime

QuickTime is Apple's multimedia technology for both Mac and Windows. When you watch a movie on your Mac (unless you're watching a DVD, of course), chances are good that it's a QuickTime file.

Chances are also good that QuickTime is already configured properly.

The QuickTime pane has five tabs: Register, Browser, Update, Streaming, and Advanced. Just check to make sure that QuickTime is set as follows and then leave this preference alone.

Register

This is where you go to upgrade your copy of QuickTime to QuickTime Pro (for $30). If you have a QuickTime Pro key, you can enter the information here and unlock the Pro features. If you don't already have a key, you can click the Buy QuickTime Pro button, which transports you to the Apple Store where you can stick a copy in your shopping cart.

Browser

This tab deals with the way your Internet browser handles multimedia files; it contains three check boxes:

- ✔ Select the **Play Movies Automatically** check box if it's not already checked if you want your browser to play movies when it encounters them.

✔ Select the **Save Movies in Disk Cache** check box to save QuickTime movies in the browser's cache folder (in your Home/Library/Preferences folder; if you use Internet Explorer, they're in Explorer/Temporary Items.)

Don't rely on this feature. Some movies don't download at all when you view them in your browser; others only download the first frame. If you need to harvest QuickTime movies from the Web, you'll be better off buying the $30 QuickTime Pro upgrade, which, among other things, lets you save QuickTime movies from within your browser.

✔ Select the **Enable Kiosk Mode** check box to hide the QuickTime controller (Play/Pause/Volume/and so on) within your browser.

The Allow Multiple Simultaneous Streams check box lets you have more than one QuickTime movie or file streaming into your Mac over the Internet (or local-area network) at a time.

If streaming movies or sounds are stuttering or not playing properly, try unchecking this option.

Update

Change settings in the Update tab to update your QuickTime software automatically (if you have an Internet connection). Because each successive version of QuickTime has added cool and useful features, I suggest you select the Check for Updates Automatically check box. After you do, your Mac will check for new versions of QuickTime whenever you connect to the Internet. As Martha Stewart says, "It's a good thing."

Streaming

This tab is where you select the speed of your Internet connection by choosing the appropriate option from the Streaming Speed pop-up menu. If you're not sure what your connection speed is, ask your ISP. (If you're not sure what an ISP is, I suggest you give Chapter 9 a read.)

The Enable Instant On check box lets you adjust how quickly streaming movies and sounds start playing. Alas, turning this feature on may degrade streaming-media performance.

Advanced

I strongly suggest you ignore the Advanced tab. I have yet to need the features on it even though they've been available in QuickTime for years. If you want to use a music synthesizer (other than the built-in QuickTime Music Synthesizer) or if someone sends you a secured media file (or you download one), you'll have to play with these settings — but I've never had to touch either one.

The Transport Setup pop-up menu offers advanced options for receiving files over the Internet. I suggest you leave this alone unless you're instructed to change it by someone highly knowledgeable, such as your ISP.

The MIME settings button at the bottom of this pane offers advanced options for receiving files over the Internet. I suggest you leave this alone unless you're instructed to change it by someone highly knowledgeable, such as your ISP.

Sharing

This is another option that you'll use when networking your Mac. There are two facets of Sharing — sharing a single Mac with other users and sharing files via an office network or the Internet. Read all the gory details in Chapter 14.

System System preferences (kind of redundant)

This section examines the preference panes displayed in the System category for administering your, um, system. (That still sounds weird.)

Accounts (formerly Users)

This pane, which is only fully useful to users with Administrator access, is where you create and administer user accounts on your Mac. About the only actions those non-Admin users can take in the Accounts pane are to

✔ Change their passwords

✔ Change their login pictures

✔ Specify applications to run and documents to open when they log in

I cover administering user accounts in greater detail in Chapter 14, but (true to my promise) here I show you how to get rid of logging in entirely if you don't like it. Here's what to do: If you don't have any reason to worry about someone else logging on and making mischief (or if you don't share your Mac), you can disable the login screen by clicking the Login Options button beneath the list of accounts.

When you disable logging in, you also affect all the preferences set by anyone else who shares your Mac. (Yikes.) So, if your Desktop pattern, keyboard settings, and so forth are different from those of someone else who uses your machine, those preferences won't be properly reflected unless each of you has a separate, individual login account. Even if you're not worried about security, consider keeping logging in enabled if any other users have accounts on your machine.

To disable the logging-in requirement, you may first need to unlock the Accounts System Preference. (For more on unlocking a preference, see the "Using System Preferences" section earlier in this chapter.)

To disable login, select yourself in the list of users, click the Login Options button below the list, check the Log In Automatically As check box, and then choose your account from the pop-up menu.

Note that only one account is allowed to use auto-login. If another user wants to use this Mac, you need to choose Log Out from the menu or press ⌘+Shift+Q or have Fast User Switching enabled. And if you've disabled automatic login in the Security System Preference pane, you can't enable it here.

For non-automatic logins, the Login Options pane has additional choices. You can choose to have your login window display just two fields — user name and password — or show the flashier list of users of this Mac, complete with those cute little pictures.

The Show Restart, Sleep, and Shut Down buttons and Show Password Hint check boxes do just what their names imply.

The Show Input Menu in Login Window check box is handy if you're using non-Roman input methods, such as Japanese or Chinese. The Use VoiceOver at Login check box turns on the new VoiceOver functionality (described later in this chapter) at login.

One cool feature you'll find in Login Options is the Enable Fast User Switching check box. It lets you switch your Mac from one user to another without first logging out. Just choose the account you want to switch to from the Fast User Switching menu (which appears when this option is enabled, as shown in Figure 13-12).

Figure 13-12:
Fast User Switching is much faster than logging out and back in under another account.

Classic

Open the Classic System Preferences pane to choose the drive or drive partition that contains a Mac OS 9.2.2 System Folder to use when working in the Classic environment. I dig deep into the Classic environment in Chapter 12. Suffice to say that if you have Mac OS 9 applications (or if you're nostalgic for the way things were in Mac OS 9), you need to use the Classic System Preferences pane.

Having multiple Mac OS operating systems isn't *quite* as bewildering as having multiple personalities, but I'll repeat what I said in Chapter 12 about version numbers to minimize confusion:

Mac OS X (10.3) requires version 9.2.2 of Mac OS, commonly referred to as Mac OS 9.2.2, to provide the Classic environment. But most (if not all) programs don't distinguish between different versions of Mac OS 9. So when I call a program a *Mac OS 9 program,* what I mean is that it's *not* an OS X program and that it will run under any version of Mac OS 9. In other words, when I talk about stuff that works with (or appears in) all versions of Mac OS 9, I say *Mac OS 9.* When I'm talking about Classic or another feature or program that *requires* OS 9.2.2, I say *Mac OS 9.2.2.*

Date & Time

Within the Date & Time System Preferences pane, you can configure your Mac's internal clock (which many programs use) and the clock that you see in the menu bar. Three tabs appear: Date & Time, Time Zone, and Clock.

Date & Time

To change the date, click a day in the current month's calendar (or click the date field above the calendar and use the up- and down-arrows that appear to the right of this field).

To set the time, type in the correct values in the Current Time field that appears above the clock face, or click the number that you want to change and use the up- and down-arrows that appear to the right of this field.

You can also use the arrow keys on the keyboard to increase or decrease the number. Or you can type a new number right over the selected number.

When you have the time set the way you want it, click the Save button. Or, if you mess up, click the Revert button to return to the way it was before you began.

Use the Tab key to move from number to number. The settings for the hour, minute, and second are selected in sequence when you press the Tab key. If you want to move backward through the sequence, press Shift+Tab. As long as you hold the Shift key down, you cycle through the numbers in reverse order when you press Tab.

You won't be able to set the date or time if you've already checked the Set Date & Time Automatically check box.

Network time servers are very cool, enabling you to synchronize your Mac's clock to a super-accurate time server on the Internet. To use a time server, however, you must be connected to the Internet when your Mac checks the time.

To set up access to a time server, just click the Set Date & Time Automatically check box, and then choose a network time server from the pop-up menu.

Apple's Network Time Server is `time.apple.com`. You're allowed to use it, of course.

If you have trouble with the network time-server feature, Apple posts a technical note that lists dozens of alternative network time servers. You can find this tech note (and several other tech notes you may find useful) by going to the Apple Knowledge Base (`http://kbase.info.apple.com`) and searching for *network time server*.

Time Zone

This tab lets you set your machine according to what time zone you're in. Click your part of the world on the map that appears or choose a time zone from the pop-up menu. The map is updated to show your time zone when you do.

Clock

This tab controls the display of the clock in the right corner of your menu bar. Each of the seven options in this tab has a check box to turn it on or off. Those options are as follows:

- ✔ The Show the Date and Time in the Menu Bar or in a Window radio buttons let you choose to see a clock on the right side of the menu bar or in a floating window.

- ✔ The View As radio buttons let you choose to see your clock (in the menu bar or window) as an analog or digital version. (If you choose analog, the next four options in this list aren't available.)

- ✔ The Display the Time with Seconds check box determines whether the time is displayed with seconds (04:20:*45*).

- ✔ The Show AM/PM check box determines whether you see AM or PM after the time (4:20 *PM*).

- ✔ The Show the Day of the Week check box determines whether the day is included before the time (*Monday* 4:20 PM). If this check box is not marked, all you see is the time (4:20 PM).

✔ The Flash the Time Separators check box determines whether the separating colons (:) between the hours and minutes (and seconds if you select the Display the Time with Seconds check box) blink on and off. If you deselect this check box, you still see the colons but they don't blink.

✔ The Use a 24-Hour Clock check box does what it says. If you're military, travel a lot, or have lived abroad, you may prefer the 24-hour clock (which expresses 1:00 p.m. as 1300 hours and so on). If so, mark this check box.

You can also have your Mac play town crier and announce the time at preset intervals (quarter hour, half hour, or hour).

Software Update

Occasionally, Apple releases a new version of some of the software that's part of a Mac system. Such releases may be a patch for the system software, a bug fix for a utility program, or even a new version of Safari, iTunes, iCal, or any other Apple-labeled software. You can set Software Update to check for new software, as well as to notify you of changes and download the fresh, hot files to your Mac. (***Note:*** You must have an Internet connection to use this feature.) Software Update has two tabs:

Update Software: Use this tab to choose to update your software automatically by marking the check box on the Update Software tab in this preference pane. If you do, you can choose how often your Mac checks for updates from the pop-up menu. If you select the Check for Updates check box, you can also select the Download Important Updates in the Background check box. Checking this latter check box just downloads the Installer file for the update, but doesn't install it until you give Software Update the go-ahead. Bottom line: You don't have to wait while a 30MB (or whatever) update downloads after you decide you want to install it.

Click the Check Now button at the bottom of the window to check manually for updates any time you like, even if you've selected the Automatically radio button.

Installed Updates: This tab shows which updates, if any, you've already installed. Click the Open as Log File button, and the installed update log will open in the Console application for you to review or save.

Speech

This pane lets you configure your desired Speech settings. It offers two tabs, which I discuss following.

Speech Recognition

This is where you set up *speech recognition* — the capability to talk to your Mac and have it understand you. Alas, I'm going to have to use another weasel-out here — I just don't have a chapter's worth of space left to explain all the other Speech goodies. Sigh. Well, okay, here are a few more tips, hints, and rants.

You'll need a decent microphone to use this feature. Unfortunately, Macs don't come with one, and (in my experience) the mike that's built into iMacs and some notebooks aren't quite good enough. Even worse, many Mac models, including some PowerBooks, don't even have an audio-in port, so you have to use a microphone that connects via your Universal Serial Bus (USB) port. Luckily, USB microphones — and converters for connecting standard microphone connectors to USB — are fairly common these days.

Dr. Bott is a great little Mac-only company that specializes in little items like USB microphones and analog-to-USB converters. Its Web address is www.drbott.com, or you can call 877-611-2688. Eric Prentice is the CEO; tell him that Bob sent you.

You can't use this feature to dictate text to your Mac — you'll need Mac-Speech's iListen, or similar software to do that. But you can use it to launch programs ("Computer, open Microsoft Word") and other stuff, like emptying the Trash, when you say to. Frankly, I haven't used it for more than a few minutes — it just doesn't work well enough yet. Still, it's kind of neat — and worth playing with, if you have the time and a decent Mac microphone.

Text to Speech

Use this tab to set the voice your Mac uses to communicate with you. Choose from the list of voices on the left side of the pane to select the voice your Mac uses when it reads to you. After you make a selection, you can click the Play button to play a sample of the voice you selected.

Use the Rate slider (bottom-right of the window) to speed up or slow down the voice. Then click the Play button to hear this voice at its new speed.

I like Fred, who says, "I sure like being inside this fancy computer."

These options are where you choose to have your Mac speak the text in alert boxes and dialogs, such as, "The application Microsoft Word has quit unexpectedly" or "The Finder requires your attention."

Two additional (and quite useful) settings are the Announce when an application requires your attention and the Speak Selected Text when the Key is Pressed check boxes. You assign the key by clicking the Set Key button.

If you want to have the clock announce the time, click the Open Date & Time Preferences button and you'll be whisked to that preference pane (which I describe earlier in this chapter).

If you want to change your VoiceOver settings, click the Open Universal Access Preferences button.

Startup Disk

This pane lets you select which hard drive, server volume, or hard-drive volume (if you've partitioned your single hard drive or have more than one) should act as the startup disk when more than one drive with system software is connected to the Mac. To use it, first unlock the Startup Disk preference if you have to (for more on unlocking a preference, see the "Using System Preferences" section earlier in this chapter) and then click the icon for the drive that you want to start up the Mac the next time that you restart.

This feature is very useful if you have both a Mac OS X startup disk *and* a startup disk with another version of Mac OS on it (such as Mac OS 9 or Mac OS 8.6). If you want to start up with the older operating system, just click that disk's icon in the Startup Disk System Preferences pane and restart your Mac; doing so makes it start up with the selected OS.

If you have OS 9.2.2 installed on the same volume as OS X, you can set this preference to choose which OS you boot from. You see two System Folder icons at the top of the pane — one with OS 9.2.2 and the other with OS X. Click the one that you want to boot from and then restart.

When you've selected the OS with which you want to restart, click the Restart button in the window.

For more information on using the Startup Disk System Preference pane, skip to the end of my discussion of the Classic environment in Chapter 12.

As I mention elsewhere in this book, Macs sold after January 1, 2003 may not be able to boot into OS 9. They will still run Classic, but won't be capable of booting into 9.

Making it easier than ever before to restart your Mac in FireWire Target Disk Mode is the Target Disk Mode button. Now you don't have to plant your finger on the T key when rebooting if you want to be in Target Disk Mode.

Universal Access

Many years ago, Apple pioneered Easy Access to assist computer users who had disabilities or difficulty in handling the keyboard and mouse. Universal Access is the OS X implementation of that assistance. This pane has a check box and four tabs.

Mark the Enable Access for Assistive Devices check box to use special equipment to control your computer.

The VoiceOver section lets you turn VoiceOver on and off via ⌘+F5. It also includes a button that will open the VoiceOver utility for you so that you can customize VoiceOver to your heart's content. I discuss VoiceOver in Chapter 11 — it's a really cool new Tiger technology that provides a verbal English interface to Mac OS X. When VoiceOver is on, your Mac tells you what you have selected, where the cursor is located, and a load of other information about what is being done, including typing.

The Seeing tab also lets you turn on a terrific feature: *hardware zoom*. Turn it on and off with the shortcut ⌘+Option+8. Zoom in and out using the shortcuts ⌘+Option+= (equals key) and ⌘+Option+– (minus key), respectively. Try this feature even if you're not disabled or challenged in any way; it's a great feature for everyone.

You can also display the screen as white-on-black (like a photographic negative), as shown in Figure 13-13. The shortcut is ⌘+Option+Control+8; use the same keyboard shortcut to toggle back to normal. If you're in the normal black-on-white mode, you can desaturate your screen into a *grayscale display* (so it works like a black-and-white TV).

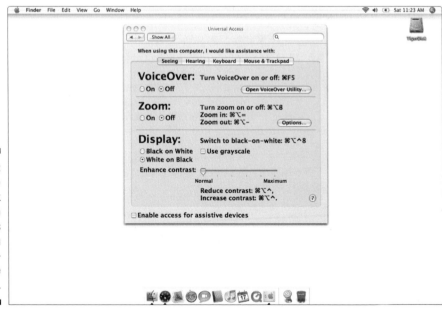

Figure 13-13:
The White on Black option reverses what you see on-screen like this.

Finally, the Zoom Options button lets you specify minimum and maximum zoom levels, display a preview rectangle when zoomed out, and toggle image smoothing on or off.

The Hearing tab lets you choose to flash the screen whenever an alert sound occurs.

This feature, created for those with impaired hearing, is quite useful if you have a PowerBook or iBook and want to use it where ambient noise levels are high.

The Keyboard tab offers two types of assistance: Sticky Keys and Slow Keys. The Sticky Keys application treats a *sequence* of modifier keys as a key combination. In other words, you don't have to simultaneously hold down ⌘ while pressing another key. For example, with Sticky Keys enabled, you can do a standard keyboard shortcut by pressing ⌘, releasing it, and then pressing the other key. There are check boxes to tell you (with a beep and/or an on-screen display) what modifier keys have been pressed.

As useful as Sticky Keys can be, they're really awkward in applications like Photoshop that toggle a tool's state when you press a modifier key. So if you're a big Photoshop user, you probably don't want Sticky Keys enabled.

Slow Keys lets you adjust the delay between when a key is pressed and when that keypress is accepted.

Finally, the Mouse tab lets you specify that you want to use the keys on the numeric keypad instead of the mouse. In this situation, everything centers on the numeric keypad's 5 key (which means clicking the mouse): 8 is up; 2 is down; 4 is left; 6 is right; and 1, 3, 7, and 9 are diagonal movements. Pressing 0 (zero) is the same as holding down the mouse button so the other numeric keys can now drag in the indicated directions. You can also increase the cursor size from the normal setting (16×16) to about 64×64.

Part IV
Networking & Troubleshooting

The 5th Wave   By Rich Tennant

"I tell you, it looks like Danny, it sounds like Danny, but it's NOT Danny!! I think the MAC has created an alias of Danny! You can see it in his eyes - little wrist watch icons!"

In this part . . .

*H*ere I get into the nitty-gritty underbelly of Mac OS X. In this part, I cover semi-advanced topics — including sharing (files, that is). That's followed by the all-important troubleshooting chapter, which takes you on a quick tour of Dr. Mac's (okay, Dr. Bob's) top troubleshooting tips for those times when good software goes bad.

Chapter 14

Mine! Miiiiine! Sharing Your Mac and Liking It

*H*ave you ever wanted to grab a file from your Mac while you were halfway around the world or even around the corner? If so, I've got good news for you — it's not difficult with OS X (believe it or not) even though computer networking in general has a well-deserved reputation for being complicated and nerve-wracking. The truth is, you won't encounter anything scary or complicated about sharing files, folders, and disks (and printers, for that matter) among computers as long as the computers are Macintoshes. And, if some of the computers are running Windows, Mac OS X version 10.4 Tiger even makes that (almost) painless. Your Macintosh includes everything that you need to share files and printers. Everything, that is, except the printers and the cables (and maybe a hub). So here's the deal: You supply the hardware, and this chapter will supply the rest. And when you're done hooking it all up, you can take a rest.

Mac OS X is a multiuser operating system. After you create a user account for someone to share your Mac, that user can log in to your Mac two different ways with the same username and password. They can log in while sitting at your Mac or they can log in to your Mac from a remote location via the Internet or a local-area network (LAN).

The first sections of this chapter provide an overview and tell you everything that you need to know to set up new user accounts and share files successfully. I won't show you how to actually share a file, folder, or disk until the "Consummating the Act of Sharing" section later in this chapter. Trust me, there's a method to my madness. If you try to share files without doing all the required prep work, the whole mess becomes confusing and complicated — kind of like networking a pair of PC clones.

One last thing: If you're the only one who uses your Mac and you don't intend to share it or its files with anyone else, you can safely skip this whole chapter if you like.

Introducing File Sharing

Macintosh file sharing enables you to use files, folders, and disks from other Macs on a network — any network, including the Internet — as easily as if they were on your own local hard drive. If you have more than one computer, file sharing is a must. It's fun, it's easy, and it's way better than SneakerNet (an ancient technology that moved files from one computer to another via floppy disk or other hand-carried media such as CD-R, DVD-R, USB Flash drives, and so on, according to the unpublished epic, "The Dr. Macintosh Unabridged Dictionary").

Before diving in and actually sharing, first check out a few necessary terms:

- **Network:** For our purposes, a network is two or more Macs connected by Ethernet cables or AirPort wireless networking.

- **Ethernet:** A network protocol and cabling scheme that lets you connect two or more computers so they can share files, disks, printers, or whatever.

- **Ethernet ports:** Where you plug an Ethernet cable into your Mac.

 Be careful. On your Mac and printer, the Ethernet ports look a lot like phone jacks, and the connectors on each end of an Ethernet cable look a lot like phone cable connectors. But they aren't the same. Ethernet cables are typically thicker, and the connectors (RJ-45 connectors) are a bit larger than the RJ-11 connectors that you use with telephones. (See examples of both types of connector ends in the margin.) When you connect an Ethernet cable to your Mac, you won't be able to put it into your RJ-11-friendly modem port (and you shouldn't try). Standard phone cables fit (very loosely) into Ethernet ports, but you shouldn't try that either — they'll probably fall out with the slightest vibration. It's unlikely that either mistake will cause any permanent damage, but it won't work and will frustrate you to no end.

✔ **Local devices:** Devices connected directly to your computers, such as hard drives or CD-ROM drives. Your internal hard drive, for example, is a local device.

✔ **Remote devices:** Devices you access (share) over the network. The hard drive of a computer in the next room, for example, is a remote device.

✔ **Protocols:** Kinds of languages that networks speak. When you read or hear about networks, you're likely to hear the words AppleTalk, EtherTalk (or Ethernet), SMB, and TCP/IP bandied about with great regularity. These are all protocols. Macs can speak several different protocols, but every device (Mac or printer) on a network needs to speak the same protocol at the same time in order to communicate.

Support for the AppleTalk protocol is built into every Mac. Your Mac includes all the software that you need to set up an AppleTalk network; the hardware that you need to provide comprises Ethernet cables and a hub (unless you use crossover cables) or an AirPort base station. I'm using *hub* here generically — its more powerful cousins, switches and routers, will also work. The AirPort base station, by the way, is a member of the router class.

Although you can use Transfer Control Protocol/Internet Protocol (TCP/IP) to do a lot of the same things that you can with AppleTalk, I concentrate on Apple's protocol, AppleTalk. By learning how to activate and use it, you'll master the basics that you need to dig into the language of the Internet.

AppleTalk is particularly useful when you have all Macs on your network. It's the easiest to configure and doesn't require additional information such as IP addresses. If you want to use the Internet to connect to another computer (or have it connect to yours), however, you have to use TCP/IP.

Mac OS X version 10.2 Jaguar added support for a protocol called Bluetooth, and this support was enhanced in OS X 10.3 Panther and again in OS X 10.4 Tiger. Bluetooth offers wireless connectivity with devices such as cell phones in addition to other computers; however, it only works over very short ranges and at lower speeds than Ethernet or AirPort. Unlike AppleTalk and TCP/IP, Bluetooth support is not included with most Macs as standard equipment. You can order Bluetooth support as a build-to-order option on some Macs, and you can use a USB adapter, known as a *dongle,* on Macs that don't offer built-in Bluetooth support. The bottom line is that while you could use Bluetooth for networking Macs, due to its slower speed and shorter range, I limit the rest of this discussion to the protocols all Mac OS X users already have on their Mac — AppleTalk and TCP/IP.

Portrait of home office networking

A typical Mac home office network consists of two Macintoshes, an Ethernet hub, and a network printer (usually a laser printer, although networked inkjet printers are becoming more common). Check out Figure 14-1 to see the configuration of a simple network. In the figure, the black lines between the devices are Ethernet cables; the rectangular device with those cables going into it is a hub. (I tell you more about cables and hubs in the section "Three ways to build a network" later in this chapter.) You need enough Ethernet cable to run among all your devices.

Figure 14-1:
Two Macs and a printer make up a simple Mac network.

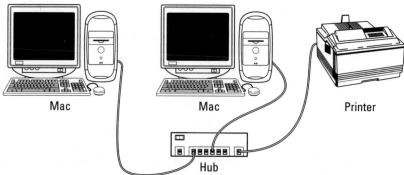

Mac   Mac   Printer

Hub

With the setup shown in Figure 14-1, either Mac can use the other Mac's files, and both Macs can print to the same printer.

A network can and often does have, however, dozens or hundreds of users. Regardless of whether your network has 2 nodes (machines) or 2,000, the principles and techniques in this chapter apply.

Three ways to build a network

Back when you could connect a whole bunch of Macs and printers by simply running cables among them, most small Mac networks were pretty much the same. You attached a small device (a LocalTalk connector) to the first Mac, and then ran plain old telephone cable to the next Mac, which also had a LocalTalk connector. By stringing more phone cable and more LocalTalk connectors, you had yourself a little network.

Today, building a Mac network is a little more complicated. Macs that support Mac OS X Tiger don't include LocalTalk ports — and Ethernet and wireless networks require a little more setup.

To cross over, or not?

The type of Ethernet cable required to connect two Macs without a hub or other middle-device has changed over time. In the old days, you absolutely had to have a crossover cable or the Macs wouldn't be able to see each other.

The basic rule had always been that to connect two Macs, you had to use a crossover cable. And if you had a hub or router or other intermediary device, you had to use regular Ethernet cables.

That's less true today because many Macs built in the past couple years — and every Mac sold today — has new and improved Ethernet that

can determine what type of cable (regular or crossover) you're using and then automatically adjust itself so cable works properly.

These days, you may encounter three possibilities: If you want to connect two older Macs, you need a crossover cable. If you want to connect an older Mac to a newer Mac, you may or may not need a crossover cable. And if you want to connect *two* late-model Macs, you can use either a regular Ethernet cable or a crossover cable.

When in doubt, check Mac OS Help in the Help menu (press ⌘+Shift+?).

In this chapter, I assume that you're working on a small network, the kind typically found in a home or small business. If you're part of a mega-monstrous corporate network and you have questions about your particular network, talk to the PIC (*person in charge,* also known as your *network administrator*). If you're trying to build one of these mega-networks, you'll need a book a lot thicker and harder to understand than this one.

The following list gives you three common ways to build a modern network:

✔ **AirPort:** If all your Macs are equipped with AirPort wireless cards and if you have the AirPort Base Station, you don't need cables at all. Just plug in the base station, and Macs with AirPort cards can communicate with each other. If you use an Ethernet printer (connected to your Mac by Ethernet cable), you need to connect it to the base station before you can print from your wireless Macs. Both the Base Station and printer have Ethernet ports, so you can use a crossover cable to make the connection.

Although this setup is more expensive than Ethernet cables and a hub, it's also more flexible because you can move your devices anywhere. (Well, almost anywhere; you're limited to 150 feet per AirPort and that's assuming that there's nothing in the way to block your signal.)

For more information about wireless networking, check out the Apple AirPort Web page at www.apple.com/airport/.

✔ **Small Ethernet:** If you have only two devices to network (two Macs, or a Mac and an Ethernet printer, in most cases), you can use an Ethernet crossover cable to connect them directly to one another via the Ethernet ports. You can purchase a crossover cable (which looks just like a standard Ethernet cable) at your local electronics store. ***Note:*** Be sure to ask for a crossover cable, or your network might not work (see the sidebar "To cross over, or not?"). Plug one end of the crossover cable into one device, and the other end into the other device.

An Ethernet crossover cable won't work with a hub; a regular Ethernet cable won't work without one in many Macs (as explained in the sidebar "To cross over, or not?"). Therefore, it makes sense to label your crossover cable(s) as such because they look exactly like regular Ethernet cables, and it's easy to become confused if you have a bunch of similar-looking cables.

✔ **Traditional Ethernet:** All modern Macs have an Ethernet port. To connect your Mac to a network, you need Ethernet cables for each Mac and a little device called a *hub*. (A hub is like the center of a wagon wheel; the wires coming out of it are the "spokes.") A typical Ethernet hub includes two to eight Ethernet ports. You plug the hub in to an electrical outlet and then connect Ethernet cables from each of your Macs and printers (from their Ethernet ports) to the hub. Voilà! — instant network. Hubs are pretty cheap, starting below $10; cables start at a few bucks, increasing in price as the length (and quality and shielding) of the cable increases.

If you have a cable modem or Digital Subscriber Line (DSL) as your Internet connection, you may need a router or switch instead of a hub. They're similar but cost a bit more and have additional features that you may or may not need. Your ISP can tell you whether you're going to need one. For what it's worth, I have a cable modem, but it works fine with a cheap hub; I didn't need a more expensive router until I wanted to have more than one of the Macs talking to the Internet at the same time.

Setting Up File Sharing

Before I get into the nitty-gritty of sharing files, you must complete a few housekeeping tasks, such as turning on file sharing, turning on AppleTalk (if you want to share files with an AppleTalk-enabled file server or print to an AppleTalk printer), and enabling sharing over TCP/IP (that is, over the Internet) if you plan to share that way.

Turning on file sharing

Before you can share files, you have to turn on Mac OS X's built-in File Sharing feature. Follow these steps to do so:

1. **From the menu, choose System Preferences (or click the System Preferences icon on the Dock) and then click the Sharing icon.**

   The System Preferences Sharing pane appears. Unless you've changed it, your long user name appears by default as the Computer Name.

2. **If you want to change the computer name at this time, do so in the Computer Name text field at the top of the Sharing pane.**

   In Figure 14-2, you can see that I named mine G4iMac. You can name yours anything you like.

3. **On the Services pane, mark the sharing services that you want to use (such as Personal File Sharing) and then click the Start button (beneath the heading Personal File Sharing Off).**

   Alternatively, you can just click inside the check box in the On column to activate file sharing (see Figure 14-2).

   Why does it say Personal File Sharing Off above the button? Because it *is* off. After you click the Start button, the button name changes from *Start* to *Stop,* and the text above the button changes to Personal File Sharing On, indicating that file sharing is on.

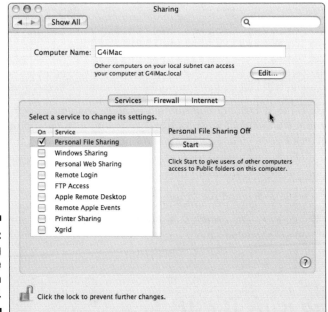

Figure 14-2:
Turning
personal file
sharing on
and off.

Starting AppleTalk

If you want to share files with an Apple file server or print to a networked printer that requires AppleTalk, as many do, you have to enable AppleTalk. (See the "Introducing File Sharing" section earlier in this chapter for a definition of AppleTalk.) Here's how:

1. **From the menu, choose System Preferences (or click the System Preferences icon on the Dock).**

   The System Preferences window appears.

2. **In the System Preferences window, click the Network icon (located in the toolbar and also in the main part of the window).**

   The Network System Preferences pane appears.

   You can get here in one step by choosing ⌘⇨Location⇨Network Preferences.

3. **If the pane is locked, click the lock icon (bottom-left corner) to unlock the Network System Preferences, type an Administrator name and password, and then click OK.**

   If your Mac is set up for multiple users, only users with administrative privileges (or, at least, knowledge of the Administrator password) can unlock these locks. Those with such privileges are the first user (created when you installed OS X) and any other user to whom you've given administrative privileges in the Accounts System Preferences pane (which I discuss in the "Access and Privileges: Who Can Do What" section later in this chapter).

4. **Choose Built-in Ethernet or AirPort (whichever you use) from the Show pop-up menu (if it isn't already chosen) and then click the AppleTalk tab.**

   The AppleTalk view of the Network System Preferences pane appears in all its glory — on-screen and in Figure 14-3.

5. **Mark the Make AppleTalk Active check box.**

6. **Click the Apply Now button in the lower-right corner of the AppleTalk tab to confirm your action.**

   That's it. You can quit the System Preferences application now.

Sharing with TCP/IP

TCP/IP is the network protocol used on the Internet. It's also the protocol used by OS X for sharing files. It enables Macs, PCs, and other computers to communicate with each other (sometimes, but not always, via the Internet), even if they're running different operating systems. TCP/IP is always on, so you don't have to do anything further about it.

If you want remote users to be able to use an File Transfer Protocol (FTP) client program (instead of using File Sharing on another Mac) to upload and download files to and from this computer, mark the FTP Access check box in the Sharing System Preferences pane's Services pane. If you want to enable Windows or Linux — or users of other operating systems to share files with you — this check box needs to be marked. (I talk more about FTP and FTP clients in Chapter 19.) Windows users can also share files if you turn on Windows File Sharing in the Sharing pane's Services pane. This feature, introduced in Mac OS X version 10.2 Jaguar, takes most of the pain out of working with people using Microsoft Windows systems.

Mac users could use an FTP client to access your Mac, but they'll probably want to use File Sharing instead because it's easier.

Security risks are involved in allowing FTP access. I strongly suggest that you go to Apple's Web site (www.apple.com) and read about them before you enable this feature.

Computers connect to one another by using a number-based addressing system *(an IP address)* that's standard all over the world. You can (and most big companies do) use this system to communicate in offices and over the Internet. If you need to know more about using TCP/IP to connect to computers on your network than I've told you here, talk to the system administrator or the network geek in charge of these things where you work.

Figure 14-3:
The
AppleTalk
tab of the
System
Preferences
Network
pane.

I touch more on TCP/IP in the "Connecting to a shared disk or folder on a remote" section later in this chapter where you can read how to use it to connect to a Mac or other server that's running it.

Bonjour (previously known as Rendezvous), the relatively new, zero-configuration network protocol included in Mac OS X version 10.2 Jaguar (and later versions, of course) makes networking simple. If two devices (and this includes all Macs running version 10.2 Jaguar or later) speak Bonjour, you don't have to do any configuration (besides turning on the sharing capability). Bonjour queries the other available networked devices to see what services they offer and support and then configures the connections for you automatically.

Access and Privileges: Who Can Do What

Before you can share your Mac with other users or share files over a network, you need to tell your Mac who is allowed to do what. Luckily for you, this process just happens to be what I cover in this section.

Users and groups and guests

Macintosh file sharing (and indeed, Mac OS X as well) is based on the concept of users. Shared items — drives or folders — can be shared with no users, one user, or many users, depending on your needs.

- ✔ **Users:** People who share folders and drives (or your Mac) are *users*. A user's access to items on your local hard drive is entirely at your discretion. You can configure your Mac so only you can access its folders and drives or so only one other person (or everyone) can share its folders and drives.

  When you first set up your Mac, you created your first user. This user automatically has administrative powers, such as adding more users, changing preferences, and having the clearance to see all folders on the hard drive.

  For the purposes of this book, I assume that some users for whom you create identities won't be folks who actually sit at your Mac, but rather those who only connect to it from a remote location when they need to give or get files. But they *could* use the same name and password to log in while sitting at your desk.

  For all intents and purposes, a remote user and a local user are the same. In other words, after you create an account for a user, that user can log in to this Mac while sitting in your chair in your office or log in to this Mac from a remote location via AppleTalk/Ethernet or the Internet.

✔ **Administrative users:** Although a complete discussion of the special privileges that a user with administrator privileges has on a Mac running OS X is far beyond the scope of this book, note two important things:

- The first user created (usually when you install OS X for the first time) is automatically granted administrator (admin) powers.

- Only an administrator can create new users, delete some (but not all) files from folders that aren't in his or her Home folder, lock and unlock System Preference panes, and a bunch of other stuff. If you try something and it doesn't work, make sure you're logged in as a user with admin privileges.

You can give any user administrator privileges by selecting that user's account, clicking the Password tab, and then selecting the Allow User to Administer This Computer check box in the Password pane. You can set this check box when creating the user account or subsequently.

✔ **Groups:** *Groups* are UNIX-level designations for privilege consolidation. For example, there are groups named `staff` and `wheel` (as well as a bunch of others). Your main account, for example, is in the `wheel` group.

If you're wondering whether you can create *your own* groups, as you could under OS 9 and earlier Mac operating systems, the answer is, well, yes and no. If you want to delve into the intricacies of the NetInfo Manager application to do it yourself, then "Yes;" but if you don't, then the answer is "No, please don't." UNIX-related tasks such as this are far beyond the scope of this book. Very far beyond. . . .

✔ **Guests:** Those who access public folders on your Mac via file sharing are *guests.* They don't need a username or password. If they're on your network, they can see and use your public folder(s), unless you or the public folder's owner has altered the permissions on one or more public folders. If they're on the Internet and know your IP address, they can see and use your Public folder(s). Public folders are all that guests can access, luckily.

Creating users

Before users can share folders and drives (or share your computer for that matter), you need to create user identities for them. You perform this little task in the Accounts System Preferences pane.

Guests can use your public folder(s) — but no other folders — without having a user account.

To create users for the purposes of file sharing, you need to add the user as a user of your computer, too. In other words, giving a user access to certain folders on your system means that that user also has folders of his or her own on the Mac. When you add (create) a user, you need to tell your Mac who this person is. This is also the time to set passwords and administrative powers of this new user. Here's the drill:

1. **From the menu, choose System Preferences (or click the System Preferences icon on the Dock), click the Accounts icon, and then make sure that the Password pane is selected.**

   The Accounts System Preferences pane appears. In this pane (shown in Figure 14-4), you can see the name of the first user (`boblevitus`) and the administrative control that this user has (look beneath the user's name).

   As I mention previously, the first user created (usually at the same time you installed OS X) always has administrator privileges.

2. **Click the + button beneath the list of users.**

   All the text fields in the Password pane empty out, waiting for you to fill in the new user's account information.

   If the + button is dimmed, you'll need to first click the lock (lower-left), supply an admin user name and password in the resulting dialog, and then click OK.

   A sheet appears in which you enter the new user's information.

3. **In the Name text box, type the full name of a user you want to add.**

   In the Short Name text box, your Mac inserts a suggested abbreviated name (or *short name,* as it's called). Check out Figure 14-5 to see both.

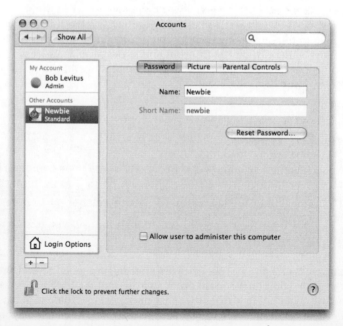

Figure 14-4:
The Accounts System Preferences pane shows who can use this Mac.

In Figure 14-5, I added **Steve Jobs** as a user, typing the full name in the Name field. You don't really need to type the user's full name, but I do so in this example to show you the difference between a name and a short name.

The name of each user's folder (in the Users folder) is taken from the short name that you enter when you create a user.

4. **Press the Tab key to move to the next field.**

   Mac OS X suggests an abbreviated version of the name in the Short Name field (as shown in Figure 14-5). Because he's the only Steve that matters around here, I'll change the suggested *stevejobs* to just plain *steve,* which is shorter than the short name recommended by OS X. (In other words, I type **steve** into the Short Name field, replacing the suggested *stevejobs.*)

Users can connect to your Mac (or log in to their own Macs, for that matter) by using the short name, rather than having to type their full names. The short name is also used in environments in which usernames can't have spaces and are limited to eight or fewer characters. Although OS X Panther allows longer user names (but no spaces), you may be better off keeping your short name shorter than eight characters, just in case.

5. **Tab to the New Password field and enter an initial password for this user.**

   The small, square button with the key to the Password field's right, when clicked, displays the Password Assistant (Figure 14-6). You can use the Password Assistant to help generate a password that should be fairly easy to remember but hard for a cracking program to guess or meet other requirements.

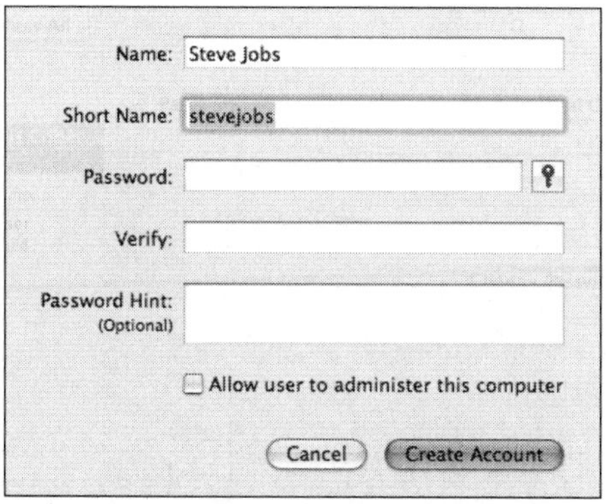

Figure 14-5:
Name the
new user;
your Mac
suggests a
short name.

Name:	Steve Jobs
Short Name:	stevejobs
Password:	
Verify:	
Password Hint: (Optional)	

☐ Allow user to administer this computer

(Cancel) (Create Account)

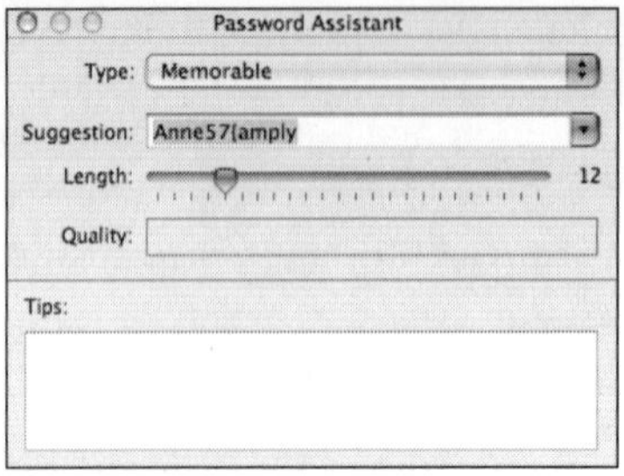

Figure 14-6:
The
Password
Assistant
dialog helps
you create
passwords.

	Password Assistant
Type:	Memorable
Suggestion:	Anne57[amply
Length:	———————— 12
Quality:	
Tips:	

6. **Press the Tab key on your keyboard to move your cursor to the Verify text field.**

7. **In the Verify text box, type the password again to verify it.**

8. **(Optional) To help remember a password, type something to jog the user's memory in the Password Hint text box.**

If a user forgets his or her password and asks for a hint, the text that you type in the Password Hint field will pop up, hopefully causing the user to exclaim, "Oh yeah . . . *now* I remember!" A password hint should be something simple enough to jog the user's memory but not so simple that an unauthorized person may guess. Perhaps something like "Your first teddy bear's name backwards" would be a good hint.

9. **Click Create Account.**

The sheet closes, returning you to the Password pane.

10. **If you want this user to administer the Mac (that is, have access to preferences, be able to create users, and so forth, select the Allow User to Administer This Computer check box.**

11. **(Optional) Click the Picture Tab to assign a picture to the user.**

OS X will suggest one from its default collection, but you can select a different one from the scrolling row, drag one in from the Finder (or iPhoto), or take one with an attached camera (such as an iSight).

The new user now appears in the Accounts System Preferences pane's Users list.

Changing a user

Circumstances might dictate that you need to change a user's identity, password, or accessibility, or perhaps delete a user. Follow these steps to change a user's name, password, or administration privileges:

1. **From the menu, choose System Preferences (or click the System Preferences icon on the Dock).**

The System Preferences window appears.

2. **In the System Preferences window, click the Accounts icon.**

   The Accounts System Preferences pane appears.

3. **Click the user's name in the scrolling list to select it.**

   The information for that person appears in the Password view.

4. **Make your changes by selecting the existing username or short name and then replacing the old with new text or a different setting.**

   • If you want to change the password, click the Change Password button and make your changes in the sheet that appears.

   • To change the picture or other capabilities, click the Picture, Login Items, or Parental Control tabs and make the appropriate changes.

   In order to change a user, you must be logged in using an account that has administrator powers.

5. **Quit the System Preferences application or choose a different System Preference pane.**

Your changes are saved when you leave the Accounts pane.

Removing a user

To delete a user — in effect, to deny that user access to your Mac — select the user you want to delete in the list of accounts and then click the – button. You will be asked to confirm that you really want to delete the user. Click OK to delete the user but save their Home folder files in the Deleted Users folder or click Delete Immediately to delete the user *and* his or her Home folder.

To remove a user from your Mac, you must be logged in using an account that has administrator privileges. When you delete the user, the files and folders that user owned will now be in the Deleted Users folder in a Disk Image file.

Limiting a user's capabilities

Sometimes — especially with younger children or computer-phobic family members — you want to limit what they can access. For example, you might want to make certain programs off-limits. With Mac OS X version 10.4 Tiger, you do this via the Parental Controls tab in the Accounts System Preferences pane.

1. **From the menu, choose System Preferences (or click the System Preferences icon on the Dock).**

   The System Preferences window appears.

2. **In the System Preferences window, click the Accounts icon.**

   The Accounts System Preferences pane appears.

3. **Click the user's name once to select it, and then click the Parental Controls tab.**

   The access information for that person appears, as shown in Figure 14-7. Note that you can't limit an account with administrator privileges.

4. **Select the check box corresponding to a user capability you want to restrict, then click that capability's Configure (or Info) button.**

   - **Mail:** Provide a list of approved mail correspondents.

   - **Finder and System:** Determine which applications the user may access, whether they can print, burn optical discs, modify the Dock, access System Preferences, or be restricted to a very limited and simplified Finder interface. Figure 14-8 shows the sheet where you can limit access.

   - **iChat:** Provide a list of approved iChat communicants.

   - **Safari:** Limit the Web sites the user can visit.

   - **Dictionary:** Limited Dictionary access reduces the number of words that can be looked up, eliminating such things as profanity.

In order to change a user's capabilities, you must be logged in using an account that has Administrator powers.

Figure 14-7:
You can control an account's access in five categories.

Figure 14-8:
Limiting
some user
capabilities
and
program
access is
easy.

5. **Quit the System Preferences application or choose a different System Preference pane.**

Your changes are saved when you leave the Accounts pane.

Mac OS X knows best: Folders shared by default

When you add users in the Accounts System Preferences pane as I describe earlier in this chapter, Mac OS X automatically does two things behind the scenes to facilitate file sharing: It creates a set of folders, and it makes some of them available for sharing.

Each time you add a user, Mac OS X creates a folder hierarchy for that user on the Mac, as I describe in Chapter 6. The user can create more folders (if necessary) and also add, remove, or move anything inside of these folders. Even if you open a user account solely to allow him or her to exchange files with you, your Mac automatically creates a folder for that user. Unless you, as the owner of your Mac, give permission, the user can't see inside — or use folders outside the Home folder (which has the user's name) — with only three exceptions: the Shared folder in the Users folder, the top level of other user account folders, and the Public and Shared folders in every other user's folder. A description of the latter follows:

✔ **Public:** A Public folder is located inside each user's folder. That folder is set up to be accessible (shared) by any user who can log in to the Mac. Furthermore, any user can log in (as a guest) and copy things out of this folder as long as he knows your Mac's IP address, even if he doesn't have an account on this Mac at all. Files put into the Public folder can be opened or copied freely.

Inside each user's Public folder is a Drop Box folder. Just like the name implies, this folder is where others can drop a file or folder for you. Only the owner can open the Drop Box to see what's inside or to move or copy the files that are in it. Imagine a street corner mailbox — after you drop your letter in, it's gone, and you can't get it back out.

✔ **Shared:** In addition to a Public folder for each user, Mac OS X creates one Shared folder on every Mac for all users of this Mac. The Shared folder *isn't* available to guests, but it's available to every person who has an account on this machine, when they're logged in at the machine. You find the Shared folder within the Users folder (the same folder where you find folders for each user). The Shared folder is the right place to put stuff that everyone with an account might want to use. In Figure 14-9, you can see a Users folder where drc and spenser have user folders. You can also see the Shared folder that both of them can use.

Here's an example of how all this works. If Dennis R. Cohen (my rockin' technical editor on this book) has a user account called drc on his Mac, he can log in and work with any item in his user directory — the drc Home folder. He can also put files in his Shared folder that he wants to share with others users who sit at this particular Mac. Or he can put them in the Public folder if he wants them available to everyone with an account as well as guests logged in remotely via a LAN or the Internet. If drc wants to share a file with just spenser, he can put it in the Public folder under the spenser user account; or, if he wants to be sure that no one but spenser sees it, he can put it into the Drop Box folder inside the Public folder for spenser. The privileges that okay all this activity are set up when the user account is created — you don't have to lift a finger.

Sharing a folder or disk by setting privileges

As you might expect, access privileges control who can use a given folder or any disk (or partition) other than the startup disk.

Why can't you share the startup disk? Because OS X won't let you. Why not? Because it contains the operating system and other stuff that nobody else should have access to.

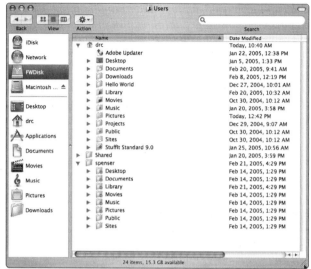

Figure 14-9:
Each user
has a folder
and can
open or
copy items
from the
Shared
folder.

Throughout the rest of this chapter, whenever I talk about *sharing a folder,* I also mean *sharing disks and disk partitions other than your startup disk* (which, when you think of it, are nothing more than big folders anyway). Why am I telling you this? Because it's awkward to keep typing "a folder or any disk (or partition) other than your startup disk." So anything that I say about sharing a folder also applies to sharing any disk (or partition) other than your startup disk. Got it?

You can set access privileges for the folder's owner, for a subset of all the people having accounts on the Mac (a group), or for everyone who has the Mac's address whether they have an account or not (guests). To help you get a better handle on these relationships, a closer look at privileges, owners, and groups is coming right up.

Contemplating privileges

When you consider who can use which folders, there are three distinct kinds of users on the network. I describe each of them in this section. Then, in the "Useful settings for access privileges" section later in this chapter, I show you how to share folders with each of them.

✔ **Owner:** The owner of a folder or disk can change the access privileges to that folder or disk at any time. The name you enter when you log in to your Mac — or the name of your Home folder — is the default owner of shared folders and drives on that machine. Ownership can be given away (more on that in the "Useful settings for access privileges" section later in this chapter). Even if you own the Mac, you can't change access privileges for a folder on it that belongs to another user (unless you get UNIX-y and do so as root). The owner must be logged in to change privileges on his or her folders.

OS X is the owner of many folders outside the Users folder. If OS X owns it, you'll see that system is its owner, as shown in Figure 14-10. Folders that aren't in the User directories generally belong to System.

You *can* change those access privileges without resorting to third-party utilities or using the Terminal (which I describe briefly in Chapter 11), as was necessary in OS X versions before Jaguar. But be careful: It's not a good idea to change them unless you know exactly what you're doing and why. Unfortunately, that discussion is far beyond the purview of this book.

✔ **Group member:** In UNIX systems, all users belong to one or more *groups*. The group that includes everyone who has an account with administrator privileges on your Mac is called admin. Everyone in the admin group has access to Shared and Public folders over the network as well as to any folder that the admin group has been granted access to by the folder's owner.

✔ **Others:** This category is an easy way to set access privileges for everyone with an account on your Mac at once. Unlike the admin group, which includes only users with administrative privileges, others includes, well, everyone (everyone with an account on this Mac, that is).

If you want people without an account on this Mac to have access to a file or folder, it needs to go in your Public folder, where they can log in as a guest.

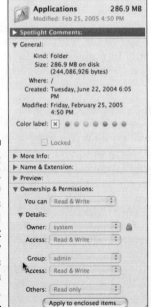

Figure 14-10: Mac OS X (system) owns this folder, and you can't easily change its access privileges.

Whatever happened to users and groups?

Mac OS X users who have used Mac OS 9 might wonder what's happened to the Users and Groups feature, which enabled you to create any number of user groups on a Mac. Because Mac OS X is based on the UNIX operating system, which deals very differently with permissions and access privileges than older versions of Mac OS did, it can't support old-style users and groups.

If you're brave or knowledgeable enough to dig into UNIX, you can make your own groups in Mac OS X. Creating a UNIX group confers identical access privileges and powers on all its members. Although the process of creating a group is beyond the scope of this book, the process basically involves either gaining `root` access to the UNIX system and working from the Terminal command line or tinkering with the

groups directory by using NetInfo Manager (which requires Administrator access).

If you feel adventurous and know a little UNIX, try this: Open the Terminal program (in the Utilities folder inside the Applications folder) and type **man group**. Terminal will display the manual pages for the topic *group*. Press Space as many times as needed to scroll through the entire document. It probably won't help you create a group, but reading it won't hurt anything.

The `admin` group includes every user of a given Mac who has administrative privileges. Although it's not as flexible as the old Users and Groups feature (in OS 9 and earlier), it's better than no groups at all and is a lot more secure than the OS 9 group functionality.

Sharing a folder

Suppose you have a folder you want to share but it has slightly different rules than those set up for the Public folder, the Drop Box folder within, or for your personal folders. These rules are *privileges,* and they tell you how much access someone has to your stuff.

Actually, the rules governing Shared and Public folders are privileges, too, but they're set up for you when Mac OS X is installed.

I suggest that you only share folders located within your Home folder (or a folder within it). Because of the way UNIX works, the UNIX permissions of the enclosing folder can prevent access to a folder for which you *do* have permissions. Trust me, if you only share folders in your Home folder, you'll never go wrong. If you don't take this advice, you could wind up having folders that other users can't access, even though you gave them the appropriate permission.

You can set access privileges for folders within your Public folder (like the Drop Box folder) that are different from those for the rest of the folder.

I said this before, but it bears repeating: Whenever I talk about sharing a folder, I also mean disks and disk partitions other than your startup disk (which you just can't share, period). So don't forget that anything I say about sharing a folder also applies to sharing any disk (or partition) other than your startup disk. Though you can't explicitly share your startup disk, anyone with Administrator access can mount it for sharing from across the network (or Internet).

To share a folder with another user, follow these steps:

1. **Select (single-click) the folder or drive icon and then choose File⇨ Get Info (or use the keyboard shortcut ⌘+I).**

   The Info window for the selected item opens.

2. **Click the triangle to the left of the Ownership & Permissions panel near the bottom of the window, and then click the Details disclosure triangle.**

   The privileges options appear, as you see in Figure 14-11.

3. **Set access privileges for this folder by using the Access Privileges pop-up menus to control how much access each type of user has to the shared folder or drive.**

   When you click one of these pop-up menus, you see the privilege description.

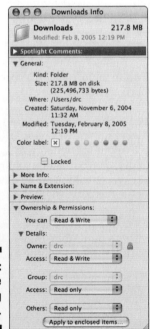

Figure 14-11: Set file sharing here.

You can choose from three types of access for each user or group, as shown in Table 14-1.

If you are the folder's owner (or have Administrator access), you can click the padlock icon and change the owner and/or group for the file or folder.

Table 14-1	Access Privileges
Access Privilege	*What It Allows*
Read & Write	A user with read-and-write access can see, add, delete, move, and edit files just as if they were stored on his or her own computer.
Read Only	A read-only user can see and use files that are stored in a shared folder but can't add, delete, move, or edit them.
Write Only (Drop Box)	Users can add files to this folder but can't see what's in it. The user must have read access to the folder containing a Write Only folder.
No Access	With no privileges, a user can neither see nor use your shared folders or drives.

Useful settings for access privileges

The following sections show you just some of the more common ways that you can combine access privileges for a folder. You'll probably find one option that fits the way you work and the people you want to share with.

Allow everyone access

In Figure 14-12, I configure settings that allow access for everyone on a network. Everyone can open, read, and change the contents of this shared folder. Do this by choosing Read & Write for Others in the Access pop-up menu in the Ownership & Permissions section of the folder's Get Info window.

Owner privileges must be at least as expansive as Group privileges and Group privileges must be at least as expansive as Others privileges. So, to set Others to Read & Write means that Group and Owner must also be set to Read & Write.

Allow nobody but yourself access

The settings shown in Figure 14-13 reflect appropriate settings that allow owner-only access. No one but me can see or use the contents of this shared folder. Choose No Access in both the Group Access and the Others pop-up menus to do it yourself.

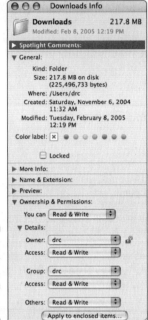

Figure 14-12:
Allow everyone access if you want.

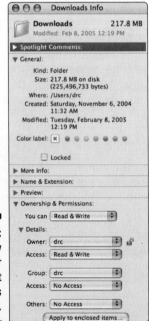

Figure 14-13:
Allow access for no one but the folder's owner.

You need to change the Others pop-up menu to No Access first because Group member privileges must be at least as broad as Others privileges.

Allow all administrative users of this Mac access

Check out Figure 14-14 to see settings that allow the group `wheel` (in addition to the owner) access to see, use, or change the contents of the shared folder. Choose Read & Write in the Group Access pop-up menu.

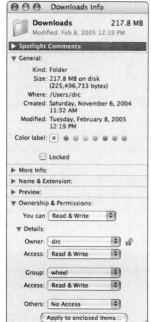

Figure 14-14: Allow access to one group.

Allow others to deposit files and folders without giving them access (a Drop Box)

The settings in Figure 14-15 enable users to drop their own files or folders without being able to see or use the contents of the shared folder. After a file or folder is deposited in a drop folder, the dropper can't retrieve it because he or she doesn't have access privileges to see the items in the drop folder. To let everyone use this folder as a Drop Box, choose Write Only (Drop Box) from both the Group Access and the Others pop-up menus.

Read-only bulletin boards

If you want everyone to be able to open and read the files and folders in this shared folder, choose Read Only from the Group Access and the Others pop-up menus. If you do this, however, only the owner can make changes to files in this folder.

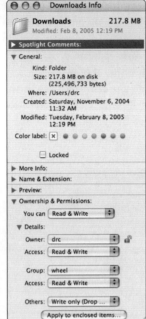

Figure 14-15: Everyone can drop files into this folder.

One more privilege

The Apply to Enclosed Items button, at the bottom of the access privileges section, does exactly what its name implies. This feature is a fast way to assign the same privileges to many subfolders at once. After you set privileges for the enclosing folder the way you like them, click this button to give these same privileges to all folders inside it.

Be careful — there is no Undo for this action.

Consummating the Act of Sharing

After you set up sharing and assign access privileges, you can access folders remotely from another computer. (Just make sure first that you have access privileges to it.)

File sharing must be activated on the Mac where the shared files/folders reside; it does not have to be activated on the Mac that's accessing the files/folders. When file sharing is turned off, you can still use that Mac to access a remote shared folder on another machine as long as its owner has granted you enough access privileges and has file sharing enabled on his or her Mac.

If file sharing is turned off on *your* Mac, though, others won't be able to access your folders, even if you've assigned access privileges to them previously.

If you're going to share files and you leave your Mac on and unattended for a long time, logging out before you leave it is a very good idea. This prevents anyone just walking up to your Mac from seeing your files, e-mail, applications, or anything else that's yours — unless you have given them a user account and granted them access privileges for your files.

Connecting to a shared disk or folder on a remote

On to how to access your Home folder from a remote Mac — a super-cool feature that's only bound to get more popular as the Internet continues to mature.

The following steps assume you've got an account on the remote Mac, which means you have your own Home folder on that Mac.

To connect to a shared folder on a Mac other than the one you're currently on, follow these steps:

1. **Make sure that you are already set up as a user on the computer that you want to log in to (DoctorMacDualG5 in this example).**

   If you need to know how to create a new user, see the "Creating users" section earlier in the chapter.

2. **On the computer that you're logging in from (TigerTiBook in this example), choose Go⇨Connect to Server.**

   The Connect to Server dialog appears.

3. **Click the Browse button.**

   A Finder window opens, set to show (aliases to) all the computers available on your local network, as shown in Figure 14-16.

   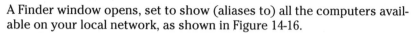

   You can combine Steps 2 and 3 by clicking Network in a Finder window sidebar.

4. **Double-click the remote Mac's name (DoctorMacDualG5) in the Finder window.**

   If the Network window is in column view, you'll also see a Connect button in the column to the right of the remote Mac's name, as shown in Figure 14-15. Clicking the Connect button serves the same purpose as double-clicking that remote Mac's icon.

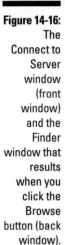

Figure 14-16:
The
Connect to
Server
window
(front
window)
and the
Finder
window that
results
when you
click the
Browse
button (back
window).

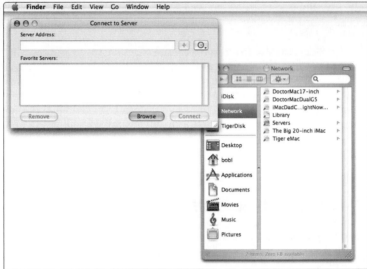

The Connect dialog appears. The name of the person logged in on TigerTiBook automatically appears in the Name field (Bob LeVitus in Figure 14-17). If that's not you, type your username in the Name field.

Figure 14-17:
The
Connect to
Server
knows it's
me but
doesn't
know my
password.
Yet.

You would mark the Guest radio button if you didn't have an account on DoctorMacDualG5.

Pressing ⌘+G is the same as marking the Guest radio button, and pressing ⌘+R is the same as marking the Registered User radio button.

As a guest user, you see only Drop Boxes for users who have accounts on DoctorMacDualG5 but nothing else. A registered user (somebody like me in this example) also sees his Home folder plus everyone else's Public folder.

If I check the Remember Password in Keychain check box in the Connect dialog, Mac OS X will remember my password for me the next time I connect to a server. Sweet!

TCP/IP must be active on TigerTiBook (the Mac I'm using in the example). If it's not, you won't see any other machines on the network — nor will you be able to use any remote shared folders. In other words, file sharing doesn't have to be turned on (on the computer you're using), but TCP/IP does.

5. **Type your password into the Password field and then click the Connect button.**

   When you log in to a Mac on which you have a user account, you see a volume with your name representing your Home folder on the Mac you're logging into. If you have Administrator privileges on that Mac, you may also see other hard drives connected to that Mac or an iDisk if one is in use.

6. **Select the volume that you want to use (such as** bob1 **in Figure 14-18) and then click OK.**

   An icon appears on your Desktop (the Desktop of TigerTiBook), as shown in Figure 14-19. This icon represents a volume named bob1, which resides on the computer DoctorMacDualG5. Notice that the icon for bob1 doesn't look like a drive or folder icon. This icon is what you see whenever a remote volume is mounted on your Desktop. You'll also see it if you add a server to your Favorites folder (more on that later) or view a server in the Finder window.

   Open the volume icon, and its folder window appears (also called bob1), as shown in Figure 14-19.

Unsharing a folder

To unshare a folder that you own, change the Group Access and Others privileges to None. After you do, nobody but you will have access to that folder.

Figure 14-18:
Selecting
the volumes
I wish to
mount.

Figure 14-19:
The finale:
My Home
directory
(bobl) on my
desktop
Mac
(DoctorMac
DualG5) as
seen when I
log in
remotely
from my
PowerBook
(TigerTi
Book).

If you're not sure how to do this, see the "Sharing a folder" and "Useful settings for access privileges" sections earlier in this chapter.

Disconnecting from a shared volume

When you finish using the shared volume, disconnect by using one of these methods:

- ✔ Drag the shared folder icon to the Eject icon in the dock.

    When a disk or volume is selected (highlighted), the Trash icon turns into a little arrow, which represents *eject*. Nice touch, eh?

- ✔ Hold down the Control key, click the volume, and then choose Eject from the contextual menu that appears.

- ✔ Select the icon and choose File⇨Eject.

- ✔ Select the icon and press ⌘+E.

- ✔ In a Finder window Sidebar, click the little Eject symbol to the right of the server's name or select the server and choose Eject from the Action pop-up.

- ✔ If you've finished working for the day, choose Shut Down or Log Out from the menu. Shutting down or logging out automatically disconnects you from shared disks or folders. (Shut Down also turns off your Mac.)

Changing your password

You can change your password at any time. Changing your password is a good idea if you're concerned about security — for example, if there's a chance your password has been discovered by someone else.

You can change the password for your Mac, or you can change the password you use to connect to your account on a remote user's Mac. I show you how to do both in the following sections.

Changing your Mac's password

To change the password on your Mac, just follow these steps:

1. **Choose System Preferences from the menu on the Finder's menu bar (or click the System Preferences icon in the Dock) and then click the Accounts icon.**

    The Accounts System Preference pane appears.

2. **Select your account in the list on the left.**

    Your account information appears in the area on the right.

3. **Click the Change Password button.**

   A sheet drops down.

4. **Type your current password into Old Password field.**

   This demonstrates that you are who you're supposed to be and not someone who just walked up to your unattended Mac.

5. **Type your new password into the Password field in the Password pane.**

6. **Retype your password in the Verify field.**

7. **Click the Change Password button.**

   Assuming you entered your old password correctly, the sheet disappears.

8. **Close the System Preferences window.**

Changing the password for your account on someone else's Mac

When you log in to a remote Mac, you can change your own password if you like. Follow these steps to do so:

1. **Log in to the remote computer on which you want to change your password.**

   See the "Connecting to a shared disk or folder on a remote" section earlier in this chapter if you don't know how to log in to a remote computer.

   The Connect to Server dialog appears.

2. **Type your username into the Connect to Server dialog if it's not already there.**

3. **Click the Action button in the Connect to Server dialog and choose Change Password from the pop-up menu.**

   A sheet for changing your password appears, as shown in Figure 14-20.

   The other choice in the Actions pop-up is Options. The sheet that appears includes several options for encrypting your password as it is sent over the network.

4. **Type your current password in the Old Password field.**

5. **Type your new password in the New Password and Verify fields.**

6. **Click OK.**

   Your password is changed, and you return to the Connect to Server dialog.

Figure 14-20:
Enter your old and new passwords.

7. **(Optional) Type your new password and click then Connect to log in to the other Mac.**

   You can skip this step by clicking the Cancel button in the Connect to Server dialog if you don't need to use anything on the remote Mac at this time. Your password is still changed, and you'll need to use the new password the next time you log in to this Mac.

Mark the Add Password to Keychain check box in the Connect to Server dialog to store your passwords in a single place on the Mac, meaning that you don't have to retype them each time you access a Mac or other remote resource. (Read more about the keychain in Chapter 11.)

Setting up shortcuts to remote volumes (and folders)

Here are three ways you can make using remote volumes and folders easier. The first is to use aliases, the second is to use OS X's Sidebar, and the third uses aliases and the Dock. The following sections describe each of these methods.

Setting up a shortcut using aliases

After you've mounted a volume for the first time, you can make it easier to use in the future by creating an alias for it. The next time you want to use that volume, just opens the alias, and the Connect dialog appears. You type your password, and the volume appears (is mounted) on the Desktop. No Connect to Server; no other dialogs; no muss and no fuss.

You can do this to any folder within the volume, too. It works just the same with one minor difference: The alias opens that folder, but it also mounts the volume that contains the folder — and opens it, too. If you find this bothersome, just close the Home folder's window. The folder within — the one for which you made the alias — remains open, and you can continue working with it.

Setting up a shortcut using the Sidebar

Here's another easy way to mount a volume: Just click the remote volume's icon (or any folder icon within that volume), and then, while it's selected (highlighted), choose File⇨Add to Sidebar (or press ⌘+T) from the Finder's menu bar. An alias to the remote volume or folder appears in the Finder Sidebar and Sidebars of all Open and Save dialogs.

Setting up shortcuts in the Dock (and on the Desktop)

If you use remote folders often, follow these steps to create a folder that sits on your Dock, ready to call remote computers at your very whim:

1. **Log in to each remote volume (or folder) you want included in the shortcut folder on your Desktop.**

2. **Create an alias for each remote volume or folder to which you want easy access.**

3. **Move the aliases that you created in Step 2 to a new folder on your Desktop (call it Remote Folders or something equally obvious).**

4. **Drag the Remote Folders folder onto the Dock.**

   Here are two easy ways to open any volume or folder in the Remote Folders folder:

   • You can open the Remote Folders folder and double-click any of the aliases in it.

   • You can click and hold (or Control+click) the Remote Folders icon in the Dock, which causes a menu to pop up that shows all the aliases in the Remote Folders folder.

   Either way, that volume or folder appears on your Desktop almost instantly.

Connecting to your own computer from a remote computer

In this section, I show you several file-sharing tricks you can use on the road. The first explains how to log in to your home Mac easily from anywhere in the world by plugging into someone else's network. The second is a trick I call *office-on-a-disk,* which is a way to take your shortcuts (see the previous section) with you, even when you use someone else's Mac. Finally, I give you a look at how to access your files remotely via modem connection.

 These techniques are especially useful for iBook or PowerBook users, or if you need to connect to your Mac from someplace other than your home or office network. The only thing you have to remember is that your Mac must be on and that you need File Sharing turned on as well.

Assume for the moment that you're on a network, perhaps at a client's office. In this section, I show how you would make the connection with a modem. For example, say you take a plane trip. You bring your PowerBook so you can work on the plane. When you get to your destination, you want to copy the files that you've been working on to your home Mac to back them up. Well, you can do that with file sharing — which is easy if you've read about file sharing in the earlier sections of this chapter and understand how to connect to a remote Mac. (If you aren't sure how to do that, please reread the previous sections of this chapter now. If you don't, the following technique will only confuse you.)

Because you are the owner of your home Mac, you have full access privileges to both your Home folder and also to the rest of your Mac, just as you would if you were working from home. Also, because you own your Mac, you don't need to make any changes to file sharing privileges in order to log in and use your stuff.

You can connect to your home Mac via an Ethernet network or a modem. I'll talk about Ethernet first, and then the nifty office-on-a-disk, and finish up with a rousing look at using a modem (screech optional).

Logging in remotely via Ethernet

Okay, so you've arrived at your destination. The first thing to do is plug your PowerBook's Ethernet cable into the network and find out what TCP/IP address info you need to use this network (by asking the PIC, or *person in charge;* also sometimes known as the network administrator, IT person, or resident geek). With those tasks completed, you're ready to do some sharing.

To connect to your home Mac from a remote computer, follow these steps:

1. **Choose Go⇨Connect to Server (on your PowerBook or other remote Mac, of course).**

2. **Type in the TCP/IP address of your Mac at home in the Address field and then click the Connect button.**

   The Connect to Server dialog appears.

3. **Type your username (it might be the same on the PowerBook as on your home Mac) and password and then click the Connect button.**

   The Volume Selection dialog appears. You see your Home folder, your startup hard drive, and any other disks or partitions that appear on the Desktop of your home machine.

4. **Choose a volume and then click OK.**

   The volume mounts on your PowerBook Desktop, and you're in business!

Logging in remotely via office-on-a-disk

Here's an even easier way to use your hard drive while working at someone else's Mac. Before leaving your computer, make an alias of your hard drive and copy it to a USB Flash drive, put it on an iPod, burn it onto a CD-R, or copy it to your PowerBook's hard drive. At a remote computer, open the alias of your hard drive. The Connect dialog appears, and as long as you type the correct password and your Mac can be found through the network connection, your hard drive mounts on that Mac's Desktop. Neat!

This technique is often called *office-on-a-disk*. If you work in a largish office and find yourself trying to connect to your hard drive from someone else's computer, carry one of these office-on-a-disk, um, *disks* with you at all times. And if you're using a PowerBook, keep the aliases to your Mac (and any others you use on the road) on the Desktop for quick access. You could also put them in a folder and drag the folder to the Dock. Then all the aliases are available in a pop-up menu when you click and hold (or Control+click) the folder's Dock icon.

If you have no USB Flash drive or other removable-media disk drive, don't despair — you can still use a disk alias. The first time you mount your hard drive on a remote Mac (see the preceding section, "Logging in remotely via Ethernet"), make an alias of the mounted drive. Leave it on the Desktop or some other convenient location, and you can use it to mount the drive immediately.

Logging in remotely via a modem

Mac OS X includes Point-to-Point Protocol (PPP) software — Internet Connect — that enables you to connect to another computer or the Internet by modem.

With Internet Connect, you can access your home hard drive from a remote Mac when you're at another location. You do need a modem — and you also need to configure this modem for remote access (which luckily is a pretty simple process). Because remote access uses the same Accounts and File Sharing tools as network file sharing, you should probably bone up on file sharing (in the sections earlier in this chapter) if you haven't already.

To use a modem to log in remotely, follow these steps:

1. **Choose System Preferences from the menu or click the System Preferences icon in the Dock.**

2. **Click the Network icon.**

   The Network pane appears.

   You can consolidate Steps 1 and 2 by choosing ⬛⇨Location⇨Network Preferences.

3. **Choose Internal Modem from the Show pop-up menu, unless you have an external modem; in that case, choose that option.**

   If you've been using Ethernet rather than a modem, notice that two new tabs appear after you choose Internal Modem from the menu: the PPP tab and the Modem tab.

4. **Click the PPP tab.**

   PPP options appear, as shown in Figure 14-21.

5. **(Optional) Type a name for this connection in the Service Provider field.**

   Doing so gives a name to the connection information you're creating, which enables you to reuse it easily later. It's handy if you need to use this modem connection again.

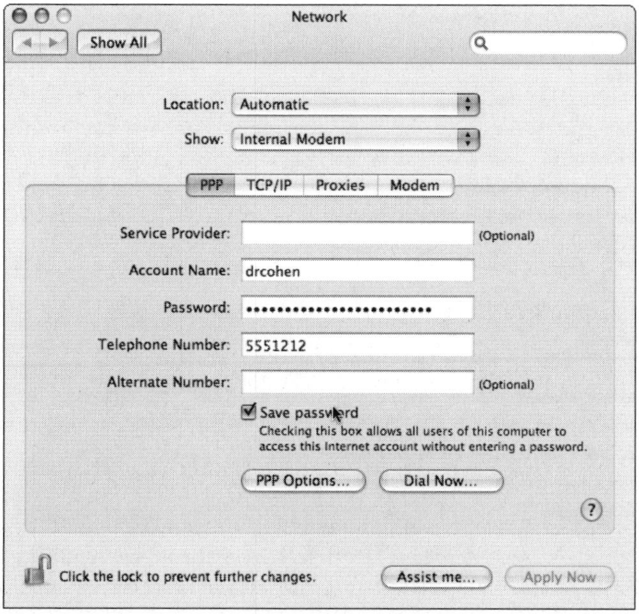

Figure 14-21: The PPP tab of the Network pane is where you set up for remote access via a modem.

6. **Type your account name (Internet username) in the Account Name field.**

7. **Type your password in the Password field.**

8. **Type the phone number that you want to dial (including any dialing prefix and area code) into the Telephone Number field.**

9. **(Optional) Type an alternate phone number, if there is one, in the Alternate Number field.**

10. **(Optional) If you want to log in without having to enter your password each time, select the Save Password check box.**

    Selecting this check box means that someone with access to your Mac can log in to your account, so be careful — especially if you're working on an iBook or PowerBook.

11. **Click the PPP Options button to set preferences for how your connection is made and maintained.**

    The PPP Options sheet appears, as shown in Figure 14-22. Of the many options you find here, I point out a few of the most useful in the following list:

    • Select the Connect Automatically When Needed check box if you want your modem to connect to the Internet when you launch your browser, connect to a remote server, or retrieve e-mail. This check box must be marked, or your Mac won't connect to the Internet automatically when you choose Go⇨Connect to Server.

Figure 14-22:
Use PPP options to set PPP connects and stays connected.

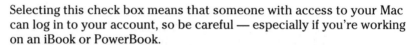

Session Options:
- ☐ Connect automatically when needed
- ☐ Prompt every 30 minutes to maintain connection
- ☑ Disconnect if idle for 10 minutes
- ☑ Disconnect when user logs out
- ☑ Disconnect when switching user accounts
- ☑ Redial if busy
    - Redial 1 times
    - Wait 5 seconds before redialing

Advanced Options:
- Terminal Script: None
- ☑ Send PPP echo packets
- ☑ Use TCP header compression
- ☐ Connect using a terminal window (command line)
- ☐ Prompt for password after dialing
- ☐ Use verbose logging

(Cancel) (OK)

- Leave the Prompt Every *x* Minutes to Maintain Connection check box selected if you're paying long distance charges or Internet access charges. If you don't set this auto-disconnect timer, you could rack up a lot of toll charges if you forget you're connected and online. If you choose this option, set the number of idle minutes by clicking within the number box and typing the number you want.

- Select the Redial If Busy check box to do just that. You can choose the number of attempts that your modem will make and how long it should wait between attempts if it gets a busy signal instead of connecting.

12. **When you're done setting PPP options, click OK to close the PPP Options sheet.**

13. **(Optional) Click the Modem tab in the Network pane.**

   Your modem should be selected in the Modem pop-up menu. If you're having problems connecting, use the menu to find your particular modem and select it. You won't need to do much with these settings unless you're having a problem connecting with the modem, but you can set little options here, too. Some options of note are

   - Some modems, such as the Apple 56K modems included in most Macs, are capable of performing some error checking and data compression. It's not industrial-strength compression, but it can speed up data transfer.

   - You can tell the modem to wait until it detects a dial tone before dialing. In less-friendly environs, you have to know to insert commas into the phone number to get that pause.

   - Choose whether to turn your speaker sound off (to rid yourself of that horrid modem-screech).

   - Choose tone or pulse dialing, if you need the latter for some strange reason.

   And that retires the side. Just choose Go⇨Connect to Server and log in to the remote machine. (If you don't know how, read the "Connecting to a shared disk or folder on a remote" section earlier in the chapter.)

Chapter 15

Troubleshooting Mac OS X

In This Chapter

▶ Facing the dreaded Sad Mac

▶ Dealing with the flashing question mark

▶ Recovering from startup crashes

As a bleeding-edge Mac enthusiast with over 20 years of Mac experience under my belt, I've had more than my share of Mac troubles. Over those years I've developed an arsenal of surefire tips and tricks that I believe can resolve more than 90 percent of Mac OS X problems without a trip to the repair shop.

Alas, if your hardware is dead, then, sadly, neither you nor I can do anything about it because this is now a job for your friendly Mac repairman and your fat checkbook.

But if your hardware is okay, you have a fighting chance of using the suggestions in this chapter to get your machine up and running.

Dem Ol' Sad Mac Chimes of Doom Blues

Although you usually see a stylish Apple logo when you turn your computer on, once in a blue moon you might see the dreaded Sad Mac icon (shown in the left margin) and hear that melancholy arpeggio in G minor (better known as the *Chimes of Doom*), or the sound of breaking glass or a car wreck, or any of the other horrible sounds that Macs make when they're dying.

The Sad Mac usually indicates that something very bad has happened to your Mac; often some hardware component has bitten the dust. But Sad Macs are rather uncommon — many Mac users go an entire lifetime without seeing one. If you ever have a Sad Mac experience, don't despair immediately. Before you diagnose your Mac as terminally ill, disconnect any external FireWire and USB devices (everything except your keyboard and mouse), and try booting from CD-ROM to bring it back to life. If you've installed third-party memory (RAM from a vendor other than Apple), remove all non-Apple RAM chips and try booting from CD-ROM to bring it back to life.

If you have your OS X installation CD-ROM ready, you can skip to the section "Booting from CD-ROM" later in this chapter. If you're not sure about your OS X installation CD-ROM, see the next section.

The ultimate startup disk: The OS X installation CD

I bet you have a copy of the ultimate startup disk right there on your computer table — the installation CD that came with your computer or (if you purchased a boxed retail copy of Tiger) Install Disk 1.

You see, in addition to the system software that you need to make your Mac work, all OS X installation disks are bootable and include a working copy of Disk Utility, which I discuss in the section "Step 1: Run First Aid" section later in this chapter.

If you see a flashing question-mark-on-a-folder (top left in Figure 15-1), prohibitory sign (top center), a spinning-disk cursor (top right), or a kernel panic alert (bottom) that doesn't go away when you start up your Mac, the first thing to do is attempt to repair hidden damage to your hard drive with the Apple Disk Utility program's First Aid feature.

Figure 15-1:
If you see any of these things at startup, it's troubleshooting time.

Another of Disk Utility's features lets you verify and repair disk permissions, which is a handy thing to do if your Mac is telling you that you don't have the correct permission to do things that you *used* to be able to do, such as move a file or folder into the Applications (or other) folder, or move an icon to the Trash.

Better safe than Mac-less

The bootable Mac OS X CD-ROM is soooo important — try to have more than one copy around. That way, if one gets misplaced, damaged, eaten by the dog, scuffed, scratched, or otherwise rendered useless, you won't be out of luck. I keep the Mac OS X CD in my middle desk drawer and several other bootable CDs on the bookshelf. An older version of Mac OS and the CD that came with your computer are examples of extra bootable CDs that you might have hanging around. The Mac OS X installation CD is bootable as well. All these will boot your Mac in an emergency, which is why they're so important to have handy.

One thing I'd do — if I only had one of these valuable CDs — is to use Apple's Disk Utility (in Applications/Utilities) to create a disk image of the CD and then burn a copy or two as spares. Don't forget to test the burned disks to ensure that they work and are bootable.

You get a brass-tacks view of using these utilities throughout the rest of this chapter.

If you don't have a bootable CD-ROM, preferably a Mac OS X Install CD-ROM, you can't do most of the rest of the stuff in this chapter. So if you don't have it handy, go find it now. If you really can't find one, consider calling Apple or your Apple dealer to arrange for a replacement — you really shouldn't be without it.

Booting from CD-ROM

To boot your Mac from a CD-ROM installation disk, follow these steps:

1. **Insert a bootable CD-ROM (the Mac OS X installer CD is a good choice).**

   If your Mac uses a tray to hold the CD, make sure that it retracts and that the disk is in.

   If you have a tray-loading CD-ROM drive and it's closed, you can get it to open by restarting (or starting up) your Mac while pressing the mouse button. Continue pressing until the drive tray pops out; then release.

2. **Shut down or restart your Mac.**

   If you shut it down, wait a few seconds and then start it up the usual way.

3. Press and hold down the C key immediately and keep it pressed until your Mac either boots from the CD or doesn't.

If it boots, you see a Welcome screen; if it doesn't, you see a flashing question mark, prohibitory sign, spinning wheel-of-death, anything but the first screen of the OS X Installer, the login window, or the Finder.

If your Mac doesn't boot from the CD when you hold down the C key, hold down the Option key while booting to display the built-in Startup Manager (Figure 15-2). It displays icons for any bootable disks that it sees and allows you to select one (including the installation CD).

Figure 15-2:
Hold down the Option key during startup to bring up the built-in Startup Manager.

Click the CD-ROM icon to select it (on the right in Figure 15-2, unselected), and then click the right-arrow button to boot from it.

This technique is quite useful if your usual boot disk is damaged or having an identity crisis during startup.

If you can boot from CD-ROM . . .

If you see the Mac OS startup (Welcome) screen when you boot (start up) from your CD-ROM, hope flickers for your Mac. The fact that you can boot from another disk (a CD-ROM in this case) indicates that the problem lies in one of two places: your hard drive and/or Mac OS X itself. Whatever the tangle, it will probably respond to one of the techniques I discuss throughout the rest of this chapter.

So your Mac boots from the installation CD-ROM, but you still have this little problem: You prefer that your Mac boot from your (much faster) hard drive than the system software CD-ROM. Not to worry. All you need to do is rein-stall Mac OS X (as described in the Appendix at the end of this book).

If you can't boot from CD-ROM . . .

If the techniques in this chapter don't correct your Mac problem or you still see the Sad Mac icon when you start up with the CD, your Mac is probably toasted and needs to go in for repairs (usually to an Apple dealer).

Before you drag it down to the shop, however, try calling 1-800-SOS-APPL, the Apple Tech Support hotline. The service representatives there may be able to suggest something else that you can try. If your Mac is still under warranty, it's even free.

Another thing you might consider is contacting your local Macintosh user group. You can find a group of Mac users near you by visiting Apple's User Group Web pages at www.apple.com/usergroups.

Or check out my new company, Doctor Mac Direct, at www.doctormac direct.com or call us toll-free at 877-DrMac4U. Our team of Mac experts does nothing but provide technical help and training to Mac users, via telephone, e-mail, and/or unique Internet-enabled remote control software, in real time and at reasonable prices.

If you get the Sad Mac immediately after installing random-access memory (RAM) — and this is quite common — double-check that the RAM is properly seated in its sockets. Don't forget to power-down your Mac first.

Follow the installation instructions that came with the RAM chips or the ones in the booklet that came with your Mac. But even if they don't say to, you should get rid of the spark, either by using an anti-static strap (available from most RAM sellers) or by touching an appropriate surface (such as the power-supply case inside your Mac) before you handle RAM chips.

If problems occur immediately after installing RAM (or any new hardware, for that matter), remove and reinsert the RAM chips to make sure that they're seated properly. If you still have problems, remove the RAM temporarily and see whether the problem still exists.

Question Mark and the Mysterians

When you turn on your Mac, the first thing that it does (after the hardware tests) is to check for a startup disk with Mac OS 9 or X on it. If your system doesn't find such a disk on your internal hard drive, it begins looking elsewhere — on a FireWire or Universal Serial Bus (USB) disk or on a CD or DVD.

If you have more than one startup disk attached to your Mac, as many users do, you can choose which one your Mac boots from in the Startup Disk System Preference pane. (See Chapter 13 for details.)

At this point, your Mac usually finds your hard drive, which contains your operating system, and the startup process continues on its merry way with the happy Mac and all the rest. If your Mac can't find your hard drive (or doesn't find on it what it needs to boot OS X), you encounter a flashing-question-mark icon or the prohibitory sign.

Don't go cryin' *96 Tears.* Those icons just mean that your Mac can't find a startup disk — a hard drive, or bootable CD-or-DVD-ROM disk with valid system software (either Mac OS X or a previous version supported by your particular Mac).

Think of the flashing question mark or prohibitory sign as your Mac's way of saying, "Please provide me with a startup disk."

If Apple can figure out a way to put a flashing question mark or prohibitory sign on the screen, why the heck can't the software engineers find a way to put the words `Please insert a startup disk` on the screen as well? The curtness of these icons is one of my pet peeves about the Macintosh. I know — you're clever and smart (but of course — you're reading *Mac OS X Tiger For Dummies,* aren't you?), so you know that a flashing question mark or prohibitory sign means you should insert a startup disk. But what about everyone else?

If you encounter any of these warning icons, go through the steps I outline next in this chapter. There are different options you can try, such as using Disk Tools and First Aid, zapping the parameter RAM (PRAM), and performing a Safe Boot. Try them in the order listed, starting with Step 1. Then, if one doesn't work, move on to the next.

Step 1: Run First Aid

In most cases, after you've booted successfully from the OS X CD, the first logical troubleshooting step is to use the First Aid option in the Disk Utility application.

Every drive has several strangely named components such as B-trees, extent files, catalog files, and other creatively named invisible files. They are all involved in managing the data on your drives. Disk Utility's First Aid feature checks all those files and repairs the damaged ones.

Here's how to make First Aid do its thing:

1. **Boot from your Mac OS X CD by inserting the CD and restarting your Mac while holding down the C key.**

   The OS X Installer appears on your screen.

2. **Choose Installer⇨Open Disk Utility to launch the Disk Utility application that's on the CD.**

3. **When the Disk Utility window appears, click the First Aid tab to select that function of Disk Utility.**

4. **Click the icon for your boot hard drive at the left of the Disk Utility window (*Tiger* in Figure 15-3).**

   Your boot drive is the one with OS X and your Home folder on it. I call this one *Tiger*.

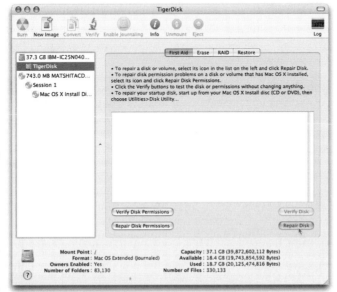

Figure 15-3:
First Aid,
ready to
perform its
magic on
the disk
named
Tiger.

5. **Click the Repair Disk button.**

   Your Mac whirs and hums for a few minutes, and the results window tells you what's going on. Ultimately, First Aid tells you (you hope) that the drive has been repaired and is now okay, as shown in Figure 15-4. If so, go back to work.

6. **Quit Disk Utility by choosing Disk Utility⇨Quit Disk Utility or by pressing ⌘+Q.**

7. **Reboot without holding the C key down.**

If First Aid finds damage that it can't fix, a commercial disk-recovery tool, such as Alsoft's DiskWarrior or MicroMat's TechTool Pro, may be able to repair the damage. And even if First Aid gave you a clean bill of health, you may want to run DiskWarrior anyway just to have a second opinion. Make sure you're running a current version; older versions were not Mac OS X-compatible.

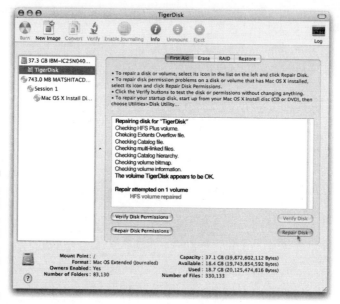

Figure 15-4:
First Aid
repaired the
disk and
gives it a
clean bill of
health.

DiskWarrior has resurrected more dead and dying hard drives for me than every other disk-repair utility I've ever tried, or all of them combined. If you're only going to buy one utility, make sure it's DiskWarrior. It's almost like magic.

If everything checks out with First Aid, eject the CD and try to boot from your hard drive again. If you still get the flashing question mark or prohibitory sign, proceed to the next section to try a little dance called zapping the PRAM (coming up in Step 3).

Step 2: Safe Boot into Safe Mode

Booting your Mac in Safe Mode may help you resolve your startup issue by not loading non-essential (and non-OS X) software at boot time. You do it by holding down the Shift key during startup, as shown in Figure 15-5.

Keep holding down Shift until the Finder loads completely. If your Mac is set up so you don't have to log in, keep pressing the Shift key until the Finder loads completely. If you do log in to your Mac, type your password as usual, but before clicking the Log In button, press the Shift key again and hold it until the Finder loads completely.

Figure 15-5:
Your Mac
lets you
know you're
booting into
Safe Mode
by adding
the words
Safe Boot to
the bottom
of the
startup
screen, as
shown.

You'll know you held the Shift key long enough if your Startup Items don't load (assuming you have Startup Items; you can create them in the Accounts System Preference pane, although some programs create them for you).

Booting in Safe Mode does three things to help you with troubleshooting:

✔ It forces a directory check of the startup (boot) volume.

✔ It loads only required kernel extensions (some of the items in /System/ Library/Extensions).

✔ It runs only Apple-installed startup items (some of the items in /Library/ Startup Items and /System/Library/Startup items). Note that the startup items in the Library folders are different from the Startup Items in the Accounts System Preference pane.

Taken together, normally these changes can work around issues caused by software or directory damage on the startup volume.

Some features do not work in Safe Mode. Among them are DVD Player, capturing video (in iMovie or other video-editing software), using an AirPort card, using some audio input or output devices, or using an internal or external USB modem. Use Safe Mode only if you need to troubleshoot a startup issue.

If your Mac boots in Safe Mode, you may be able to determine what is causing it — usually a damaged Preference file (in Home/Library/Preferences) or one of your Startup Items (in the Accounts System Preference pane).

If your Mac still has problems, try Step 3.

Step 3: Zapping the PRAM

Sometimes your *parameter RAM (PRAM)* becomes scrambled and needs to be reset. PRAM is a small piece of memory that's not erased or forgotten when you shut down; it keeps track of things such as printer selection, sound level, and monitor settings.

PRAM stores these settings:

- ✔ Time zone setting
- ✔ Startup volume choice
- ✔ Speaker volume
- ✔ Recent kernel panic information, if any
- ✔ DVD region setting

To reset (often called "zapping") your PRAM, restart your Mac and press ⌘+Option+P+R (that's four keys — good luck; it's okay to use your nose) until your Mac restarts itself. It's kind of like a hiccup. You may see the flashing question mark or spinning-disk cursor for a minute or two while your Mac thinks about it — then the icon disappears, and your Mac chimes again and restarts. Most power users believe you should zap it more than once, letting it chime two, three, or even four times before releasing the keys and allowing the startup process to proceed.

Now restart your Mac without holding down any keys.

If the PRAM zap didn't fix your Mac, move on to Step 4.

Remember that your chosen startup disk, time zone, and sound volume are reset to their default values when you zap your PRAM. So after zapping, open the System Preferences application to reselect your usual boot disk and time zone, and set the sound volume the way you like it.

Unlike prior versions of the Mac OS, Mac OS X does not store display or network settings in PRAM. If you are having problems with video or networking, resetting PRAM will not help.

Step 4: Reinstalling OS X

I present the procedure to reinstall the system software last in this section because it takes the longest and is the biggest hassle. I detail this procedure at great length in the Appendix.

Read the Appendix and follow the instructions. If you're still unsuccessful after that point, you'll have no choice but to consider Step 5 . . .

Step 5: Take your Mac in for repair

If none of my suggestions work for you and you're still seeing anything you shouldn't when you start up your Mac, you have big trouble.

You could have any one of the following problems:

- ✔ Your hard drive is dead.
- ✔ You have some other type of hardware failure.
- ✔ All your startup disks and your system-software CDs are defective (unlikely).

The bottom line: If you still can't start up normally after trying all the cures I list in this chapter, you almost certainly need to have your Mac serviced by a qualified technician.

If You Crash at Startup

Startup crashes are another bad thing that can happen to your Mac. These crashes can be more of a hassle to resolve than flashing-question-mark problems, but are rarely fatal.

You know that a *crash* has happened when you see a System Error dialog, a frozen cursor, a frozen screen, or any other disabling event. A *startup crash* happens when your system shows a crash symptom any time between flicking the power key or switch (or restarting) and having full use of the Desktop.

Try all the steps in the previous section before you panic. The easiest way to fix startup crashes (in most cases) is to just reinstall OS X from the CD using the Archive and Install option. I detail this procedure at great length in the Appendix. Read the Appendix and follow the instructions. If you're still unsuccessful after that point, come back and reread the "Step 5: Take your Mac in for repair" section.

Part V
The Part of Tens

The 5th Wave   By Rich Tennant

"Wow, I didn't know OSX could redirect an email message like that."

In this part . . .

These last chapters are a little different — they're kind of like long top-ten lists. Although I'd like for you to believe I included them because I'm a big fan of Dave Letterman, the truth is that Wiley always includes The Part of Tens section in its *For Dummies* books. This book continues the tradition. And because Wiley pays me, I do these chapters how I'm asked. (Actually, it's kind of fun.)

First, I tell you how to speed up your Mac experience. I then move on to a subject near and dear to my heart — awesome things for your Mac that are worth spending money on. Stay tuned for a collection of great Mac-related Web sites and a discussion of cool OS X applications that you may need someday.

Chapter 16

Ten (Or So) Ways to Speed Up Your Mac Experience

. . . .

This chapter is for speed demons only. At some time in their Mac lives, most users have wished that their machines would work faster — even those with Power Macintosh models or iMac G5s. I can't help you make your processor faster, but here I cover some ways to make your Mac at least seem faster, and most of these tips won't cost you a red cent.

Use Those Keyboard Shortcuts

Keyboard shortcuts (see Table 16-1 for a way-groovy list of the more useful ones) can make navigating your Mac a much faster experience compared to constantly using the mouse, offering these benefits:

- ✔ By using keyboard shortcuts, your hands stay focused on the keyboard, reducing the amount of time that you remove your hand from the keyboard to fiddle with the mouse.

- ✔ If you memorize keyboard shortcuts with your head, your fingers will memorize them, too.

- ✔ The more keyboard shortcuts you use, the faster you can do what you're doing.

Trust me when I say that learning the keyboard shortcuts for commands that you use often will save you a ton of time and effort.

Make a list of keyboard shortcuts and tape it to your monitor or somewhere where you'll see it all the time when using your Mac. (Heck, make a photocopy of Table 16-1!)

Table 16-1		Great Keyboard Shortcuts
Keyboard Shortcut	**What It's Called**	**What It Does**
⌘+O	Open	Opens the selected item.
⌘+. (period)	Cancel	Cancels the current operation in many programs, including the Finder. Also the keyboard shortcut for the Cancel button in most dialogs. The Esc key at the upper-left corner of your keyboard usually (but not always) does the same thing as the shortcut ⌘+. (period).
⌘+P	Print	Brings up a dialog that enables you to print the active window's contents. (See Chapter 10 for info on printing.)
⌘+X	Cut	Cuts whatever you select and places it on the Clipboard. (I cover the Edit menu and the Clipboard in Chapter 3.)
⌘+C	Copy	Copies whatever you select and places it on the Clipboard.
⌘+V	Paste	Pastes the contents of the Clipboard at the spot where your cursor is.
⌘+F	Find	Brings up a Find window in the Finder; brings up a Find dialog in most programs.
⌘+A	Select All	Selects the entire contents of the active window in many programs, including the Finder.
⌘+Z	Undo	Undoes the last thing you did in many programs, including the Finder.
⌘+Shift+?	Help	Brings up the Mac Help window in the Finder; usually the shortcut to summon Help in other programs.
⌘+H	Hide	(Usually) Hides the current application. Use the Application menu (the one that reads *Finder* when you're in the Finder) to Show All applications again. Some applications, such as BBEdit and Illustrator, have long used ⌘+H for something else — and hiding the application would really confuse their long-time users (so they don't use this shortcut).

Keyboard Shortcut	What It's Called	What It Does
⌘+Q	Quit	Perhaps the most useful keyboard shortcut of all — quits the current application (but not the Finder because the Finder is always running).
⌘+Shift+Q	Log Out	Logs out the current user; the login window appears on-screen until a user logs in.
⌘+Delete	Move to Trash	Moves the selected item to Trash.
⌘+Shift+Delete	Empty Trash	Empties the Trash.

Learn to Type Better

One way to make your Mac seem faster is to make your fingers move faster. The quicker you finish a task, the quicker you're on to something else. Keyboard shortcuts are nifty tools, and improving your typing speed and accuracy *will* save you time. Plus, you'll get stuff done faster if you're not always looking down at the keyboard or up at the screen when you type.

You'll also find that as your typing skills improve, you spend less time correcting errors or editing your work.

The Mac is not a typewriter

The Macintosh is more of a typesetting machine than a typewriter. So when you use a Macintosh, you should follow the rules of good typography, not the rules of good typewriting. If you want your documents to look truly professional, you need to understand the difference between inch and foot marks (" and ') and typographer's quotation marks " and " or ' and ', in addition to putting single spaces after punctuation. You also need to know where and how to use a hyphen (-), an en dash (–), and an em dash (—).

For more on making your documents look more elegant and professional, get a hold of an excellent book by Mac-goddess Robin Williams, *The Mac Is Not a Typewriter* (published by Peachpit Press).

The speed and accuracy that you gain has an added bonus: When you're a decent touch typist, your fingers fly even faster when you use those nifty keyboard shortcuts. (I list a gaggle of these in the preceding section, in Table 16-1.)

Resolution: It's Not Just for New Year's Anymore

A setting that you can change to potentially improve your Mac's performance is the resolution of your monitor. Most modern monitors and video cards (or onboard video circuitry, depending on which Mac model you use) can display multiple degrees of screen resolution. You change your monitor's display resolution in the same place where you choose the number of colors you want: the Display System Preference pane. Click your resolution choice from the Resolutions list on the left side of this tab.

In Displays System Preferences, check the Show Displays in Menu Bar box to change resolutions and color depth without opening System Preferences. You can then select your resolution from the Displays menu that appears near the right end of your menu bar, as shown in Figure 16-1.

Figure 16-1:
Use the handy Displays menu to switch resolutions right from the menu bar.

Here's the deal on display resolution: The smaller the numbers that you use for your monitor's resolution, the faster your screen refreshes. For a computer monitor, *resolution* is expressed as a dimension-type set of numbers (*number* x *number*). The first number is the number of pixels (color dots) that run horizontally, and the second number is the number of lines running vertically. Fewer pixels refresh faster. Therefore, a resolution of *640* x 480 updates itself faster than a resolution of *832* x 624; *832* x 624 updates faster than *1,024* x 768; and so forth.

This isn't always true if you have an LCD (flat-panel) monitor or a PowerBook. In that case, the native resolution is usually faster. Which is the native resolution? Depends on the monitor. For the Apple Studio Display 15-inch, and most older iBooks and PowerBooks, it's 1024 x 768. For newer PowerBooks, it's usually 1280 x 854. And for my 22-inch Apple Cinema Display, it's 1600 x 1024. Check the documentation that came with your display to determine what resolution(s) the vendor recommends.

On the other hand, the speed difference between resolutions these days is relatively minimal. In fact, I can almost never tell the difference between one and the other. Furthermore, because you can see more onscreen at higher resolutions, a higher resolution reduces the amount of scrolling that you have to do and lets you have more open windows on the screen. Therefore, you could say that higher resolutions can speed up your Mac as well.

Bottom line: Choose a resolution based on your preference, rather than one you think might be faster. That said, if your Mac seems slow at a resolution setting of 1,600 x 1024, try a lower resolution and see whether it feels faster.

Although you can use Mac OS X at resolutions of less than 1024 x 768, Apple has designed the OS X windows and dialogs on the assumption that your resolution will be at least 1024 x 768. So if you choose a lower resolution, some interface elements may be drawn partially or completely off-screen. Just keep that in mind if you choose a resolution below 1024 x 768.

A Mac with a View — and Preferences, Too

The type of icon display and the Desktop background that you choose affect how quickly your screen updates in the Finder. You can set and change these choices in the View Options windows. From the Finder, choose View➪Show View Options (or use the keyboard shortcut ⌘+J).

The View Options window, like our old friend the contextual menu, is . . . well . . . contextual. Depending on what's active when you choose it from the View menu, you see one of four similar versions (shown in Figure 16-2) — from left to right: folders in Icon view, folders in List view, folders in Column view, and the Desktop.

The All Windows and This Window Only radio buttons in the View Options window display identical options. You choose the All Windows radio button to set the default appearance for all your Finder windows, and you choose the This Window Only radio button to set up just the current window. These buttons appear only for the Icon and List view windows; Column windows are one-size-fits-all.

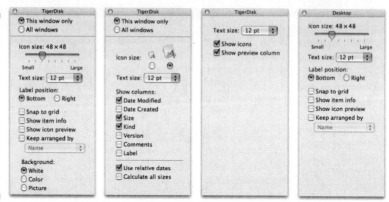

Figure 16-2:
Your
choices in
the View
Options
windows for
Icon view,
List view,
Column
view, and
the Desktop.

When bigger isn't better

The smaller the icon, the faster the screen updates. In the Icon view of the View Options windows, moving the Icon Size slider to the left makes icons smaller (faster); moving it to the right makes them bigger (slower). In List view, select one of the two Icon Size radio buttons to choose smaller (faster) or larger (slower) icons. The difference is greater if you have an older Mac.

Calculated moves

I recommend that you deactivate Calculate All Sizes (that is, deselect, or clear, its check box). If you activate this option, the Finder calculates the size of every folder of every open window in List view and displays that number in the Size column. At least to me, the screen feels as if it redraws faster with this feature turned off. This feature is offered only for windows using the List view.

The Finder is kind of smart about the Calculate All Sizes option. If you try to do anything in the Finder while folder sizes are calculating — say, make a menu selection, open an icon, or move a window, for example — the Finder interrupts the calculation so you can complete your task before it resumes calculating. So (in theory) you should never notice a delay when Calculate All Sizes is selected.

Try the Calculate All Sizes option both on and off. I don't know about you, but I find any noticeable delay unacceptable, and I notice a delay when this option is turned on, even on fast Macs. Maybe this feature is just annoying and not actually slowing things down, but I can't stand having it on. If you want to know how big a folder is, just click it and choose File➪Get Info (or use the keyboard shortcut, ⌘+I).

Getting ahead-er and other stuff

The Show Columns check boxes in the View Options window for List view — Date Modified, Date Created, Size, Kind, Version, and Comments — have a slight impact on screen update speed when you open a Finder window in List view. The Finder has to draw everything that you select here: With fewer items checked, the Finder updates windows faster.

The effect of these items on screen updating is pretty small, so your choice should be made according to the specific information you want to see in Finder windows, not on whether choosing them slows down your Mac. Play around with these options if you like, but unless your Mac is very slow, you probably won't notice much (or any) difference between on and off.

Get a New, Faster Model or Upgrade Yours

Apple keeps putting out faster and faster Macs at lower and lower prices. But many Mac models still ship with a paltry 256MB of RAM, not enough to run Tiger at its best.

Check out the latest iMacs and eMacs — they're an excellent value. Or, if you crave portability, iBooks and PowerBooks are rocking good computers and have never sold for less. You might even consider a used Mac that's faster than yours. The big-time honcho of auction Web sites, eBay (`www.ebay.com`), has hundreds of used Macs up for auction at any given time. Shopping on eBay might just get you a better Mac at an outstanding price. Give it a try!

Or, for a lot of bang for the buck, upgrade your Mac's RAM. Get an additional 512MB, 768MB, heck, even a gigabyte or more of the stuff — you can never have too much. Your Mac will run better with at least 512MB of RAM, which will cost you well under $100 in most cases and can be installed by anyone. Yes, anyone — the instructions are right there in your User Guide booklet or you can find them at Apple's Technical Support pages (`www.apple.com/support/`; search for **RAM upgrade** and your Mac model).

Unless, that is, you own a Mac mini. The Mac mini, you see, is exceedingly difficult to open without the proper and very specialized tool (a putty knife). And Apple frowns upon mere mortals applying such a tool to said Mac mini. Therefore, those of you with a Mac mini might want to opt for the services of an authorized, certified Mac cracker-opener to perform your RAM upgrade.

Get an Accelerator

An *accelerator* is a card that replaces the processor (CPU) in your Mac with a faster one. Even if you have a G4 in your Mac already, you might be able to upgrade to a faster one.

But before you plunk down the cash for an upgrade, be sure that it's compatible with Mac OS X. Some upgrades work only with older versions of Mac OS — and those won't help you.

Visit www.macworld.com for information on the various upgrade options available and how they compare with each other. Upgrades start at a few hundred dollars and go up to more than a thousand clams. The older your Mac, the more bang you'll get for your G4 upgrade buck.

Get an Accelerated Graphics Card

An *accelerated graphics card* is designed to speed up one thing: the screen update rate. Accelerated graphics cards blast pixels onto your screen at amazing speeds. They're extremely popular with graphic-arts professionals who would otherwise suffer slower screen redraws while working with 24-bit graphics. Most accelerators are also awesome for playing 3-D games. And because OS X's Quartz Extreme imaging architecture hands off part of its load to the processor on an accelerated graphics card, it might even make other tasks faster because it does some of the work that your Mac's main processor (CPU) used to do.

You can use a graphics accelerator only if your Mac has a slot for it; that's where you install one. Currently, you need a PowerMac G4 or G5 to use a graphics accelerator with OS X.

Visit www.macworld.com for information on the various graphics cards available and how they compare with each other. Cards start at around a hundred dollars and go up from there. And remember, the older your Mac, the more of a performance boost you'll see for your graphics-card-upgrade buck.

Get a New Hard Drive

Depending on how old your Mac is, a faster hard drive could provide a substantial speedup. If you have a relatively new Mac — any Mac with a G4 or G5 processor — the internal hard drive that came with it is pretty fast already. Unless you also need more storage space, a new hard drive may not be the best way to spend your bucks. On the other hand, if you have an older G3 model, a faster (and larger) FireWire or USB 2 hard drive could be just the ticket.

Add Storage with FireWire or USB 2 Drives

FireWire and USB 2 are the fastest *busses* (or data pathways) you can use for external devices on most Macs.

FireWire, the current state of the art in connecting devices that need fast transfer speeds, is used to connect devices that require high-speed communication with your Mac — hard drives, CD burners, scanners, camcorders, and such.

FireWire is the fastest, easiest way to add storage to Macs that include it.

If you must use USB, make sure you get USB 2 and not plain old USB (Universal Serial Bus). Plain ol' USB will work, of course, but it's as slow as molasses by comparison. (Plain ol' USB runs at about three percent of the speed of FireWire.)

USB 2, on the other hand, transfers data at roughly the same speed as FireWire. So if you have the need for speed, be sure you opt for a FireWire or USB 2 hard drive model and not a plain ol' USB model.

The good news is that whatever you choose, you can usually just plug it in and start using it. Ninety-nine percent of the time, there's nothing more to it!

Chapter 17

Ten (Or So) Ways to Make Your Mac Better by Throwing Money at It

● ●

*T*his is one of my favorite chapters. As you've probably figured out by now, I love souping up my Macs. I live to find ways of working smarter, saving time or hand motion, and coaxing my Mac to do more work in less time. So it gives me great pleasure to share in this chapter my personal top ten things that you can buy for your Mac to tweak it and make it faster, easier to use, and (I hope) more fun.

The items listed in this chapter are things I have, use every day, love dearly, and would (and probably will!) buy again.

RAM

RAM, or *random-access memory,* is your computer's primary working memory. The more you have, the smoother your Mac runs — period. If you have anything less than 512MB in your Mac, you'll like your Mac *a lot* better if you upgrade to 512MB or more. If you like to do a few things at once, more megabytes of RAM will make you a happier camper. (For what it's worth, RAM has never been cheaper than it is today — it's worth every penny.)

It's also easy as pie to install RAM into most Macs made this decade. Chances are the manual that came with your Mac includes step-by-step instructions simple enough for a nine-year-old to follow. I know because I once asked my (then) nine-year-old son do it. Which he did — and with no trouble, either.

Backup Software

The only two kinds of Mac users are those who have lost data and those who are going to. If your work means anything to you, get something that helps automate the task of backing up your files. Retrospect Desktop, Workgroup, or Server, all from Dantz Development (`www.dantz.com`), are the names to trust. And please, please read Chapter 8, which is titled (appropriately) "Back Up Now or Regret It Later." It may well be the most important chapter in this book.

A Better Monitor (or a Second One)

If you have a tiny monitor, get a bigger one. With a larger monitor, you spend less time scrolling and rearranging windows and more of your time getting actual work done — which is a good thing, right? For example, my main computer setup includes two monitors: a 22-inch Apple Cinema flat-panel LCD display, and an old fashioned CRT display, a 24-inch NEC MultiSync. It's an awesome setup — one that I highly recommend. With two monitors, you can have the menu bar and Finder windows on the first monitor, and document(s) that you're working on displayed on the second monitor. Or, when using a program like Photoshop (which has lots of floating palettes), you can put the palettes on one monitor and a document that you're working on can be displayed on the big one. And so on.

Flat-panel LCD displays, such as the Apple Studio and Cinema Displays, have come down dramatically in price over the past year. In my humble opinion, LCD displays are brighter and easier on the eyes than traditional CRT (glass picture tube) monitors. Apple must agree, because they no longer sell CRTs other than the ones built into eMacs. If you can afford one, that's what you really want. Alas, owners of older iMacs, as well as most iBook owners, are out of luck on this tip — it's not possible to add a second monitor to those models. If you've got a more recent iMac that includes a video port, however, you can get a bigger second monitor.

A Fast Internet Connection

High-bandwidth (that is, fast-Internet-access) connections just *rock.* By adding a high-speed Internet connection, such as digital subscriber line (DSL) or cable modem, your capacity to communicate electronically will increase tenfold. With this add-on, you can join an online service, surf the Internet, e-mail your friends, and much, much more, at speeds ten or more times faster than a 56Kbps modem. Web pages that once took minutes to load appear onscreen almost instantly. And it's fast enough that you can listen to streaming audio or watch streaming video without (many) hiccups. If you can afford cable/DSL ($25-$50/month in most places) and are in an area where you can get cable modem or DSL (not all places can, yet), it will change the way you view the Internet.

Additional Hard/Removable/Optical Drive (s)

Apple stopped including floppy disk drives with new Macs long ago. So now the only ways you can load new files (programs, documents, games, or whatever) onto your Mac are by copying files from some other kind of removable medium (such as a Zip drive, CD, or DVD, as described in Chapter 7), or by downloading from the Internet.

If you want to back up your Mac or hand your buddy a disk with files on it, you'll need some kind of external drive that uses removable media.

The most common is a CD-R (recordable CD-ROM) drive — or a CD-RW drive (with unlimited writing capabilities), like those built into almost every Mac, which let you create CDs that contain files, music, or both! Both kinds of drives let you *burn* CDs (CD-RWs just let you burn 'em again and again).

An even better choice (if you have the dough) is an Apple SuperDrive, which not only burns CD and CD-RW discs, but also lets you burn DVDs with 4.7GB of data (or video) each. If you don't already have a burner, SuperDrive's the way to go; if you're getting a new Mac soon, get one with a SuperDrive — you won't regret it.

If you have a relatively new Mac, you may have a built-in CD-RW, or SuperDrive drive. If you do (or if you get an external one), for goodness sake — use it to back up your stuff!

Games

Gaming on the Mac has never been better, and the game developers are getting better and better at coaxing even more performance out of OS X.

Some of the games I *love* include *Halo, Unreal Tournament 2004,* and every pinball game LittleWing (www.littlewingpinball.com/) has ever created. Try one — you'll be amazed at how far computer gaming has come.

Multimedia Titles

Many great games, references, and educational titles come on CD-ROM or DVD-ROM these days. My favorite is *World Book*, which makes use of many Mac features to deliver an encyclopedia that's both authoritative and fun to use. You'll love it and so will your kids. Remember, your Mac is more than just a computer — it's a full-blown multimedia player. Enjoy it.

Don't forget that most Macs can also play video DVDs like those you rent at Blockbuster Video or NetFlix. . . .

Some Big Honking Speakers with a Subwoofer

Face it: Most Macs have crummy speakers (or worse, only one crummy speaker). With a decent set of speakers, games are more fun, music sounds like music instead of AM radio, and the voiceovers in your multimedia titles suddenly become intelligible. If you're into sound, you'll enjoy your Mac much more if you add a set of window-rattling speakers, preferably one with a massive subwoofer to provide that booming bass that sound lovers crave. So crank it up! I'm partial to RSL Digital Fidelity One (www.rslspeakers.com), which gives you killer sound for well under $100, but any good speakers kick the stuffing out of the speakers built-into any Mac.

If you have a DVD-ROM drive, a killer set of speakers makes watching movies on your Mac a zillion times better.

A New Mouse and/or Keyboard

If you're still using that hockey-puck mouse that came with your iMac, G3, or G4, do yourself a favor and beat it to death with a hammer. Then buy a real mouse. You'll be so much happier if you upgrade to a mouse that's easier to move around and maybe even has two or more buttons or a scroll wheel.

You'll be amazed at how much easier it is to work with a mouse that fits your hand. OS X knows about multi-button mice and scroll wheels. With a two-button mouse, you no longer have to hold down the Control key while clicking to display a contextual menu — just click with the right-hand button.

Also, consider ditching that silly Chiclet keyboard if you're stuck with one (you know, those curved, tiny-keyed annoyances that first came with iMacs and that Apple continued to foist on users for many years). Third-party Mac keyboards on the market today are also a huge improvement over what probably came with your Mac — and the new Apple Pro keyboard is an excellent product.

I'm partial to so-called ergonomic keyboards, which I find more comfortable for prolonged writing sessions. I also think I type faster with this kind of keyboard. My current axe is a Microsoft Natural Keyboard Pro. Even though it's a Windows keyboard and the modifier keys are mislabeled (the Command key says Alt and the Option key has a Windows logo on it), Microsoft offers excellent Mac drivers for OS X. Although this particular model has been discontinued, sadly, Microsoft offers other ergonomic keyboards in the Natural line of products. Shop around to find one that works for you.

Look into the clear Apple Pro keyboard and Pro Mouse if they didn't come with your Mac, or their wireless Bluetooth keyboard and mouse Both are cool and have decent tactile response (but still only one button on the mice — phooey).

A PowerBook or an iBook

You need a laptop because one Mac is never enough. With a portable Mac, you can go anywhere and continue to compute. And both iBooks and PowerBooks come with Apple's AirPort wireless networking, so you can surf the Net, print, and share files from the couch or pool, or the Airport (the kind with planes and a small "p") or Starbucks for that matter.

A New Mac

If you have any money left, consider upgrading to a newer, faster Mac. They've never been faster, cheaper, or better equipped; if yours is getting a bit long at the tooth, consider a newer, faster model. The iMac G5, for example, delivers a ton of bang for the buck.

Timing can be everything when shopping for a new Mac. Historically, new models are announced at Macworld Expo in January (in San Francisco) and at the Apple Worldwide Developer Conference in the summer (in San Francisco). So it's usually a bad idea to buy a new Mac in December or June because chances are good that what you buy will be discontinued in a month or two. On the other hand, Apple occasionally lowers prices the month before Macworld Expos to clear out old inventory before introducing new models. Keeping that in mind, *my* advice is to wait until after a Macworld Expo to choose your new Mac. But if a December or June deal is so good you can't pass it up, go for it. Bear in mind, however, that the model you're buying might be discontinued shortly and replaced with a faster, better model at around the same price (especially if you'd have to upgrade last year's model).

One great truth of computer shopping is that no matter when you hop on the highway, a faster and less expensive ride will be along pretty soon. You just have to realize that if you wait for the ultimate machine at the ultimate price, you're never going to have a computer or get anything done with it.

Caveat emptor.

Chapter 18

Ten (Or So) Great Web Sites for Mac Freaks

As much as I would love to think that this book tells you everything you need to know about using your Mac, I know better. You have a lot more to discover about using your Mac, and new tools and products come out almost daily.

The best way to gather more information than you could ever possibly soak up about all things Macintosh is to hop onto the Web. There you'll find news, freeware and shareware software to download, troubleshooting sites, tons of news and information about your new favorite OS, and lots of places to shop. So make sure that you read Chapter 9 to get set up for the Internet — because this chapter is all about finding cool stuff on the Web to help you use your Mac better (while having lots of fun).

The sites in this chapter are the best, most chock-full-o'-stuff places on the Web for Mac users. By the time you finish checking out these ten Web sites, you'll know so much about your Mac and Mac OS X that you'll feel like your brain is in danger of exploding. On the other hand, you may just feel a whole lot smarter. Happy surfing!

MacFixIt: www.macfixit.com

Frequent *Macworld* contributor and consultant Ted Landau put together an excellent troubleshooting site to help users solve common problems and keep current on compatibility issues with new system software and third-party products.

Alas, Ted has taken a less active role in the site of late, and there is now a surcharge to search the archives. This site isn't quite as useful as it once was if you don't purchase a Pro membership (currently $25 a year). But even without paying, it's worth checking this site when you have any problem with your Mac. Chances are MacFixIt has a solution.

But I encourage you to go Pro if you can afford the $2 a month. It's worth more than that to have unlimited access to MacFixIt's extensive troubleshooting archives and special reports.

Don't tell the MacFixIt gang, but I'd consider it a bargain at twice the price.

VersionTracker.com: www.versiontracker.com

For free or shareware stuff, try VersionTracker. It's one of the best sites to search for software — for any version of Mac OS — by keyword. And it's terrific for getting the latest version of any kind of software: commercial, shareware, and/or freeware. It's a virtual treasure trove of software and updates, and is worth visiting even when you aren't looking for anything in particular. So check it out and download some useful utilities or games or something. I love this site and visit daily.

MacInTouch: www.macintouch.com

For the latest in Mac news, updated every single day, check out MacInTouch. com. Authored by longtime *MacWeek* columnist Ric Ford and his staff of newshounds, this site keeps you on the bleeding edge of Mac news, including software updates, virus alerts, and Apple happenings. I consider this site essential to keeping up with Mac OS X.

MacMinute: www.macminute.com

Here's another great source of up-to-the-minute Macintosh news. It's a great site, updated many times a day with lots of useful stories, links, and other Mac info.

Apple Knowledge Base: www.apple.com/support

Do you have a technical question about any version of Mac OS or any Apple product — including OS X? March your question right over to the Knowledge Base, Apple's searchable archives of tech notes, software update information, and documentation. The Knowledge Base is especially useful if you need info about your old Mac — Apple archives all its info here. Choose from a preset list of topics or products and type a keyword to research. You're rewarded with a list of helpful documents. Click any one of these entries (they're all links) to take you right to the info you seek. The site even has tools that can help narrow your search.

The Mac OS X Home Page: www.apple.com/macosx

Part of Apple's main Web site, this section is all about Mac OS X, its cool features, how to get the most from it, what applications are available for it, and so on. Check in here to see what Apple has cooking; think of it as one-stop-shopping for your Mac.

ramseeker: www.macseek.com

One of the best ways to make your Mac better is to buy more random-access memory (RAM). *RAM* is the readily available memory that your computer uses; the more you have, the smoother programs run. Although Mac OS X may run on a Mac with only 128 MB of RAM, officially Tiger requires 256MB and works even better and faster with more than that — at least 512MB in my opinion. As cheap as RAM is, the price that you pay for it can vary quite a lot. The best way I know to get the lowdown on RAM prices is using the `ramseeker` feature of this site, which organizes memory prices by Mac type.

Outpost.com: www.outpost.com

Recently taken over by Fry's (the great electronics retailer), Outpost.com is all about buying stuff — and what big kid doesn't love his toys? Here you can find lots and lots and lots of Mac products, including Apple CPUs, memory, drives, printers, scanners, and other miscellaneous accessories. You'll love the prices, as well as the massive selection of Mac and non-Mac electronics products.

EveryMac.com: www.everymac.com

The author of this site claims that it is "the complete guide of every Macintosh, Mac Compatible, and upgrade card in the world." You can't argue with that (unless you've done a staggering amount of research). Become a member (it's free) and sign up for forums. Check out the Forums and Q & A sections, too, for your Mac-related questions.

Inside Mac Games: www.imgmagazine.com

This is the best of the Mac gaming sites on the Web (at least in my humble opinion). Order CDs of game demos, download shareware, check out game preview movies, or shop for editors and emulators. Find forum camaraderie and troubleshoot gaming problems, too.

dealmac: www.dealmac.com

Shopping for Mac stuff? Go to `dealmac` ("Because cheap Mac stuff rocks," this site boasts) first to find out about sale prices, rebates, and other bargain opportunities on upgrades, software, peripherals, and more.

Doctor Mac Direct: www.DoctorMacDirect.com

Doctor Mac Direct is (in all due modesty) my cool new troubleshooting, training, and technical-support site, designed just for Mac users. With the aforementioned Ted Landau (the world's premier Mac troubleshooting guru) in charge of our team of expert technicians, Doctor Mac Direct provides jargon-free expert technical help at a fair price, regardless of your location — usually on the same day. Let our experts provide you with high-quality Macintosh troubleshooting, technical support, software or system training, pre-purchase advice, and more! We do our thing via phone, e-mail, iChat, and/or our unique Web-enabled remote-control software, which lets us fix many common Mac ailments in less than an hour.

The next time you need help, and none of the aforementioned sites does the trick, why not let Doctor Mac Direct make the mouse call? (So to squeak.)

Note: This crass commercial message is the only time in the whole book where I blather on about my "day job." So if there's something you want to know about your Mac, or something you would like examined or fixed, we can probably help you in less than an hour. I hope you'll give it a try.

And now, back to our regularly scheduled programming.

Chapter 19

Ten (Or So) Mac OS X Apps That You Might Need Someday

. . . .

Dig around the Mac OS X Applications folder — or take a gander at the System Preferences application's main window — and you'll run across some programs and preferences that you may not use every day, but are still kind of cool.

In this chapter, I tell you what some of these items do (and whether you're likely to get much from them). Space limitations forbid delving into these potentially useful goodies elsewhere in this book — and they'd overflow that space if I gave them the detailed how-to treatment here. So, to save space and restore order in the galaxy, I briefly describe each one and then provide some insights on whether you need it or not.

Almost everything I mention in this chapter includes a Mac OS Help feature. Use it to discover more about how these goodies work. Just search Mac OS Help for the item you're interested in, and you'll get an eyeful.

Web Sharing

Web Sharing enables others to share documents on your computer through the Web. You can set up a Web site just by adding HyperText Markup Language (HTML) pages and images to the Sites folder in your home folder, and then activating Web Sharing in the Sharing pane of System Preferences.

Web Sharing works only while your Mac is connected to the Internet or an internal network. In other words, if you use a modem and connect to the Internet by dialing up, this application won't be a lot of use to you because your server (your Mac) will only be on the Internet when you've dialed up and made a modem connection. When you're not connected, your server won't be available, except to other computers on your local network. That's not to say that Web Sharing can't be used this way, but you'll have to tell remote users when they'll be able to find it — and then make sure you dial up and make a connection at just that time. Another downside to this method is that almost without exception, dial-up users will have a different IP address every time they connect, so you would have to tell folks your new address every time.

Furthermore, even if you keep your modem connected to the Internet 24 hours a day with a digital subscriber line (DSL) or cable-modem connection, using this feature could violate your agreement with your Internet Service Provider (ISP) because some ISPs prohibit you from running a Web site. Also, most cable and DSL connections use dynamic IP address assignment through Dynamic Host Configuration Protocol (DHCP), which means your IP address will change from time to time.

On the other hand, some ISPs don't care whether you run a Web site. Check with yours if you're concerned.

I do turn on this feature occasionally, but (because I don't use it 24/7) I never bothered to check with my ISP. Do me a favor and don't rat me out.

FTP Access

File Transfer Protocol (FTP) is kind of like Web Sharing: It allows folks on the Internet to have access to files on your Mac. The difference is that FTP access is specifically designed to let you make files available for download, and Web Sharing is designed to let people view Web pages.

When you activate FTP by selecting the Allow FTP Access check box in the Sharing pane of System Preferences, users on the Internet have the same access to the contents of your Mac that they would if they were using file sharing. (See Chapter 14 for more on file sharing.) People who don't have accounts on your Mac can access Public folders and Drop Boxes — or any folder to which you grant everyone access, as I describe in Chapter 14.

Internet users can connect to your Mac with any FTP client application.

An *FTP client* is a program that offers FTP features — uploading files, downloading files, and so on. Better FTP clients can also do stuff like rename and delete remote files. On the Mac, Transmit (my personal fave), Interarchy, and Fetch are probably the best-known FTP clients. You can also find FTP clients for Windows, Linux, and most other operating systems (but because I use only Macs, I don't know the names of the good ones).

Most Internet browsers can serve as FTP clients as well as browsers (although they're mostly good only for downloading, and not much use for uploading, deleting, renaming, and other such useful functions).

ColorSync Utility

ColorSync helps ensure color consistency when you're scanning, printing, and working with color images. This package includes ColorSync software as well as pre-made ColorSync profiles for a variety of monitors, scanners, and printers.

A *ColorSync profile* is a set of instructions for a monitor, scanner, or printer, which tells the device how to deal with colors (and white) so the device's output is consistent with that of other devices (as determined by the ColorSync profiles of the other devices). In theory, if two devices have ColorSync profiles, their output (on-screen, on a printed page, or in a scanned image) should match perfectly. Put another way, the red (or green or blue or white or any other color) that you see on-screen should be exactly the same shade as the red that you see on a printed page or in a scanned image.

To calibrate or not to calibrate?

One thing you might want to try, even if you never plan to use ColorSync, is to calibrate your monitor. This process adjusts the red, green, blue, and white levels, and could make what you see on your screen look better than it does now.

To calibrate your monitor, follow these steps:

1. **Open the Displays System Preferences pane.**

2. **Click the Color tab and then write down the Display Profile that your Mac is currently using (it's highlighted in the Display Profile list).**

3. **Click the Calibrate button.**

The Display Calibrator Assistant appears.

4. **Follow the simple onscreen instructions to calibrate your monitor and create a custom display profile.**

5. **Give your profile a name and then click the Continue button.**

If you decide that you don't like the results of your calibration, just click the Display Profile that you wrote down in Step 2 from the Display Profile list in the Displays System Preference pane, and your monitor will go back the way it was before you calibrated it.

You'll find the ColorSync Utility in /Applications/Utilities; use it to pick a profile or check to see that the profile ColorSync is using is the right one for your display, input, output, or proof device.

If you're not a graphics artist working with color files and calibrating monitors and printers to achieve accurate color matching, you probably don't need ColorSync (unless you've gotten hooked on iPhoto and want your printed inkjet color pictures to match up correctly).

Image Capture

Image Capture is a nifty little application that you can use to download images from a digital camera (or from a variety of scanners) to your Mac. You can also use it to tell your Mac what program to launch when a digital camera or scanner is connected to it. (It's preset to open iPhoto unless you've told it otherwise.)

You'll find it in your Applications folder. You can use it with many kinds of digital cameras and a number of different scanner models, so if you have more than one, you may be able to avoid having to install a separate application for each.

Unfortunately, Image Capture doesn't work with every digital camera. For example, Image Capture did not recognize my relatively new Olympus digital camera. To find out whether Image Capture works with your digital camera, plug the camera into one of your Mac's USB ports and open Image Capture. If the Camera menu at the top of the window reads No devices found, you're out of luck. The same steps apply to your scanner, except that you'll be checking the Scanner menu.

Image Capture can automate some parts of the image-downloading process. For example, you can set it up to download all images from the camera into a preselected folder, or to open automatically when you connect your camera to your Mac.

You may not want to use Image Capture if you prefer the program that came with your digital camera (the program you use to import pictures from the camera) or iPhoto. On the other hand, you may have to use Image Capture if the program that came with your digital camera doesn't work (or does work but kinda sucks). And if your scanner lacks working software, Image Capture might still work for you.

If Image Capture doesn't support your scanner, a shareware program for Mac OS X called VueScan from Hamrick Software (www.hamrick.com) supports scanning images with many different scanners, including ones that don't work with Image Capture. Its $60 price tag ($100 for the "Pro" version) is a small price to pay if your scanner is just going to collect dust otherwise.

Finally, if the program that came with your camera doesn't run under Classic and Image Capture doesn't work with your camera, you may have to reboot with OS 9 to run the program. (For more info on running Classic and OS X, and rebooting under OS 9.2.1, read through Chapter 12.)

Text to Speech

Use Text to Speech to convert on-screen text into spoken words from your Mac. This application is pretty much unchanged from earlier versions of Mac OS. With a whole slew of voices to choose from, you can have Text-to-Speech read dialogs, or even documents, aloud.

Sometimes hearing is better than reading. For example, I sometimes use Text to Speech to read a column or page to me before I submit it. If something doesn't sound right, I give it a final polish before sending it off to my editor.

You can activate this feature in the Speech System Preferences pane. Click the Text to Speech tab to check it out.

VoiceOver

The camera pans back — a voice tells you what you've just seen, and suddenly it all makes sense. Return with us now to those thrilling days of the off-camera narrator. . . .

Mac OS X 10.4 Tiger introduces a new feature called VoiceOver, designed primarily for the visually impaired. You'll find it in the Universal Access System Preferences pane, where it's the first item in the Seeing tab. When it's turned on (keyboard shortcut: ⌘+F5), your Mac talks to you about what is on your screen. For example, if you clicked on the Desktop, your Mac might say something along the lines of, "Application, Finder; Column View; selected folder, Desktop, contains 8 items." It's quite slick. For example, when you click a menu or item in a menu, you hear its name spoken at once, and when you close a menu you hear the words, "closing menu." You even hear the spoken feedback in the Print, Open, and Save (and other) dialogs.

VoiceOver is kind of cool (talking alerts are fun), but having dialogs actually produce spoken text becomes annoying (real fast) for most folks. But check it out! You might like it and find times when you want your Mac to read to you.

Speech Recognition

Speech Recognition enables your Mac to recognize and respond to human speech. With this feature, you can issue verbal commands such as, "Get my mail!" to your Mac and have it actually get your mail. You can also create AppleScripts and then trigger them by voice.

An *AppleScript* is a series of commands, using the AppleScript language, that tells the computer (and some applications) what to do.

You create AppleScripts with the Script Editor program, which you'll find in the AppleScript folder in the Applications folder.

You'll need a microphone (some Macs have them built in) to use Speech Recognition. And you'll only be able to talk to your Mac when you're using applications that support Speech Recognition.

You'll find the Speech Recognition tab to the Default Voice tab's left in the Speech pane of System Preferences.

This application is clever and kind of fun, but it's also slow on all but the fastest Macs, and requires a microphone. I've never been able to get Speech Recognition to work well enough to continue using it beyond a few hours at best. Still, it's kind of neat (and it's a freebie), and I've heard more than one user profess love for it. So you might want to check it out.

NetInfo Manager

NetInfo is a hierarchical database that contains much of the configuration information needed to manage what goes on behind the scenes of Mac OS X. NetInfo knows all your settings, who has an account on your Mac, what network addresses you're using, and lots, lots more. With NetInfo Manager, which you'll find in Applications/Utilities, you can view and edit some of this information. Although it has a Mac interface, the database info displayed there will be pretty much incomprehensible to most folks.

NetInfo is a central location for a lot of important information. With NetInfo Manager, a savvy Mac user can do cool things that can't be done with the Network or Sharing System Preferences panes. But most average users won't want to play here. One suggestion: If you're at all curious about the internals of the UNIX operating system on which Mac OS X is based, start by learning a bit about NetInfo before you dive into the hard-core UNIX stuff (see the next section for a quick briefing).

UNIX Tools: Terminal, Console, and Activity Monitor

Mac OS X is based on the UNIX operating system, although its UNIX under-pinnings are mostly hidden. While most Mac users are grateful that they can ignore UNIX, you'll find that if you know UNIX (or think you might like to), you can do a lot of very geeky things with the UNIX tools included in Mac OS X.

You'll find all three programs in the Utilities folder within your Applications folder.

UNIX is not for the inexperienced or faint of heart. Before you even begin experimenting with it, you should get yourself a good UNIX primer and learn the ropes. And as usual, be very careful. Mucking around in the Mac OS X UNIX files gives you access to lots of stuff that isn't ordinarily available to you, which can very quickly lead to major problems if you're not absolutely sure what you're doing. If you want more info on UNIX, check out *Unix Bible,* 2nd Edition, by Yves Lepage and Paul Iarrera (Wiley).

Terminal

Basically, UNIX is a *command-line* operating system: Instead of clicking buttons and dragging icons around the Desktop, you type commands (not in English, by the way) at a command line. To do this in Mac OS X, you use a program called Terminal, which you'll find in the Utilities folder in the Applications folder.

Terminal is nothing more than a single window with a line (or many lines) of very geeky-looking text — there are no menus or buttons to make your life easier. So Terminal is mostly useless unless you speak a decent amount of UNIX.

Console

Console is another UNIX tool that's used to show you technical messages from Mac OS X — in UNIX-speak, of course. It shows what UNIX processes are running, what devices are in use, and logs messages from applications, processes, and Mac OS X. Think of it as a UNIX troubleshooting and status-checking tool. Unfortunately (as with Terminal), Console's only window is a wall of super-geeky-looking text — still no menus or buttons to make your life easier. Like Terminal, Console is mostly useless unless you speak a decent amount of UNIX.

Activity Monitor

Activity Monitor might be more useful than Console for seeing what's going on under the hood, because it has a Mac interface (or at least it has some menus), a Find text field, and columns that you can sort. Think of it as another, somewhat fancier, UNIX troubleshooting and status-checking tool. Unlike Terminal and Console, which are entirely text-based, Activity Monitor gives you information in an easier-to-digest and far more visual manner, as shown in Figure 19-1.

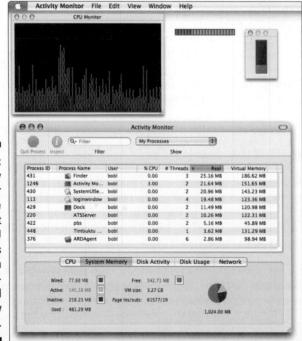

Figure 19-1:
Activity Monitor offers three different CPU Monitors (top) plus an information-packed window (bottom).

Appendix

Installing or Reinstalling Mac OS X 10.4 Tiger (Only If You Have To)

. . . .

In This Chapter

▶ Installing (or reinstalling) Mac OS X Tiger

▶ Setting up OS X Tiger with Setup Assistant

▶ Running OS X Tiger and OS 9 on the same Mac

. . . .

*Y*ou'll probably never need this Appendix. Some of you will get Mac OS X 10.4 Tiger pre-installed on a new Mac, and others will have installed it long before buying this book. And so, I expect few of you will have to refer to this Appendix to install OS X on your Mac for the very first time.

But (and there's always a *but*, isn't there?), someday something unexpected might happen to your Mac. You could have a hard drive crash or a problem starting up from your hard drive, or maybe you'll see the prohibitory sign when booting — all meaning that you'll need to *reinstall* OS X. And so, I expect some of you (I hope not many) will have to refer to this Appendix for instructions on reinstalling OS X.

A Mac OS X reinstallation is a pain-in-the-buttocks final step. Be sure you've tried all the stuff in Chapter 15 before even thinking about reinstalling OS X. If nothing else fixes your Mac, reinstalling Mac OS X could well be your final option before invasive surgery (that is, trundling your Mac to a repair shop). I save this solution for here at the very end of the book because it's the biggest hassle, and you don't *want* to reinstall OS X if something easier can correct the problem. So if you have to do a reinstallation, realize that this is more or less your last hope (this side of the dreaded screwdriver, anyway).

In this Appendix, you'll discover all you need to know to install or reinstall OS X, if you should have to. I say reinstalling is a hassle because although you won't lose the contents of your Home folder, Applications you've installed, or the stuff in your Documents folder (unless something goes horribly wrong or you have to reformat your hard drive), you could lose the settings for some System Preferences — which means you'll have to reconfigure those panes manually after you reinstall. And you may have to reinstall drivers for third-party hardware such as mice, keyboards, tablets, and the like.

It's not the end of the world, but it is almost always inconvenient. That said, reinstalling OS X almost always corrects all but the most horrifying and malignant of problems. And, as you'll soon see, the process is (compared to root-canal work or income taxes) relatively painless.

I'll stay with you through it all, though; don't you worry about a thing.

How to Install (or Reinstall) Mac OS X

In theory, you should have to install OS X only once. And in a perfect world, that would be the case. But you may find occasions when you have to install/reinstall it, such as

- ✔ If you get a new Mac that didn't come with Mac OS X pre-installed
- ✔ If you have a catastrophic hard-drive crash that requires you to initialize (format) your boot drive
- ✔ If any essential Mac OS X files become damaged, corrupted, or are deleted, or renamed

The following instructions do double duty: They're what you do to install OS X for the first time on a Mac — and they're also what you do if something happens to the copy of OS X that you boot your Mac from. That is, the following describes both the process for installing and the process for *re*installing OS X. The only difference is the choice you make in the Options window in Step 4.

If you've backed up or duplicated your entire hard drive, you might prefer to reinstall from your backup disks, CDs, DVDs, or tapes rather than reinstalling OS X from the Install Mac OS X DVD. That way, you'll be certain that anything you've tweaked on your Mac will be just the way you left it — your System Preferences will be the way you like them and you won't have to bother with reinstalling drivers for your third-party hardware.

Here's how to install (or reinstall) OS X, step by step:

1. **Boot from your Install Mac OS X DVD by inserting the DVD into your machine's DVD drive and then restarting your Mac while holding down the C key.**

When Mac OS X has finished booting your Mac, the Install program launches automatically. Here is where you begin the process of installing or reinstalling Mac OS X.

2. **Unless you want to use a language other than English for the main language of Mac OS X, click the Continue button (a blue arrow pointing to the right) in the first screen you see.**

   If you do want to use another language, select the language by clicking its name, and then click the Continue button.

3. **Read the Welcome and Software License Agreement screens, clicking the Continue button after each.**

   A sheet drops down, asking whether you agree to the terms of the license agreement. If you don't, you can't go any farther, so I advise you to go ahead and click the Agree button.

   If you're currently using any version of Mac OS except version 9.2.2, you might next see a dialog with the warning that you can't run Classic applications unless you have Mac OS 9.2.2 or a later version installed. Of course, you can't install Mac OS 9.2.2 right now (you're installing OS X!), but you *can* click OK and install 9.2.2 later. (Mac OS X, version 10.4 Tiger does not come with a Mac OS 9.2.2 Install CD, so you're on your own here.) If you have Mac OS 9.2.2 installed, you won't see this dialog.

4. **Choose the disk on which you want to install (or reinstall) Mac OS X by clicking its icon once in the Select a Destination screen.**

   At the bottom of the Select a Destination screen is the Options button; click it and a sheet drops down with three mutually exclusive choices:

   a. Upgrade Mac OS X: Choose this option to upgrade an earlier version of OS X installed on the disk you choose in Step 4. Your Home and other files are left undisturbed; after the upgrade, things will be (more or less) as they were before, except you'll be running a newer version of OS X.

   b. Archive and Install: Choose this option to move all the System components from your existing OS X installation into a folder named Previous System and then install a fresh new copy of OS X. The Previous System folder cannot be used to boot — but it does contain any and all files that were in any of the OS X folders before you upgraded.

   If you select this option, a check box for a second option — Preserve Users and Network Settings — becomes available. Mark it if you want to import all the existing users of this Mac, their Home folders, and their network settings — but still archive all the old System stuff into the Previous System folder.

   If you choose this option, you skip the Setup Assistant discussed later in this Appendix.

c. **Erase and Install:** Choose this option if you want to completely erase the disk that you selected in Step 4, starting completely from scratch — which gives you a factory-fresh installation.

If you choose the Erase and Install option, the disk you selected in Step 4 will be erased — and all your files will be deleted immediately! You should only choose this option if you've backed up all your documents and applications. In most cases, erasing the startup disk is not necessary.

If you select this option, the Format Disk As pop-up menu appears. Your choices are Mac OS Extended (Journaled), which is the one you want, or Unix File System (the one you don't want).

Unix File System is not a good choice for most OS X users. Suffice it to say that 99.9 percent of you should absolutely and positively *avoid* Unix File System like the proverbial plague (the other tenth-of-one-percent know who they are — and why they need a UFS disk). 'Nuff said.

After you make your selection in this window, click OK to return to the Select a Destination screen and then click Continue.

Now you have a choice of which installation to perform — easy or customized:

• **Easy Install** copies all Mac OS X onto your chosen hard drive (as you choose in Step 4).

• **Custom Install** (click the Customize button at the bottom of the screen) enables you choose to install only the items that you want to install.

In almost all cases, whether you're either doing a complete installation or reinstallation, Easy Install is the right way to go — so that's what I assume you'll choose for the rest of these steps.

5. **To begin the installation, click the Install button.**

The installer first checks your installation DVD for errors, and then installs the operating system which takes 10 to 20 minutes. So now might be a good time to take a coffee break (unless your machine is slow — installation takes about an hour on a 400 MHz G4, and that's enough for lunch). When it's done installing, your Mac will restart itself, and you can begin using Mac OS X . . . hopefully trouble-free.

After your Mac reboots, the Setup Assistant appears, *unless* you've chosen Archive and Install and also selected the Preserve Users and Network Settings option, which would obviate the need for the Setup Assistant (your settings from before the installation would be intact).

6. **Work your way through all the Setup Assistant screens.**

You have to do that housekeeping before you can begin working in OS X, and I show you how in the next section.

Getting Set Up with Setup Assistant

Assuming that your installation (or reinstallation) process goes well and your Mac restarts itself, the next thing you should see (and hear) is a short, colorful movie that ends by transforming into the first Setup Assistant screen, fetchingly named *Welcome*.

To tiptoe through the Setup Assistant, follow these steps:

1. **When the Welcome screen appears, choose your country from the list by clicking it once, and then click the Continue button.**

   If you need to hear instructions for setting up your Mac, press the Escape key now to learn how to use VoiceOver to set up your computer.

   If your country doesn't appear in the list, select the Show All check box, which causes a bunch of additional countries to appear in this list. Choose yours by clicking it and then click the Continue button.

   The Do You Already Own a Mac screen appears.

2. **If you own another Mac, you can choose to transfer your date from it to this Mac now by clicking the appropriate radio button — Transfer My Information from Another Mac; Transfer My Information from Another Partition on This Mac; or Do Not Transfer My Information — and then clicking the Continue button.**

   If you choose to transfer your information, just follow the on-screen instructions and wait for the transfer to complete — which could take an hour or longer.

   The Select Your Keyboard screen appears next.

3. **Choose a keyboard layout from the list by clicking it once; then click the Continue button.**

   If you're an American (or want to use an American keyboard setup), click the U.S. listing. If you prefer a different country's keyboard layout, select the Show All check box, and a bunch of additional countries (as well as a pair of Dvorak keyboard layouts) appears in the list. Choose the one you prefer by clicking it — and *then* click the Continue button.

   If the Setup Assistant detects more than one wireless network available, you might see a screen enabling you to choose which one to use. If so, choose the appropriate wireless network and then click the Continue button.

   The Enter Your Apple ID screen appears.

4. **If you have an Apple ID, type your user name and password in the appropriate fields and then click the Continue button. If you don't have an Apple ID or don't want to provide yours at this time, leave both fields blank and click the Continue button.**

Click the Learn More button to find out more about an Apple ID and what it can do for you. In a nutshell, it lets you make one-click purchases at the iTunes Music Store, iPhoto, or the Apple Store. If you get one now, you'll also get a free, limited 60-day trial account with .Mac.

When you're finished reading, click OK, and then click the Continue button.

The Registration Information screen appears.

5. **Fill out the fields (name, address, phone number, and so on) and then click the Continue button.**

   If you're interested in what Apple will and will not do with this informa-tion, click the Privacy button on this screen and read the Privacy Policy.

   The Thank You screen appears.

6. **Click the Continue button.**

   The Create Your Account screen appears.

7. **Fill in the Name, Short Name, Password, Verify, and Password Hint fields, and then click the Continue button.**

   This first account that you create will automatically have administrator privileges for this Mac.

   Each of these fields has an explanation beneath it.

   You can't click the Continue button until you've filled in all five fields.

   The Extend Your Mac Experience Online screen appears.

8. **Select one of these four radio buttons and then click the Continue button:**

   ✔ I've Already Purchased a .Mac Box and Want to Enter the Activation Key

   ✔ I Want to Purchase .Mac Online Now

   ✔ I'm Already a .Mac Member

   ✔ I Don't Want to Purchase .Mac Right Now

   When you've completed this selection, you're essentially done though you might see one or more of the following screens before you're taken to the OS X desktop.

9. **If you want to set up the Mail program now, click the appropriate radio button — Use My Mac.com Account Only or Add My Existing Email Account — fill in the blanks, and then click the Continue button.**

   The Select Time Zone screen appears.

10. **Click your part of the world on the map, click to choose a city from the pop-up menu, and then click the Continue button.**

    The Set the Date and Time screen appears.

TECHNICAL STUFF

Two ways to run two systems

Some folks have compelling enough reasons to use older software that they're willing to put up with the extra complexity of running two operating systems — Mac OS X and Mac Classic. If you're planning on using Classic applications at all, I need to tell you a little about how Mac OS X and Classic (Mac OS 9.2.2) co-exist on the same computer. (If you'd rather just learn how to use Classic, you can skip this section and read Chapter 12 instead.)

Both Mac OS 9.2.2 and OS X can either be installed on the same volume — usually the single hard drive in your Mac — or on separate volumes. If they're installed on a single volume, as they would be if you got your Mac with Mac OS X pre-installed, the files that make up Mac OS 9.2.2 are buried within the complicated hierarchy of Mac OS X components. You probably won't have much to do with them, other than customizing some preferences. If you've used any version of Mac OS 9 (9.0.1, 9.0.4, or even 9.1), you won't find the familiar System Folder or be able to work with its files in the way that you're used to.

In some cases, Mac OS 9.2.2 and Mac OS X are installed on separate volumes on your Mac.

Volumes can be individual hard drives, or they can be partitions of a single hard drive. A *partition* looks and behaves like a hard drive, but it's actually just a section of the disk that is completely separate from the rest of the drive. In this arrangement, Mac OS X and Mac OS 9.2.2 each have their own partitions on the same hard drive. That means that you can install and customize a Mac OS 9.2.2 drive without affecting Mac OS X. They behave as if they were completely separate drives. When you launch Classic while running Mac OS X, Mac OS 9.2.2 launches from the other partition, and you have access to its System Folder, just as you would on a Mac with Mac OS 9.2 as the primary operating system.

If you're installing Mac OS X from scratch and you're comfortable with concepts such as drive partitioning and the like, I recommend that you install Mac OS 9.2.2 on two partitions or hard drives. In other words, install 9.2.2 on both partitions and then install OS X on one of them. Let the copy of OS 9.2.2 on the same disk (or partition) as OS X be the one that you use for Classic. Use the other copy of OS 9.2.2 to boot from when you need to run Classic apps or use Classic extensions/control panels that aren't supported by Classic (such as DVD Player, CD Audio Player, some CD burning software, full functionality for iTunes, and so on). You'll have more flexibility when using Mac OS 9.2.2 if you follow this advice, and you'll be able to troubleshoot both operating systems more easily if you keep them on separate drives. You'll also find that Classic starts up faster because it won't have all the extra control panels and extensions to load. You might also find it more convenient to store all your Classic applications on the partition or drive with OS 9.2.2 only rather on the OS X drive or partition. That's how I have the Mac I used for writing this book arranged (check the screen shots).

If you have multiple partitions or drives — each of which has a copy of Mac OS 9.2.2 — you can choose which copy to use when launching Classic. Make this choice in the Classic pane of System Preferences. (Read more about this in Chapter 12.)

In addition to running Classic applications under OS X, you can choose to boot from Mac OS 9.2.2 any time you like. After you've installed OS X, you can switch between it and OS 9.2.2 quickly and easily, assuming your Mac allows you to boot into Mac OS 9. (Read about this process in detail at the end of Chapter 12.)

If you've got two copies of OS 9.2.2, boot from the one that's *not* on the same drive or partition as OS X.

11. **Set today's date and the current time, and then click the Continue button.**

12. **When the next screen appears, click the Done button.**

    The assistant will quit and in a few moments, the Mac OS X Desktop will appear. That's it. You're done.

For the very last time in this book (and it bears repeating): Don't forget that Macs sold after January 1, 2003 aren't able to boot into Mac OS 9 *at all*. Classic is the only option for running OS 9 software on Macs made in 2003 and beyond.

Index

Symbols

^ (caret), for Control key, 69
... (ellipses) after menu command, 59, 71

• A •

About Finder command, Application menu, 75
About This Mac command, Apple menu, 17, 72
accelerated graphics card, 368
accelerator card, 368
access privileges
 guidelines for setting, 329–332
 list of, 329
 setting for folders or disks, 324–329, 335–336
 types of users for, 325–326
accessibility
 Universal Access preferences, 302–304
 VoiceOver Utility, 254–255, 297, 303, 385–386
accounts. See .Mac account; users
Accounts preferences, 296–297
Action button in toolbar, 55, 66, 99–100
actions, in Automator, 226
active window, 58–59
Activity Monitor, 245–246, 388
Activity Monitor icon, in Dock, 245
Add Bookmark button, Safari, 184
Add Printer command, Printers menu, 207
Add to Sidebar command, File menu, 81
Address Book
 adding sender to, 197
 Buddy List using, 200
 creating entries in, 195–196
 definition of, 195, 224
 spam filtered with, 197
 synchronizing with other devices, 241
Address Book icon, in Dock, 30, 195
Address field, Safari, 185

administrative users, 317
AIM (AOL Instant Messenger), 240
airline flights, tracking, 234
AirPort Admin Utility, 246
AirPort base station, 309
AirPort network, 311
AirPort Setup Assistant, 247
alert sound, screen flash for, 304
aliases
 advantages of, 42–43
 badge (arrow) below, 43
 creating, 43–44, 81
 definition of, 22, 41, 42
 deleting, 44–45
 parent icon of, 43, 45, 81
 to remote folders and disks, 339–340
 when to use, 144
Alsoft's DiskWarrior utility, 353–354
Always Open With command, File menu, 79–80
Ambrosia Software, Snapz Pro X utility, 250–251
animation, for minimizing windows or opening applications, 39
anti-aliasing of fonts on screen, 277–278
antivirus programs, 173–174, 198
Anti-Virus service, 198
AOL (America Online), 182
AOL Instant Messenger (AIM), 240
Appearance preferences, 276–278
Apple Graphing Calculator, 224
Apple Knowledge Base, 378
Apple - Mac OS X icon, in Dock, 31
Apple menu. See also System Preferences
 About This Mac command, 17, 72
 in Classic Environment, 263
 customizing, 71–72
 Dock command, 38
 Force Quit command, 73
 Log Out command, 74
 Mac OS X Software command, 73
 Restart command, 74
 Shut Down command, 18, 74

• *K* •